DATE			

SuperMotivation

A Blueprint for Energizing Your Organization From Top to Bottom

Dean R. Spitzer

amacom

American Management Association

New York • Atlanta • Boston • Chicago • Kansas City • San Francisco • Washington, D. C.
Brussels • Mexico City • Tokyo • Toronto

This book is available at a special
discount when ordered in bulk quantities.
For information, contact Special Sales Department,
AMACOM, a division of American Management Association,
135 West 50th Street, New York, NY 10020.

Library of Congress Cataloging-in-Publication Data

Spitzer, Dean R.
      Supermotivation / a blueprint for energizing your organization
   from top to bottom / Dean R. Spitzer.
         p.   cm.
      Includes bibliographical references.
      ISBN 0-8144-0286-0
      1. Employee motivation.   2. Organizational effectiveness.
   I. Title
   HF5549.5.M63S665   1995
   658.3'14—dc20   95-18428
                                                            CIP

SuperMotivation™ is a trademark of Dean R. Spitzer & Associates, Inc.

Printing number

10   9   8   7   6   5   4   3   2

For
Cynthia
and
David

Contents

Preface

If you want an organization full of high performers who consistently delight customers with innovative, high-quality products and flexible, caring service, this book will show you how to achieve it.

If you have ever been frustrated by the difficulty of motivating your employees and keeping them motivated, you will find *real solutions* in this book.

This book will help you dramatically increase motivation in your organization or department, attract and retain the best employees, and reduce motivation-related costs by eliminating enticements and entitlements that have little or no motivational value.

What would it mean to your organization, your customers, *and* your bottom line if your employees were to become 20 percent more effective? *If you use just a small proportion of the concepts and recommendations presented in this book, then a 20 percent improvement is a very conservative estimate of the benefits your company and your customers can realize.*

Believe it or not, even the most lethargic employee in your organization is a *potential dynamo* of energy and performance! *SuperMotivation* helps you to understand the mysteries of motivation, and shows you how to unlock the hidden potential that lies within each and every one of your employees.

Although many books have been written on the subject of motivation, this book presents a completely new approach. Most books focus on how *individual* managers and supervisors can motivate *individual* employees, or on how employees can motivate *themselves*. *SuperMotivation* shows how to motivationally transform an *entire organization* (or a unit within an organization).

The secret of motivation contained in this book is really quite simple: In order to be sustainable, motivation must be built into the organization itself.

SuperMotivation shows you how to create a working environment that will enable all employees to rediscover their latent self-motivation, and thereby make it possible for high motivation to exist organization-wide.

This book is organized into two parts: Part One presents an overview of the SuperMotivation approach, and Part Two provides the applications. In Part Two, there are hundreds of practical suggestions for motivationally transforming jobs, teams, meetings, suggestion systems, training, performance appraisal, compensation, benefits, and much more. Each chapter is packed with immediately applicable techniques that any organization can use to maximize the bang from its motivational bucks.

For twenty years, I have been helping organizations around the world, both large and small, maximize the potential of their employees. Now I would like to help you "SuperMotivate" *your* organization.

Acknowledgments

Writing this book has been a labor of love. It represents the culmination of a creative process that began more than twenty years ago. At that time, I realized that motivation was the key to human performance; I just didn't understand how it worked.

I am deeply appreciative of all the organizations and individuals who contributed to that discovery process and, at least indirectly, to this book. In particular, I would like to thank all my clients over the years, who afforded me the privilege of helping them and allowed me to experiment in the greatest laboratory in the world: American business. Their confidence motivated me to do my best.

I would also like to thank some special people who made significant contributions to this book: Victoria Carlyle Weiland, my San Francisco-based editor, was much more than an editor; she was a true friend. Don Longstreth of the Hewlett-Packard Company was a constant source of encouragement. Drs. Howard Scheiber, Gary English, and Tim Boone made valuable suggestions. I am also grateful to AMACOM Books, particularly Adrienne Hickey, who believed in the project when it was only a concept, and Mike Sivilli, who shepherded the manuscript through the editing process.

But, most of all, I would like to thank my wife, Cynthia (who had only half a husband during the writing of this book), and my son, David (who had only half a father), for their love, understanding, and support.

Part One
The SuperMotivation Approach

The Importance of Understanding SuperMotivation

SuperMotivation is not just a collection of isolated techniques; it is a *complete technology of motivation*. But, in order to use this technology successfully, you must *understand* the concepts and principles that underlie it. Part One of this book will give you a thorough, state-of-the-art understanding of both individual and organizational motivation.

Chapter 1 presents an overview of the SuperMotivation approach and explains why I developed it. Chapter 2 explores *self-motivation*, the enormous (and largely untapped) motivational potential that resides within every employee in your organization. In Chapter 3, you will discover how even the most routine work can become highly motivating when the environment (context) of work is "motivationally reengineered." You will also be introduced to the pivotal components of SuperMotivation: demotivators and motivators.

Chapter 4 examines *demotivators,* the all-too-frequently ignored negative factors that conspire to destroy work motivation. This chapter also identifies practical strategies for defeating demotivators in the workplace. In Chapter 5, you will find a comprehensive discussion of *motivators,* the positive, energizing factors that will later be used to "motivationally transform" organizational systems.

A careful reading of Part One will greatly enhance your understanding of motivation. This understanding will pay huge dividends when we turn our attention to the applications of SuperMotivation in Part Two.

For readers who would like to delve deeper into motivation, there are notes at the end of each chapter and a comprehensive bibliography at the end of the book.

Clyborn

1. Why we care about motivation
   NEED FOR MOTIVA
2. What is MO?
3. Mot. THEORIES

+ slides
+ fiction

1

The Need for SuperMotivation

There is a motivation crisis in American industry, and the symptoms are all around us: low productivity, quality problems, poor customer service, costly accidents, high absenteeism, increased violence in the workplace, and declining morale, to name but a few.

Survey after survey has identified "lack of motivation" as the number one human resources concern of business owners and managers nationwide. For example, personnel managers identified "lack of employee motivation" as the most troublesome problem they face,[1] 69 percent of operating managers said that "lack of employee motivation" is the most annoying problem in their organization,[2] and small-business CEOs reported that motivation is the human resources issue that takes up most of their time.[3] In fact, I don't think I've ever met a business owner or manager who wasn't frustrated by his or her failed attempts at motivating employees and keeping them motivated.

Surveys of workers have reported equally disturbing findings: 73 percent of employees said they are less motivated today than they used to be,[4] 84 percent said they could perform significantly better if they wanted to,[5] and—perhaps most shocking of all—50 percent of workers said they are putting only enough effort into their work to hold onto their jobs![6]

Walk around a typical organization, and you are likely to find employees with low energy levels "going through the motions," engaged in a high proportion of off-task behaviors, waiting to be told what to do, offering poor customer service, showing little initiative, playing it safe, and demonstrating little striving for excellence.

In these organizations, getting things done seems to require a major effort. Employees can't be bothered. They feel they are being interrupted by customers. Their attitude toward new business is: "Oh, no, not another

order!" "Oh, no, not another phone call!" "Oh, no, not another new product!" And this low motivation is not limited to low-skill employees, but
extends to managers and professionals, as well.[7]

In many organizations, the primary subject of conversation among
employees is what they are going to do during their off-hours, or how
much longer they have before retirement. And in company parking lots,
one can see cars displaying such cynical bumper stickers as I OWE, I OWE
. . . IT'S OFF TO WORK I GO; WORK SUCKS, BUT I NEED THE BUCKS; I'D RATHER BE
SAILING [or fishing, or golfing, or anything but working]; and the all too
familiar refrain THANK GOD IT'S FRIDAY!

And yet the companies employing these workers are spending millions and millions of dollars annually trying to motivate them.

Does this mean that American workers are lazy, as is so often reported in the popular media? After twenty years' experience in management and organizational improvement consulting, I can confidently
answer with a resounding no!

On the contrary, American workers at all levels of ability and responsibility are eager to be given a chance to perform well and to contribute
positively to their organizations. It is simply that they need a *different
kind of motivation* than currently exists in most organizations. People have
changed dramatically since the mid-1970s, but the prevailing motivational technology has not. What is required to energize today's workers
is a completely new approach to motivation.

This is what SuperMotivation is all about.

What Is SuperMotivation?

SuperMotivation is *self-sustaining, organization-wide, high motivation.* Let's
look at each of the three components of this definition that contributes to
making SuperMotivation such a distinctive concept.

SuperMotivation Is High Motivation

There are two major components of human performance: *ability* and *motivation.* They are related as follows:

$$Performance = Ability \times Motivation$$

Human beings are creatures of infinite possibilities, but most of us
use less than 30 percent of our abilities (some estimates put it closer to 10

percent). However, ability means nothing unless it is used. *When multiplied by motivation, ability comes alive!*

That is why, in times of urgency or crisis, ordinary human beings are somehow able to mobilize their latent capacities to accomplish remarkable feats. High motivation is what empowers a 100-pound woman to free her child from under a 3,000-pound truck. High motivation is what energizes a runner to pull away from the pack and win a race. And high motivation is what causes a work team to meet a seemingly unattainable goal. In each case, ordinary people are able to achieve extraordinary results through *the power of high motivation.*

If you examined a sample of 100 people in virtually any area of human endeavor, you would probably notice little difference among them (perhaps 10 to 15 percent) as far as ability is concerned, but huge differences in performance (sometimes 1,000 percent or more). Astonishingly, studies have found that the top one percent of employees produce nearly twenty times the per capita output of the bottom half of the workforce![8] Most of this variation in human performance is due to differences in motivation.

Consider the top salespeople in any organization. Although all the salespeople in the organization have pretty much the same innate ability and receive the same basic training, somehow the top ones generate far superior results. These top salespeople do what needs to be done, when it needs to be done; they engage in proper planning without being told to; they go out and make the sales calls; and they don't procrastinate. In short, they are *more motivated.* They don't sit around and wish or hope; they don't waste energy complaining about reticent customers; they take persistent, positive action.

For that matter, compare the top performers with the average performers in any job, profession, or organization. Why do some employees have to be constantly prodded, whereas others grab hold of the ball and run with it? What characteristic do all top performers have in common? High motivation!

Now let's take a look at some other examples in everyday corporate life. In every organization, there are some highly motivated individuals who tend to excel under the same conditions as the mediocre performers. These unsung heroes of the American workplace include the machine operator who reduced downtime to near zero by developing his own superior preventive maintenance procedures, the secretary who cut typographical errors by 90 percent by flagging the most frequently misspelled words, the customer service representative who virtually guaranteed satisfaction by using a self-developed "debriefing" procedure to ensure that all customers received the extraordinary service they deserved, and the

waiter who sold a $200,000 convention contract simply by being moti-
vated enough to tell a visitor how great his hotel was.[9] And you could
probably add many examples of your own to this list.

SuperMotivation Is Organization-Wide

High motivation, such as in the examples cited above, has typically been
viewed as a characteristic possessed by only a few rare individuals, rather
than as a quality that can exist organization-wide. Fortunately, as we see
in the next chapter, high motivation is a state that *all* employees are capable of manifesting. All people have virtually unlimited motivational potential. This innate *self*-motivation potential has simply been temporarily
suppressed because most employees are working in environments that
inhibit its expression.

SuperMotivation will result in higher levels of motivation—and performance—for virtually everyone. One way of visualizing this phenomenon is by considering the number of employees at various motivation
levels, as depicted in Figure 1–1. Curve "A" shows the distribution of
employee motivation in a typical company. In this distribution, most employees exhibit low to moderate motivation, and there is a very wide
range of motivation levels. As an organization moves toward SuperMotivation, the distribution of employee motivation will shift to the right

Figure 1-1. Shift in motivation brought about by SuperMotivation.

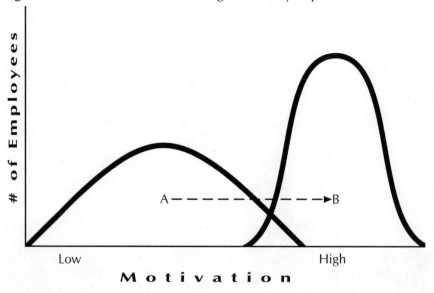

(toward higher motivation), and the range of motivation levels will be reduced (as shown by curve "B").

In a SuperMotivating environment, even those with formerly low levels of motivation will be able to excel, while those with higher levels of motivation will be able to realize their full potential.

SuperMotivation Is Self-Sustaining

Although high motivation is not difficult to *attain*, it tends to be much more difficult to *sustain*. Some organizations have been successful at mobilizing widespread high motivation—for short periods of time. We have all seen glimpses of this phenomenon when motivational speakers or charismatic leaders have been able to pump up the enthusiasm level for a short time, or when special programs have been able to arouse employees' energies to reach a short-term goal or meet an urgent deadline.[10] Too many motivational interventions leave people full of hope, energy, and enthusiasm only to have these hopes dashed when they return to the demotivating realities of the workplace.

Practically any motivational program can create a momentary surge of energy. However, these bursts of energy rarely last, and they generally leave employees feeling lower than before. The impact of short-term motivation has been described as being "much like the effect of eating a doughnut. . . . When the sugar high wears off, very little of value is left in the system."[11]

This is why motivation has been perceived mostly as a cyclical phenomenon, notorious for its volatility: up one day and down the next. According to this traditional model, individuals and organizations must be continually energized with new doses of motivation. The major problem with this approach is that when each dose wears off (as it inevitably will), another must be added. Under these circumstances, it is ridiculously difficult and exorbitantly expensive for companies to try to maintain high motivation.

The real challenge of motivation is not to mobilize energy at a particular moment, but *to sustain it for the long haul.*

Motivation can be sustained only if it is *built into* the organization itself. This way, motivation will no longer be subject to the whims of people or the initiation of new programs that come and go.

Why Motivation Has Failed

Despite tremendous effort and massive expenditures, the results of previous attempts to address the motivation crisis in American industry have not been impressive. In the sections that follow, I discuss the four major reasons why most of the earnest and well-intentioned efforts to motivate employees have failed to produce the desired results.

Theoretical Chauvinism

It has been said that "the management woods are full of theories and fads."[12] Behind everything we do is a theory, an explanation in the simplest possible terms. Although theories are valuable, American management has suffered from "theoretical chauvinism"—the tendency to adopt one theory to the exclusion of others. Whether the theory is Maslow's, Herzberg's, McGregor's, Freud's, Skinner's, or anyone else's,[13] no one theory *alone* is sufficient to explain the complexity of human motivation. Our dismal track record in motivating employees testifies to the limitations of each of these theories when used in isolation. Furthermore, most theories of motivation have proven virtually useless for practicing managers, and have had little relevance for organizational improvement.

I am convinced that the most accurate explanation of human motivation lies somewhere in the middle—where most motivational theories converge—and not inside any one of them. That is why this book has drawn upon many different theories, without adopting any of them in full.

Quick Fixes and Panaceas

The United States is a society with a compulsion for instant gratification, widely known for fast food, instant pudding, and quickie divorces. Americans love "quick fixes," fast pseudo-solutions that, unfortunately, usually do not solve the problem.

Quick fixes are seductively simple; they are usually intended to only temporarily "stop the bleeding" or "relieve the pain." The rallying cry of the quick fix is: "Ready, fire, aim!"

Quick fixes make it appear, at least for a while, that something meaningful has been done. Because many managers are evaluated on whether they are *doing something*, rather than on whether they are actually solving the problem, it shouldn't be surprising that American management has been attracted to quick fixes.

No area has been more susceptible to the quick fix than employee motivation.

Not only has employee motivation been particularly prone to the quick fix, it has also been a prime target for the panacea—the cure for all ills, the "solution" for all problems. Unfortunately, most quick fixes and panaceas are fast, convenient . . . and ineffective. Alas, quick fixes and panaceas distract managements from real solutions and consume massive amounts of time and money.

It seems as if every organization has its own motivational panaceas (which employees often deride as the "program of the month" or "program du jour"). A manager with a prominent company explained it this way: "Every few months, our senior managers find a new religion."[14] In fact, at one time or another, organizations have tried almost every panacea solution, and found every one wanting.

In one company, over a ten-year period, thirty-six new programs were embarked upon and subsequently discontinued. "Each of them began with impressive fanfare, lofty expectations, and large budgets." The result: "Most are now dead or comatose."[15] Another company sponsored so many different programs concurrently that it needed a special chart to keep track of them![16]

It isn't that motivational programs aren't valuable. Most of them can indeed be quite helpful if they are well planned and are *part* of an integrated, holistic approach. However, like the tendency to depend on isolated theories, the introduction of isolated programs is doomed to failure. No program *in itself* is going to increase productivity, improve quality, or provide long-term solutions to motivational problems.

It is going to take more than one or a few isolated tactics to overcome the crisis of motivation. That's why SuperMotivation provides an *integrated, multifaceted approach.*

Entitlement Expectations

Many organizations have tried to buy performance and loyalty by using pay and benefits. As a result, salaries, wages, and benefits have exploded, contributing significantly to the eroding competitive position of the United States vis-à-vis the rest of the world.

Rewards that are not contingent upon performance are *entitlements*.

Today, employees show up for work expecting a benefits package that comes close to bankrupting many companies. Salary increases and frequent promotions are also taken for granted. While these "golden handcuffs" *do* keep employees around, by now it is obvious that they do little to increase productivity or quality. What they do increase is the fear of job loss. Salary and benefits do get employees to show up for work, but they don't get people to work longer, harder, or smarter.

Fringe benefits are the classic example of entitlements because they are almost never performance-based. They are given to every employee "in good standing"—that is, whoever shows up for work. Because of their size, fringe benefits are no longer "fringe": In 1955, benefits given to American workers accounted for 17 percent of total compensation; in 1990, they accounted for 38 percent.[17]

Paradoxically, employees who have been conditioned to an entitlement mentality are generally *less* satisfied and *less* motivated than others who have to work harder for what they get. Rather than gratitude, the employee who feels entitled asks: What has the organization done for me lately? Why isn't it doing more?[18]

Despite compelling evidence that entitlements don't motivate, companies continue to pay enormous sums for them every day.

Six Misconceptions About Motivation

Further compounding the problems of worker motivation are a number of popular, widely held misconceptions. These misconceptions about motivation have led many companies to make serious motivational errors, all of which have contributed to the current motivational malaise of the American workforce.

Although there are probably others, the following six misconceptions have contributed significantly to the motivational crisis afflicting American industry today:

1. *Some people are motivated and some are not.* It is widely believed that motivation is a relatively fixed personality characteristic that cannot be modified. The truth is, everybody is motivated! Your employees just may not be motivated to do what *you* want them to do, when *you* want them to do it. Some people may be *temporarily* more motivated when they participate in a particular activity, but under different circumstances, this can change.

For example, we have all seen employees who appeared dead at their desks or work stations suddenly come alive when the clock strikes five, and they are off to play golf, play tennis, ski, fish, socialize at the local cocktail lounge, or engage in whatever activity excites them. As we see in Chapter 3, motivation is situational, based on the context in which people find themselves.

2. *Rewards will do it all!* The traditional American approach to motivation has been predominantly financial and materialistic: Pay, benefits, bonuses, status, and perks are the hallmark of American motivational practice.

However, real motivation is not for sale! Buying allegiance is not an effective long-term motivational strategy. There is much more to human psychology than an obsession with money and other material rewards.

Furthermore, American management has traditionally rewarded the wrong things (such as attendance, seniority, conformity, and minimally acceptable performance). The motivational message too often sent to employees is that results aren't important—*loyalty is!*

3. *Threat is the only motivation that some people understand.* When reward doesn't seem to work, many managers resort to the threat of punishment. In the short term, threat appears to be effective. Some managers and supervisors make a career out of intimidating their employees. These bullying tactics are often reinforced because, in the short run at least, they get the employees to do what their managers want them to do.

Although there may well be a time when threat is necessary, its widespread use ultimately leads to negativity, fear, and avoidance behavior, not to sustainable high performance.

4. *Happy employees are motivated employees.* This misconception is probably the most insidious of all because it has been largely responsible for the costly glut of entitlements. According to one observer, it has also led many organizations to some rather bizarre motivational programs "in search of the happy worker."[19]

A great many American companies have prided themselves on worker satisfaction and focused their motivational energies in that area, but in general these "country club" organizations are no more productive than the "sweatshop" organizations they revile. In fact, all too often, happiness leads to complacency, not to higher levels of motivation. Recently, a number of complacent "high-satisfaction" companies have had to lay off vast numbers of employees because management confused happiness with motivation.

In reality, job satisfaction and motivation are not necessarily highly correlated.[20] Although motivated people tend to be happy, happy people are not necessarily motivated!

In Chapter 2, you learn about the difference between relaxed positive emotions that don't motivate and energizing positive emotions that do. SuperMotivation focuses on creating a *more energetic* workforce, not a more relaxed one!

5. *Motivation is the personnel department's or supervisor's responsibility.* This misconception has been mainly responsible for perpetuating the lack of attention traditionally given to motivation in executive suites and board rooms across America. Unfortunately, too many managers spend their time managing processes, projects, money, and facilities—anything except people.[21] They find it easier to delegate motivation to others, rather than deal with it themselves.

Motivation cannot be perceived as a "personnel" or "supervisory" problem. It is one of the most crucial issues facing American industry today. To be effective, employee motivation must involve decisions made at the highest levels of corporate management.

6. *Motivation is common sense.* You know this misconception isn't true; otherwise, you wouldn't be reading this book! As Kilmann has explained in *Beyond the Quick Fix:* "It is time to stop perpetuating the myth of simplicity. The system of organization invented by mankind generates complex problems that cannot be solved by simple solutions."[22] Although motivation may be one of the most complex problems facing American industry, you would be surprised how many CEOs and other managers still believe that motivation can be done intuitively, just by using plain "horse sense."

SuperMotivation doesn't rely on "horse sense" or common sense. This book will give you the *technology* you need to successfully meet the motivational challenges in your organization, and motivate the new breed of employee.

Motivating the New Breed of Employee

There is no question that today's employees are different from those of a generation ago. Gone are the workers who were geared to blind obedience and hard work for salary and benefits alone. In the not-too-distant past, work was so important to employees that their lives were their work, and their work was their first priority. Today, for many employees, work is their *number three* priority (after family and leisure).

The American work ethic has not necessarily disappeared; it has just changed. A new work ethic of *self-concern* is emerging. Today's employees are more demanding, more skeptical, more individualistic, less loyal, less willing to sacrifice their personal lives for the sake of the organization, and more easily distracted from work. In short, the new breed of employees are more dedicated to themselves—and less dedicated to their organizations.

Employees also have much higher expectations for what work can, and should, be. Today's workers want their work to be enjoyable, stimulating, and challenging, not "a Monday through Friday sort of dying."[23] "New breed" employees want to *thrive* at work, not just *survive*.

Employees want to be treated by management as colleagues, not subordinates. They want to be privy to organizational planning, not occasional recipients of token information that management condescendingly gives them. They want performance-based rewards that are commensurate with their efforts and personal contributions, not the same salary and wages that everyone else gets just for coming to work in the morning.

Today's workforce is also much more varied and complex. The demographics of the American workforce are entirely different from those of twenty or forty years ago. There is a broader array of educational backgrounds and career aspirations. There is a much greater ethnic diversity, a much higher proportion of women and minority groups, and a larger number of workers who are part of a nontraditional family unit. These new demographics are creating enormous stress on employees and on the companies they work for, which makes it even more imperative for American industry to create *more motivating work environments.*

The SuperMotivation Approach

All work environments include two types of factors that powerfully influence employee motivation, one positive and the other negative. In this book, the positive factors will be referred to as *motivators,* and the negative factors as *demotivators.* As we see in later chapters, both motivators and demotivators are extremely powerful, and have a profound impact on how employees experience their work. For example, there are many employees who perform extremely interesting work, but who despise going to work because their work environments are so full of demotivators; then there are others who perform boring and tedious work, but who love going to work because their work environments are so full of motivators.

The SuperMotivation approach involves two parallel processes. The first is *reducing demotivators;* the second is *adding motivators.* The combination of these two processes will create dramatic improvements in the motivational climate of any organization willing to accept the challenge.

Reducing Demotivators

Nothing has done more to ensure the failure of previous efforts at improving organizational motivation in the American workplace than the problem of demotivators. Demotivators include all of those nagging daily occurrences that frustrate employees and drain so much of their motivational energy.

Many organizations take great pride in touting their humane treatment of employees and their employee-centered work environments. Other companies pat themselves on the back for the great salaries and benefits they offer. However, when employees find themselves being excluded from important planning and production decisions, receiving little information, attending boring meetings and training classes, and receiving very little positive feedback, these demotivating influences negate much of the hoped-for positive impact from the benevolent treatment.

No matter how generous an organization is to its employees, the demotivators will be around long after the employees have forgotten the generosity. Any approach to motivation that does not address demotivators is doomed to failure. That is why this book places so much emphasis on reducing demotivators.

Adding Motivators

The second element of SuperMotivation is to add motivators to the work environment. In this book, motivators are not people; they are *environmental conditions.*

However, as we see in Chapter 2, it isn't money or material rewards that the new breed of employee primarily seeks. Nonmonetary rewards such as involvement, freedom, responsibility, achievement, and meaning are valued most highly, and these are the rewards that will be the major focus of this book. What's more, these motivators are a great deal less expensive—and much more effective—than the traditional incentives now being offered by most companies. The impact of these motivators is often so dramatic that employees who previously appeared passive and lethargic come alive with energy and vitality even *they* didn't know they would have on the job!

By adding a variety of motivators to the organizational environment, management has an exciting opportunity to change the way employees experience their work—*permanently.* These motivators are not here today and gone tomorrow; they actually become part of the organization itself.

The Leadership Challenge

No matter who or what is to blame for the myriad of motivational problems plaguing American industry, one thing is for sure: *American management is the only hope for the solution.*

Management, especially upper management, is ultimately responsible for creating a working environment that is conducive to *self-sustaining, organization-wide high motivation.* Unfortunately, for too long, quick fixes and motivational tinkering have distracted CEOs and other corporate executives from seeking lasting solutions to employee motivation problems.

While many organizations are doing some of the right things motivationally, very few are doing so consistently and systematically. To achieve this kind of *consistent* and *systematic* motivation, there must be strong leadership from the top.

This book is an invitation to all levels of management (as well as other employees) to consider motivation as the long-term organizational priority it must become.

Toward Self-Motivation

You will notice that the focus throughout this book is on developing *self-motivation*. In fact, every aspect of the SuperMotivation approach is aimed at creating an environment conducive to high levels of self-motivation. Demotivators are important only because they present obstacles to self-motivation, and motivators are important only because they stimulate self-motivation.

Self-motivation is *real* motivation. Understanding self-motivation and the internal forces that drive it is the subject of Chapter 2.

Notes

1. D. W. Blohowiak, *Mavericks!* (Homewood, Ill.: BusinessOne Irwin, 1992).
2. L. Grensing, *Motivating Today's Workforce* (North Vancouver, British Columbia: Self-Counsel Press, 1991).
3. The Executive Committee, *Small Business Survey* (San Diego: T.E.C., 1993).
4. C. Colson and J. Eckerd, *Why America Doesn't Work* (Dallas: Word Publishing, 1991).
5. R. C. Huseman and J. D. Hatfield, *Managing the Equity Factor* (Boston: Houghton Mifflin, 1989).
6. L. H. Chusmir, *Thank God It's Monday* (New York: New American Library, 1990).
7. G. M. Prince, *The Practice of Creativity* (New York: Collier, 1970).
8. N. Augustine, *Augustine's Laws* (New York: Penguin, 1987).
9. D. R. Spitzer, "The Best Performer: Sharing the Secrets of Success," *Performance and Instruction,* December 1986.
10. There are many books that highlight peak performers and describe extraordinary organizational peak performances, such as C. Garfield, *Peak Performers* (New York: Avon, 1986), and T. Kidder, *The Soul of a New Machine* (Boston: Little, Brown, 1981).
11. A. Kohn, *Punished by Rewards* (Boston: Houghton Mifflin, 1993), p. 187.
12. H. Levinson, *The Great Jackass Fallacy* (Boston: Harvard University Press, 1973), p. 17.
13. A. Maslow, *Motivation and Personality* (New York: Harper & Row, 1954);

F. Herzberg, *Work and the Nature of Man* (New York: World, 1966); D. McGregor, *The Human Side of Enterprise* (New York: McGraw-Hill, 1960); S. Freud, *Complete Psychological Works of Sigmund Freud* (London: Hogarth Press, 1968); B. F. Skinner, *About Behaviorism* (New York: Vintage Books, 1976).

14. M. Hammer, "Reengineering Work: Don't Automate, Obliterate," *Harvard Business Review,* July–August 1990, p. 112.

15. G. A. Rummler and A. P. Brache, *Improving Performance* (San Francisco: Jossey-Bass, 1990).

16. R. H. Schaffer, *The Breakthrough Strategy* (Cambridge, Mass.: Ballinger, 1988).

17. J. R. Schuster and P. K. Zingheim, *The New Pay* (New York: Lexington Books, 1992).

18. J. Bardwick, *Danger in the Comfort Zone* (New York: AMACOM, 1991).

19. M. E. McGill, *American Business and the Quick Fix* (New York: Henry Holt, 1988), p. 115.

20. R. L. Kahn, "Productivity and Job Satisfaction," *Personnel Psychology,* vol. 13, 1960.

21. P. Crosby, *Running Things* (New York: Mentor, 1989).

22. R. H. Kilmann, *Beyond the Quick Fix* (San Francisco: Jossey-Bass, 1984), p. x.

23. S. Terkel, *Working* (New York: Avon, 1975), p. xiii.

2

Self-Motivation:
The Energizing Force

Self-motivation is the most powerful motivational force there is. It releases the latent motivational energy residing in all of us, and has the potential to energize extraordinary human performance.

The Power of Self-Motivation

There are two types of motivation: *self-motivation* and *external motivation.* Rarely is one present without the other. Motivation involves the interaction between people and their environment, and therefore it almost always results from a combination of both internal and external factors.

However, *real* motivation is essentially internal. While it usually does take something external to trigger it, no external factor alone can ever be exclusively responsible for motivation. For example, experiments have shown that people placed alone in barren rooms for long periods of time with no external stimulation whatsoever were still highly motivated.

All of us are driven to take action by powerful internal forces. These forces, referred to as *desires,* are responsible for self-motivation.

All of us are born profoundly self-motivated. The young child is the best illustration of self-motivation. Infants and toddlers tend to be inquisitive about everything—observing, touching, exploring, and constantly learning without any outside intervention. During this all-too-brief period of life, there is no need for any external reward.

But what happens to that spark of self-motivation as we proceed through life? Why do adults appear to exhibit much less self-motivation than young children do? In *Punished by Rewards,* Alfie Kohn has summarized a large body of research showing that much of our innate self-motivation diminishes (at least temporarily) as we become increasingly dependent on external motivation.[1]

External Motivation

Gradually, the power of self-motivation becomes obscured by the overwhelmingly powerful impact of external forces (such as rewards and threats). External rewards (including money, awards, and praise) begin to substitute for the simple, natural joys and curiosities of life.

As Denis Waitley has stated: "For too long . . . it has been wrongly assumed that motivation . . . can be pumped in from the outside through incentives, pep talks, contests, rallies, and sermons."[2]

After a while, learning for the sake of learning becomes learning for the sake of grades. Working for the satisfaction of it becomes working for the financial rewards that accrue. The hope we all share of pursuing an exciting and challenging career in an area of personal interest—without undue external restraint—is replaced by the reality of doing something mundane that we don't particularly like, within burdensome organizational constraints, for money.

One hundred percent self-motivation is an unrealistic expectation. Clearly some external control is necessary, but not to the extent that it currently exists in our lives. We must do some things that we don't particularly want to do. Reward (and even punishment) has its place. However, when there is too much external dependency, we become conditioned to wait for external incentives or threats before taking action.

External motivation also encourages us to stick to routine behavior patterns rather than risk more creative responses. It is extremely difficult for most of us to resist the powerful external forces controlling our lives.

By the time we reach adulthood, most of us have been thoroughly socialized to external control through the promise of rewards and the threat of punishment. At this point, self-motivation has become subordinated to potent external forces.

What happens to self-motivation is typified in the following story about several young boys who enjoyed throwing rocks at the house of an old man who lived on the outskirts of town. The old man tried many methods of stopping the boys from throwing rocks at his house. He tried yelling at them. He tried reasoning with them. He even threatened to call the police. Nothing seemed to work.

Finally, in desperation, the man came up with a bold plan. He started *paying* the boys a dollar each to throw rocks at his house. Then he reduced the payment to twenty-five cents. Although the boys complained, they continued to throw the rocks, but with less enthusiasm. Finally, he reduced the payment to a penny each. Amazingly, the boys stopped entirely, telling the old man that it was no longer worth it to throw rocks at his house! And they never returned. The explanation for this occurrence is that the formerly self-motivated (albeit negative) behavior became externally controlled. First, the rock throwing lost its intrinsic pleasure. Second, the reduced external reward was insufficient to maintain it.

This is not so different from what happens at work when self-motivation is obscured by external motivation. When behavior becomes too closely linked with external forces, self-motivation is lost. Because work motivation has traditionally depended upon particularly strong external rewards (such as pay and promotions), self-motivation at work has been difficult to sustain.

Workers quickly become habituated to external rewards, which eventually cease to have the desired motivational impact. After a while, employees work for two major reasons: to get paid and to avoid being fired. These motives do not stimulate outstanding efforts. They will never produce employees who care. They will never release high levels of energy.

Companies that depend too much on external rewards and threats to get things done do not achieve *long-term* high performance. External motivation is always temporary. It depends on the potency of the reward or threat being used. It may be possible to achieve satisfactory performance—and sometimes even short-term high performance—through external motivation, but high productivity, excellent quality, and outstanding customer service (the kind of performance that American industry so desperately needs) cannot be primarily externally motivated.

If high performance is going to be sustained, motivation must ultimately come from the inside out, rather than the outside in.

The Capacity for Self-Motivation

Even when we do not appear to be very self-motivated, the capacity for self-motivation still remains. Deep inside every human being is the yearning to be self-motivated rather than controlled by rewards, authority, or some other aspect of the external environment.

Highly motivated people possess their own internal incentives to act. They don't wait for external forces to motivate them (although external factors can enhance motivation). Highly motivated people are invariably driven by strong *internal* desires.

Every person has the capacity for high motivation. The energy is there. That energy must simply be released.

How Motivation Works

When we talk of motivation, we are really talking about the release of energy.

All human beings are essentially energy factories. Energy is continually and automatically manufactured through metabolism from the food we ingest. The energy derived from this food is then stored in the hundred billion or so cells that make up the human body. Every one of these cells becomes packed with energy, providing every person with a *virtually inexhaustible reservoir of energy,* just waiting to be used.

Unfortunately, most of this tremendous energy sits in our cells doing absolutely nothing, because it is never released. In fact, more than 90 percent of the energy stored in the human body never gets used at all. It is a great tragedy that although every employee has an *enormous internal storehouse of energy,* this energy is almost entirely wasted. When not used, energy dissipates, and is lost forever. This loss is both costly and unnecessary.

Motivation actually depends on emotions to release the pent-up energy stored inside the human body. According to Shad Helmstetter, "To motivate someone, anyone, to do anything, you must influence his emotions."[3] The strength of emotions comes from the release of hormones (most notably adrenaline) into the bloodstream.

All emotions begin with thoughts in the form of subjective, split-second evaluations of situations. Any situation can be experienced as positive or negative, depending on how the particular person interprets it. Positive emotions include such feelings as happiness, contentment, pride, interest, desire, hope, and excitement. Negative emotions include such feelings as sadness, boredom, anger, resentment, disgust, fear, anxiety, frustration, guilt, regret, and shame.

Consider a situation in which rumors of impending layoffs are circulating throughout an organization. An employee in that organization is summoned by her boss to a private meeting. What emotion do you think the employee might experience? Probably fear or anxiety. However, if a profitable new contract had just been awarded to that same organization, the employee would be more likely to greet the boss's request for a meeting with interest or excitement.

In other words, positive thoughts about a situation will trigger positive emotions and negative thoughts about a situation will trigger negative emotions.

There are two types of positive emotions. One type makes people feel good without necessarily energizing them. Happiness and contentment are examples of these positive/relaxing emotions. These emotions are triggered by thoughts that inform the person that all is well—perhaps a victory was won, a compliment was received, or some other positive event was experienced. In these circumstances, a temporary state of satisfaction has been attained. The feeling is one of relaxation, not of energy.

The second type of positive emotion is positive *and* energizing. Positive/energizing emotions include interest, excitement, and desire. When a person is feeling energetic, it is not just because of a good night's sleep. More likely it is because of positive/energizing emotions. Positive/energizing emotions make people want to do things, to be active, productive, and creative. *These emotions (especially desire) are the key to human motivation.*

When positive thoughts arouse positive/energizing emotions, large quantities of motivational energy are typically released. This, in turn, energizes productive and, most importantly, creative behavior. Creative behavior manifests itself when employees go beyond the "normal" requirements of the job and take initiative to solve a problem, improve a work procedure, or give a customer extraordinary service. This is the kind of behavior that characterizes the highly motivated employees described in Chapter 1. This motivating cycle is depicted in Figure 2-1.

Although negative emotions (such as fear and anger) can temporarily mobilize motivational energy, all negative emotions are ultimately de-energizing. Once the anger subsides, or the object of fear has been successfully avoided, people tend to feel emotionally drained.

Negative emotions cause enormous energy dissipation, making less

Figure 2-1. The motivating cycle.

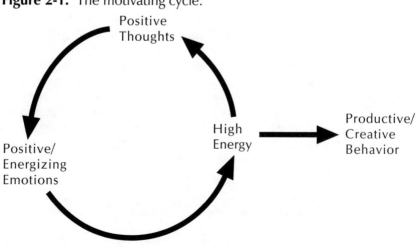

Figure 2-2. The demotivating cycle.

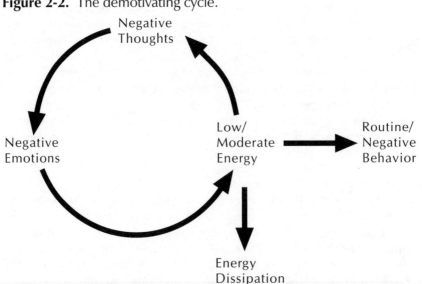

energy available to power behavior. When energy levels are low, more automatic *routine behavior* tends to be selected over creative behavior (which typically requires higher energy levels). Negative emotions also generate *negative behavior* (a destructive form of behavior to be discussed in more detail in Chapter 4). This demotivating cycle is depicted in Figure 2-2.

Clearly, positive emotions are vital to organizational effectiveness, since they are responsible for releasing so much constructive motivational energy.

In fact, it has been found that the single most important characteristic of high-performing companies is a high level of emotional energy.[4] The most successful companies in the world are emotionally charged.

There is no doubt about it: If organizations want to have highly motivated employees, they will have to put much more emphasis on emotions in the future. Organizations must recognize that emotions and motivation go hand in hand; you can't have one without the other. In particular, they will have to stimulate more positive/energizing emotions (especially desire) among their workforces. In the SuperMotivating organizations of the future, employees will be really excited about their work. They won't walk around like automatons or zombies.

Desire: The Driving Force Behind Self-Motivation

Desire is what propels us forward. It is desire that releases the tremendous motivational energy that all human beings possess. Desire has been responsible for instigating all the man-made miracles of the world, all scientific discoveries, and all commercial breakthroughs. Desire has motivated every visionary business leader to discover new products, develop breakthrough strategies, and pioneer new industries. When allowed to express itself, desire can be an incredibly creative force!

Desire differs from need. A *need* is something that is essential for the survival of a living creature. Most traditional theories of motivation have focused on the concept of need. According to these theories, human behavior is seen as governed by "need reduction."[5] When there is a need, behavior occurs to meet that need. Then homeostasis (satisfaction) takes over until the next need arises. According to this paradigm, people are rather passive and reactive.

In contrast, *desires* are things we actively want; they might make us happier and more effective, but we will not die without them. When we desire something strongly enough, we become very persistent in its pursuit. In fact, with strong enough desire, nothing is impossible. A full life requires the expression of desires.

Without desire, we would be stuck in one place. We would be completely satisfied. But we are not programmed to be satisfied. From our first breath of life, we *want*. As soon as we get what we want, we want more. Human beings are motivated by what they seek, not by what they have. "I want" is motivating; "I have" is not!

It is human nature to be dissatisfied with the status quo. Dissatisfaction gives rise to desire. Satisfaction is actually the absence of motivation. As Lawrence Miller has observed in *American Spirit*, "I have never met an excellent executive who was satisfied."[6] I would go even farther: I have never met an excellent human being who was satisfied. People may become accustomed to mediocrity, but they are never motivated by it.

The Eight Human Desires

There are eight major human desires, each of which has the potential for releasing enormous amounts of motivational energy. These are the desires for activity, ownership, power, affiliation, competence, achievement, recognition, and meaning. When these desires are allowed to find expression, great motivation is generated. When these desires are blocked, anger and frustration are the inevitable result.

In the sections that follow, each of these eight desires is described.

Desire for Activity

The desire for activity reflects the innate human orientation toward stimulation—to be active, to be engaged, and to enjoy life. Just as nature abhors a vacuum, we abhor boredom and monotony. In one experiment, subjects were paid a large sum of money to remain in a low-stimulation environment. Despite the excellent pay, not one of the subjects was able to endure more than two days of activity deprivation.

In our personal lives, we typically find extremely creative ways to avoid boredom. However, at work, there tend to be fewer options. Employees want to be active and involved. They want more variety in their work. They know that work should be more fun than it is now.

Today's workers have grown accustomed to endless hours of routine. They are willing to sit for a very long time in chairs, tapping on computer keyboards; they tolerate the mindless repetition of operating a machine or soldering connections on a circuit board; they are compelled to endure extensive bureaucratic delays; and they are conditioned to sitting (and half listening) in mind-dulling meetings without saying a word.

Many of us have become passive spectators, rather than active participants, in life and in work. We are not by nature passive and lethargic. We have just been conditioned to be that way. This is one explanation of why work motivation is so low.

Passivity, lethargy, and a sedentary lifestyle are not what the human mind and body were created for. When work fails to provide sufficient stimulation, we look elsewhere for it. That is why sports and games are so popular. They provide a motivating context of activity and a high level of involvement that work seldom does.

Desire for Ownership

From earliest childhood, we have an innate love for possessions. One of the most remarkable human activities is the propensity to collect all kinds of things, and it is utterly amazing what some people collect. From coins to stamps to homes to cars to knick-knacks, people want their piece of the pie. After a while, people learn that if they collect money, they can purchase anything else they want, and so money has become the dominant collectible in our society.

Ownership has become a measure of self-worth. Owning things makes people feel better about themselves. In fact, in contemporary society, the more a person owns, the better he or she is considered to be. How much one possesses has become the primary yardstick of human value.

When someone owns something, he or she takes much more pride in it. People will spend countless hours mowing their lawns, washing their cars and boats, and cleaning their houses. They even spend large sums of money for the equipment and related paraphernalia.

Ownership is certainly not limited to material possessions and tangible items. *Psychological ownership* may be even more important than material ownership. Consider how protective people are about their ideas, and how sensitive they are when their ideas are criticized or ignored. Human history is littered with people who fought and died to protect ideas they felt strongly about.

In the workplace, we have scarcely begun to scratch the surface in discovering opportunities for satisfying employees' potent desire for ownership. How many employees take real pride in their workspace, their equipment, the products they produce, and the company they work for? If they don't, it's only because their desire for ownership has been frustrated.

Employees want to "own" their work, and they are willing to work very long hours, even for less pay, to experience the spirit of ownership. "New breed" employees want significant input into their work. They want to feel responsible for their jobs and major projects.

The desire for ownership can release enormous energy in each and every employee if we simply create an environment conducive to it. It should not be at all surprising that in some organizations, increasing the sense of employee ownership in work has dramatically improved productivity and quality.

Desire for Power

The desire for power is also deeply rooted in human nature. Unfortunately, a great many people today feel that they are powerless over the external forces shaping their lives. There are a great many external controls, both inside and outside of work, that rob employees of a sense of personal power. People want to make choices. They desperately want control over their own destinies.

Traditionally, organizations have been highly controlling places. The conventional model of power in organizations consists of a strong manager giving orders to a weak employee, who follows obediently. According to this model, employees are expected to trade their freedom for a paycheck. Today, an increasing number of employees are demanding their freedom back. As I travel from company to company, I regularly hear employees say things like: "I want to make decisions about my work." "Why do I have to ask permission about everything?"

People naturally resist external control. Even young children rebel when parents place too many restrictions on them. Why should adults be expected to passively accept major restrictions on *their* freedom? Most employees have very few choices. They are told when to come to work, where to work, what to wear, what to do, how to do it, when to take breaks, when to leave, etc.

Enlightened organizations everywhere are beginning to address the desire for power. Empowerment has become a major organizational theme. Companies are discovering that by creating an empowering environment, they are able to release enormous quantities of previously untapped motivational energy.

Desire for Affiliation

We human beings are social creatures. We have a deep desire to interact and socialize with one another. Although some of us may desire more social contact than others, there is little doubt that the desire for affiliation exists in everyone. This is the primary reason why solitary confinement is considered to be such a severe punishment.

Work provides extremely important affiliative opportunities. It provides rich and varied social contacts and relationships. In fact, for many people, work is the major source of social interaction.

Despite the increase in home-based businesses, a recent study showed that only 7 percent of employees would work at home if they had a choice.[7] This finding further supports the importance of social interaction in the American workplace. Social support and helping relationships (especially from peers) are among the many benefits that work provides.

Work groups—from departments to unions to informal groups—provide employees with a strong sense of social identity. This sense of identity is one of the major reasons for the explosive growth of the team concept, which is truly revolutionizing the American workplace.

Desire for Competence

The quest for competence begins on the first day of life, as the infant strives for mastery over its very limited environment, and grows progressively more important throughout childhood. But it doesn't end there; recent research has shown that competence is a potent lifelong pursuit.

Competence may be the most fundamental human desire because human survival depends on it. Very little else is possible without sufficient competence. Competence is also at the very core of self-esteem. In fact, self-esteem is really nothing more than *self-perceived* competence. There is no better feeling in life than the feeling of being competent.

Competence requires learning, and human beings are natural learners. The work environment ought to be the most fertile territory for learning. There are so many opportunities to learn and so many skills to master at work.

Competence is a deep and abiding desire. Virtually all employees welcome opportunities to feel more competent.

Desire for Achievement

Another powerful human desire is the desire for achievement. Because of its centrality to work, achievement has probably been the subject of more motivational research than any other desire.

It has been said that in all people there lies the "seed of achievement," which, if used, can carry them to undreamed-of heights.[8] Achievement has also been described as one of the fundamental routes to happiness.[9]

Achievement has a lot to do with the feeling of *succeeding*. Although success means different things to different people, everybody thrives on some form of success. For some, it means creating a masterpiece; for others, it means completing a project on time; and for still others, it means just taking a step in the right direction.

Consistent with this desire for achievement, people *like* accomplishing things at work. Employees are not inherently lazy and recalcitrant. Under the right conditions, they enjoy hard work and overcoming obstacles (as long as the obstacles are not overwhelming). Easy victories are not very satisfying. The challenging life is what really motivates.

The ultimate satisfaction from achievement is pride, or a feeling of accomplishment. When people feel good about what they have accomplished, no external reward is needed. In fact, external rewards sometimes detract from the intrinsic pleasure of pure achievement.

Desire for Recognition

No desire is more clearly universal than the desire for recognition. Everyone wants to feel appreciated by others, to be positively recognized for his or her merits and contributions. The desire for recognition is deeply ingrained in human nature.

All of us have a virtually insatiable hunger for genuine positive recognition, which is amply demonstrated in our appetite for honors, medals, trophies, titles, and the like. These tokens of esteem hold great significance for the human ego.

One of the major complaints I hear from employees is that they receive too little positive recognition for their efforts (especially for their extra efforts). Employees complain that supervisors see screw-ups all the time, but rarely see the positive things employees do.

We all know how difficult it is to keep going without encouragement and appreciation. Everybody needs an occasional pat on the back and a word of encouragement from time to time. Without it, motivation diminishes rapidly. Desire for recognition is so strong that people who do not receive enough positive recognition will often seek negative recognition by provoking punishment. Some people who receive inadequate recognition become seriously depressed.

Recognition can be given in a great many diverse ways, from money to gifts to a simple "thank you." However it is expressed, recognition is one of the most powerful forces that American business can use to unleash human energy and productivity.

Desire for Meaning

"Man's search for meaning is the primary force in his life." So said Viktor Frankl—who devoted his life to studying the psychology of meaning—in his classic book *Man's Search for Meaning*.[10] All human beings want to feel that their life matters, that they are living for a reason other than just to make a living and make stockholders richer. Frankl even showed how the desire for meaning kept him and others alive in Nazi concentration camps. The desire for meaning is a powerful motivational force.

People want to feel significant, and want to feel that their efforts, however humble, are making a difference. The human spirit seeks more than a mundane life. It seeks meaning beyond survival and wealth. All people want to find something they can truly believe in and commit to—a mission that transcends the ordinary and transforms their existence into something extraordinary. The more people care about something, the more they will strive to make it happen. Many people are willing to give their lives for a cause that they deeply believe in.

Although work has unlimited potential for meaning, people are likely to find more meaning in religion, in political causes, or in charity than in the work they do.

Unfortunately, most companies have done very little to address their employees' desire for meaning. One bright light on the horizon is the quality movement. Quality is something many employees are finding meaningful and worthy of their commitment.

Resistance to Self-Motivation

If our desires are so strong, why, then, does self-motivation appear so weak? The potential for self-motivation is always there. Although there are individual differences in the strength of desires, the eight major desires are *always* present—in *everyone.*

Unfortunately, many people's desires have been frustrated by family, institutional, and societal constraints. Therefore, these desires often lie dormant, waiting to be awakened.

This resistance to self-motivation starts out as parental discipline and negativity (the well-intentioned noes, don'ts, and can'ts) and then expands into broader institutional constraints that conspire to kill the human spirit. Many organizations prefer docile, conforming employees to those who are driven by desire. Status quo–oriented managers have long found that docile employees cause fewer problems than their ambitious counterparts.

Too many institutions view desires as negative (rather than creative) forces, and have traditionally frowned upon their expression. For example, the most ambitious employees are often labeled "aggressive" and scorned by the so-called "team players" in the organization. In other words, it's all right for employees to have desires as long as they are kept under control.

Employees *want* to be active, but their work often forces them to work passively. Employees *want* to enjoy their work, but their jobs are often dull and tedious. Employees *want* to make choices regarding their work, but their work is often far too rigidly programmed. Employees *want* to work cooperatively in teams, but they are often forced into noninteractive and competitive working arrangements. Employees *want* to develop new competencies, but they are often stuck in dead-end jobs. Employees *want* to achieve more ambitious goals, but they are often punished if they set goals too high and then fail to attain them. Employees *want* more recognition, but the only recognition many of them get is being reprimanded for mistakes. Employees *want* to feel pride in quality, but they discover that management values production more than it does quality.

These and other powerful countermotivational forces exist in most organizations, blocking the self-motivating desires of the workforce and wasting the greatest resource that companies possess. When self-motivation encounters resistance, all the positive energy that could have been the source of outstanding productivity and quality is suppressed, elicits destructive behavior, or both. Organizations that frustrate employees' desires eventually find themselves full of frustrated people.

Resistance to self-motivation is cumulative. It is collected throughout life. One experience does not kill self-motivation. It is the hundreds and thousands of experiences deposited in people's memory banks that lead them to believe that their desires will not be fulfilled—and certainly not at work. But it doesn't have to be that way!

The First-Day-of-Work Phenomenon

Most of us probably remember our first day of work. We couldn't wait to get started, to meet new people, and to accomplish great things. Once we arrived at work, there were smiles all around. We were nervous, but that only added to the excitement. We came to do a great job, to set the world on fire. We expected the best from ourselves, and from the new organization we had just joined.

However, for most of us, from that promising beginning, the general trend was rapidly downhill. The hopes and excitement all too often turned into anxiety and boredom. The honeymoon was over. After a short while, things changed. We learned that it was best to just "do our job, play it safe, and not make any waves." As time passed, and other first days came and went, we learned that the tremendous promise of that first day of work would never be realized.

For some people this process takes only a few days; for others, weeks or months. But however long it takes, the saddest thing in organizational life is to see so many employees become increasingly discouraged and demotivated.

Coping Strategies

In order to reduce their frustration, some employees adopt personal coping strategies. They remove themselves from the resistance by creating a protected niche for themselves (perhaps in a technical area where they are uniquely competent) or gravitating to the top of the organization (where there is less resistance) or just giving up. Unfortunately, most employees simply give up. Furthermore, many managers (who have been able to muster greater personal resources to overcome organizational resistance) evidence very little empathy for those who possess fewer personal resources. This is why so many organizations remain as demotivating as they do.

Some organizations try to cope with this problem by using elaborate interviewing and testing methods to select employees with greater desire. Unfortunately, when these "highly motivated" people start work, they find little organizational support for their high personal motivation. Other organizations spend freely on motivational training, which does nothing to change the organization that employees return to after the training.

A more *realistic* and *permanent* solution is to create an environment that is much more conducive to self-motivation and able to release the eight human desires described in this chapter.

Chapter 3 deals with this challenge.

Notes

1. A. Kohn, *Punished by Rewards* (Boston: Houghton Mifflin, 1993).
2. D. Waitley, *The Psychology of Winning* (New York: Berkley Books, 1984), p. 65.
3. S. Helmstetter, *What to Say When You Talk to Yourself* (Scottsdale, Ariz.: Grindle Press, 1986), p. 168.
4. G. Jacobs and R. Macfarlane, *The Vital Corporation* (Englewood Cliffs, N.J.: Prentice-Hall, 1990).
5. P. T. Young, *Motivation and Emotion* (New York: Wiley, 1961).
6. L. Miller, *American Spirit* (New York: Warner Books, 1984), p. 55.
7. M. Maccoby, *Why Work?* (New York: Simon & Schuster, 1988).
8. N. Hill, *Think and Grow Rich* (New York: Fawcett Crest, 1960).
9. V. de Bono, *The Happiness Purpose* (London: Penguin, 1979).
10. V. Frankl, *Man's Search for Meaning* (New York: Pocket Books, 1963), p. 154.

3

Changing the Context of Work

In Chapter 2, we talked about the enormous potential for self-motivation (driven by the eight universal desires) that is *always* present in *every* employee. Unfortunately, this self-motivation has been consistently resisted by even more powerful countermotivational forces. In this chapter, we begin to see how work can be "motivationally reengineered" so that the power of self-motivation can be released.

The Motivating Potential of Work

No other type of activity is so broadly motivating, or has as much psychological and spiritual importance, as work. As adults, we spend most of our waking hours involved in some form of work. For many people, work is their major source of personal identity and meaning.

We don't just work for money. Even when we are not working, most of us find some kind of "work" to do, whether it is fixing up the house, tending the garden, sprucing up the yard, maintaining the car, or involving ourselves in a hobby. Without work, we would deteriorate (and, unfortunately, when we retire, many of us do). Under the right conditions, even the humblest forms of labor can be deeply satisfying. If we didn't have work to do, we would have to create it!

As a matter of fact, multimillionaires (who certainly aren't in financial need of work) are some of the hardest-working people in the world. In addition, surprisingly enough, 80 percent of all lottery winners go back to work soon after winning, despite their newly acquired financial independence.

On several occasions in my own life, I have temporarily retired, only to promptly return to work. There is something in me, and in most other people, that craves work. There are some aspects of work that we love, others that we hate, but there is something about work that seems to bring us back. As Benjamin Franklin is reputed to have said, "There's nothing wrong with retirement as long as it doesn't interfere with one's work!"

The Demotivating Reality of Work

Despite the motivating potential of work, most work is not very motivating. While some people are fortunate enough to find jobs and careers they love, for most people, work is a duty, toil, labor, something that has to be done. Work is called "work" because it has traditionally been viewed as being unpleasant. Even the Bible tells us that when Adam sinned, part of God's punishment was a lifetime sentence of work![1]

At the end of the day, most workers feel relief rather than satisfaction. At the end of a work week, they say things like "Thank God it's Friday." When was the last time you heard someone say "Thank God it's Monday"?

The truth of the matter is that most people dread Monday mornings. There are more first-time heart attacks on Monday mornings than at any other time during the week. It has even been found that couples fight most on Wednesdays because it is the farthest point from the weekend in both directions!

Early in my career as a corporate manager, I was assigned to a plant owned by a large manufacturing company in which most jobs were so boring, tedious, dirty, noisy, and tiring that the workers openly hated them. It was only the generous wages, benefits, and retirement plan that kept the employees coming back each day and kept them working (albeit at the minimum level of performance tolerated by the company).

It didn't take me long to see that their work was causing many of the workers to act in antisocial ways. There was extensive antagonism, blaming, obscene language, hostility toward management, fights among peers, sabotage of equipment, work slowdowns, and obsessive complaining. However, when I observed these very same employees outside of work, they were actively involved in, and excited about, a wide variety of leisure-time pursuits. I kept asking myself why this same level of desire and energy couldn't be tapped at work.

Deep inside, I knew that work didn't have to be demotivating. I knew that operating a machine (or any other job, for that matter) had the potential to be interesting, challenging, and meaningful. I also knew that these workers (in fact, *all* workers) possessed plenty of energy and desire. We, as management, simply weren't tapping that desire and releasing the positive energies of the workforce.

This is when I started developing the "work context" concepts I share with you in this chapter.

Task and Context

All work has two aspects: the *task* and the *context*. These two aspects of work are depicted in Figure 3-1.

A task is the *technical content* of work, that's all. The context is everything else.

Most work tasks are intrinsically boring. In fact, I would go so far as to say that virtually *all* tasks are, in themselves, boring, or will eventually become so when they are repeated often enough.

How long would you stay interested in baseball if all you did was throw the ball back and forth the same way every time? How long would you stay interested in attending meetings if each meeting was identical to the previous one? How long would you remain interested in performing

Figure 3-1. The work context model.

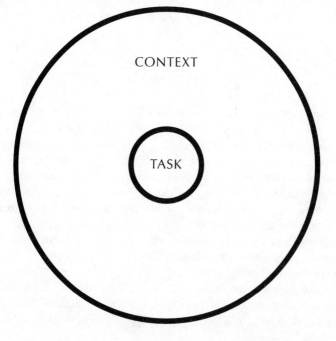

any task without some variety? Any task will become repetitive and boring unless some enhancement (such as variety) is added. In fact, strip any task down to its basics and it will be B-O-R-I-N-G.

If you want to make throwing a baseball enjoyable, after a while, you will begin to vary the trajectory and the speed of the ball. You will throw some pop-ups, some fast balls, and some grounders. You will make some balls easy to catch and others more difficult. You might even adopt a scoring system.

I doubt whether anyone could tolerate just throwing a ball back and forth, back and forth, for very long. Just think how terrible it would be if you had to perform this task all day long, day in and day out.

But that is almost exactly what I saw when I first observed the workers in the manufacturing plant. These workers had to perform the same highly structured tasks over and over again. Furthermore, the working environment added insult to injury. The plant was old, drab, and dirty; the machines were noisy; dust flew all over the place; and the temperature in the plant ranged from fifty degrees in the winter to well over ninety degrees in the summer. All the while, supervisors incessantly prodded employees to work faster and to produce more and more product.

Unfortunately, this is what I too often see when I visit factories and offices around the world: a preponderance of boring, tedious, demotivating work.

For most of my career, I had internalized the widely held management belief that not much could be done to make a boring task interesting or challenging, much less exciting.

But, as you will see, this is *not* really true.

The Context of Golf

Golf is a superb example of an *intrinsically boring* task! However, before the avid golfers reading this book jump on me, let me explain.

Most people who play golf love it. Golfers are almost fanatical about their sport. What is it about golf that is so motivating? I certainly don't think it is the repetitive behavior of walking long distances just to use various funny-looking tools to hit a small round object into a little hole, only to take out the object and put it into seventeen other identical holes. What's more, people spend huge amounts of time and money to participate in this "boring" task.

Any objective observer would have to admit that the basic, stripped-down "task" of golf is really rather silly. What could be duller than spending half a day hitting a ball into eighteen little holes? (In fact, did you realize that an average golfer swings a golf club for only about three minutes in every four hours of golf?) If that was all there were to golf, how excited do you think golfers would be about their sport?

What makes golf so highly motivating is its *contextual factors,* which have been added to the basic game, including the variety (e.g., golf course terrain, diversity of clubs and strokes), the aesthetic pleasure of the golf course, exercise (flexible enough to suit almost everyone), positive social interaction, challenges posed by the obstacles, the unique scorekeeping system, healthy competition (particularly competing against one's own score), unlimited potential for improvement, immediate feedback, the frequent recognition, and, of course, the joyous celebrations at the nineteenth hole!

The reason for golf's popularity is certainly not that the basic task is so inspiring, but that the *context* that has been built into the total game is so motivating. It is the context of golf, not the golf task itself, that releases so much motivational energy in people. The same principle applies to most of the hundreds of other sports and games that are so popular around the world. It is the context, rather than the task itself, that keeps people coming back.

One of the major premises of this book is that if a motivating context can be added to sports and games (most of which involve intrinsically boring tasks), then the same can be done for operating a machine or performing routine office duties. Any work can be made more motivating by installing contextual factors similar to those that exist in play.

Imagine, if you will, how motivating golf would be if it were designed like a typical work task. How motivated would you be if your assigned task was to drive the ball off the twelfth tee? That's all you are allowed to do: just hit the ball off the tee, over and over again, according to a predetermined "production" schedule. Once you have performed your task, someone else takes over for you. In addition, your boss tells you precisely how, when, and where you are supposed to hit the ball, with no variation allowed. You get almost no positive feedback on your performance for six months or a year, at which time your performance is subjectively ranked against the performance of others doing the same task. However, if you hit the ball incorrectly, you are immediately reprimanded. How much fun would this version of golf be?

Unfortunately, very little attention is given to the context in which work tasks are performed. The prevailing attitude is: "Work shouldn't be fun anyway!" or "That isn't what employees are being paid for!" This explains why so much work is demotivating, and why it stays that way.

The Tom Sawyer Phenomenon

In his classic novel *The Adventures of Tom Sawyer*,[2] Mark Twain tells the story of how, on one beautiful Saturday, when all the other kids were free to play, Tom Sawyer was sentenced by his Aunt Polly to a day of whitewashing her picket fence. The story tells how Tom conceived a brilliant strategy to recruit others in the neighborhood to perform the onerous task for him.

Initially, the other kids laughed at Tom for having to perform such an "awful" job on such a beautiful day. However, Tom was able to convince them that it was actually great fun to paint the fence. By the end of the day, the fence was completely painted and, according to Twain, "Tom was literally rolling in wealth," acquired from the kids who actually paid him for the privilege of doing his job!

Tom Sawyer was dreading the prospect of whitewashing his aunt's fence. After all, whitewashing fences was not very motivating to him. In fact, Tom looked forward to it about as much as most workers look forward to Monday mornings!

Tom wanted to spend his Saturday "having fun" (that's what his self-motivating desires were telling him), and, in his mind, whitewashing a fence didn't qualify as fun. Tom's dominant desire was for enjoyable *activity*, such as fishing and swimming. Tom could not have cared less about the fence or how it looked, so he didn't feel any personal *ownership* in the task. Being forced to whitewash the fence against his will didn't make Tom feel that he had much personal *power*. He was expected to perform the task alone, so it wasn't going to satisfy his desire for *affiliation*. He didn't have any aspirations for improving his *competence* as a fence painter. He didn't view whitewashing the fence as a worthwhile *achievement*. He failed to see any significant positive *recognition* accruing from this punitive assignment. In addition, the task held no real *meaning* for his life. As far as Tom was concerned, the prospect of whitewashing the fence was thoroughly demotivating.

However, Tom Sawyer was not your average boy. He possessed exceptional personal resources. Being a creative fellow, he was able to turn the situation to his advantage. Tom transformed what he thought was going to be one of the most boring days of his life into a fun and profitable adventure. He turned whitewashing the fence into a motivating "game."

The game he designed (desire for activity) was to see how many others he could get to paint the fence for him. By selling the "privilege" of painting the fence, Tom acquired money and valuable trinkets (desire for ownership). He used his leadership ability and took control of the situation (desire for power). Throughout the day, he was constantly interacting with his peers (desire for affiliation). He used his ample problem-solving skills and ingenuity (desire for competence) to devise and carry out his cunning strategy. He succeeded spectacularly in recruiting others to perform the task (desire for achievement). He received tremendous positive attention from the other kids (desire for recognition). And last but not least, Tom not only got the fence beautifully whitewashed (desire for meaning), but "elaborately coated and recoated" such that Aunt Polly's "astonishment was almost unspeakable." It was quite a day's work!

Although Tom accomplished the task in a rather unconventional manner, the fence did get beautifully whitewashed, and both Tom and his workers had a terrific time in the process. By building his own motivators into the context of the boring task, Tom Sawyer was able to satisfy both his self-motivating desires and those of his "workers."

There is a great deal we can learn from Tom Sawyer and his creative use of "motivational engineering" (although Tom didn't realize he was a motivational engineer).

Most workers are not as personally resourceful as Tom Sawyer, nor are they sufficiently empowered to independently transform boring and tedious work into enjoyment and challenge. In fact, if they attempted such a ploy in a conventional company, they would probably be severely reprimanded, and possibly fired. Because of this, research indicates that the most self-motivated workers tend to join smaller and emerging companies, which are more likely to allow them to use their personal resourcefulness.[3]

The point I am making by citing the Tom Sawyer example is this: Even without altering the basic nature of work, any task or job can be transformed from *demotivating* to *motivating* simply by changing its context.

Motivators and Demotivators

Of course, work is much more than just a single task or even a series of tasks. It is made up of a large number of other elements, including co-workers, supervisors, managers, customers, the physical environment, rules, work standards, work roles, equipment, raw materials, training, rewards, disciplinary methods, and performance evaluations.

In fact, for most workers, the actual tasks they perform are less significant than all the *contextual factors* in which those tasks are embedded. When employees talk about their jobs, they are referring as much to their peers, their supervisor, company policies, compensation, discipline, communications, social events, and so on, as to the tasks they perform. Not only do employees talk a lot about these contextual aspects of work, they also tend to feel strongly about them.

Many of these contextual aspects of work can be classified as either motivators or demotivators. A *motivator* is any aspect of work that arouses *positive/energizing emotions,* most notably desire. A *demotivator* is any aspect of work that arouses *negative emotions,* such as boredom, fear, anger, and resentment. All work contexts include a substantial number of motivators and demotivators, as depicted in Figure 3-2.

Unfortunately, in many, if not most, organizations today, the context of work tends to have a greater abundance of demotivators than of motivators. The key to fostering SuperMotivation in any organization is to *reduce the demotivators* and *add motivators* to the context of work. How to accomplish this is the subject of most of the rest of this book.

Two Approaches to Motivation

As we have seen, the real challenge of motivation is not to change the individual worker, but to change the context of his or her work. Tradi-

Figure 3-2. Motivators and demotivators.

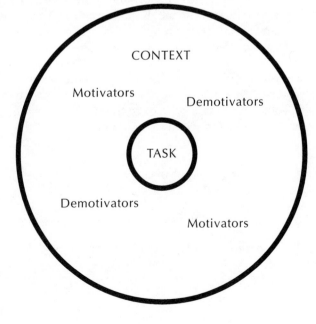

tional approaches to motivation have tended to focus on changing the individual. Many psychologists have proposed that if you can change people's thinking (especially the attitudes underlying thought), you can change their motivation. In theory, this is correct; changing thought patterns *can* increase motivation. But *permanently* changing individual thought patterns is quite difficult, time-consuming, and costly. Furthermore, when you put these newly motivated people back into their demotivating work contexts, the motivation rarely lasts.

The key to motivation, then, lies in the work context. It is also the only area where managers have any real control. Changing the context of work is, by far, the most *cost-effective* and *permanent* solution to the problem of motivation in the workplace.

Creating a more motivating work environment will ultimately help *all* employees to think and feel more positively about their work and will release enormous motivational energy—an approach that is clearly more efficient than trying to change the attitudes of each and every individual employee.

Changing the context of work is not manipulative. It doesn't compel employees to do anything in particular against their natural inclinations (which would constitute "external motivation"). What it does do is create an environment conducive to self-motivation and high performance.

Just as Tom Sawyer transformed the work of whitewashing his aunt's fence from drudgery into a fun and profitable adventure, all organizations have the opportunity to change the way employees experience their work. Every organization or department can be transformed from a place where employees "do their time" to a place where employees "do their best."

If you want to stop the tremendous drain of human energy in your organization, dramatically increase the productivity and quality consciousness of your workforce, and reduce the terrible waste of resources on motivational programs that don't work, then read on.

Notes

1. Genesis 3:17.
2. M. Twain, *The Adventures of Tom Sawyer* (New York: Bantam Books, 1966; first published in 1876).
3. S. C. Brandt, *Entrepreneuring in Established Companies* (New York: New American Library, 1986).

4

Identifying and Defeating Demotivators

Managers typically rely on rewards to motivate workers. However, unless they can reduce the *demotivators* that pervade most organizations, these rewards will not be effective. Even worse than that, rewards offered in the presence of demotivators are often met with cynicism and contempt.

Demotivators have done more to undermine motivation in the American workplace than any other force. They cause workers to reduce, consciously or unconsciously, the amount of productive energy they use in their jobs. These powerful demotivating influences have had a profoundly negative impact on both motivation and performance. They are the number one entropic force (cause of energy depletion) in organizations.[1]

Demotivators exist in every organization in one form or another, but they are not necessarily egregious wrongs. They are usually part of the normal operating practices of the organization, more the result of neglect than of design. Demotivators exist simply because they are *allowed* to exist. The prevalence of demotivators in the American workplace attests to the fact that their removal has not been considered a high priority.

One employee wistfully remarked, "If it weren't for all the demotivators, this could be such a wonderful place to work!"

How Demotivators Affect Employees

Many organizations have created a demotivating work context in which employees with enormous personal desire feel blocked from expressing those desires by what they perceive as arbitrary and unnecessary organizational constraints.

It is no secret that fear and anger, both expressed and repressed, are rampant in organizations today, and demotivators are responsible for much of this. Furthermore, employees are increasingly venting their negative emotions in the form of negative behavior (such as criticizing management, withholding effort, sabotaging the work of others, and even perpetrating criminal behavior against the company). In fact, Martin Sprouse, in his book *Sabotage in the American Workplace*, presents more than 100 first-hand accounts of negative behavior at work—most of it caused by demotivating conditions.[2] It has been estimated that these employee practices cost American businesses up to $170 billion each year![3]

Demotivators also adversely affect the health of American workers. Research has indicated that work-related ailments—in no small part due to the prevalence of demotivators—account for 100,000 deaths and 340,000 disabilities and cost American industry another $150 billion each year.[4] In addition, it has been found that 75 percent of all mental illness is at least partially work-related![5]

In companies everywhere, demotivators are often concealed or ignored. And because managers are, for the most part, isolated from the daily frustrations of the workforce, many of them simply don't appreciate how serious the demotivation problem is.

Too many managers underestimate the importance of what they consider to be minor irritations in their organizations or departments, not realizing how large these irritations loom in the subjective experience of employees. To employees stuck in the middle of them, they are not minor at all.

Although demotivators often appear to an outsider to be relatively trivial, they tend to affect people far out of proportion to their actual size. In fact, overreacting emotionally is human nature.

When there is a negative response to a situation or circumstance, a magnification effect often occurs. Negative emotions tend to enlarge the perception of problems, causing problems that might in themselves be relatively minor to become larger than life. Furthermore, since demotivators rarely exist in isolation, they interact to increase the intensity of each of the individual concerns. As a result, the negative feelings attributable to one demotivator combine with the negative feelings attributable to other demotivators to create a much larger pool of negative emotions—all of which are extremely damaging to employee morale. As one commentator described it: "Ten units of fearful thoughts and ten units of fearful feelings can continue to multiply exponentially; the net result is not twenty units of fear, but one thousand or ten thousand units of anxiety."[6]

The Need to Declare War on Demotivators

We must never underestimate the insidiously negative impact of demotivators in any organization. *This is why all organizations must declare war on demotivators!* Demotivation in the workplace *must* be defeated. In fact, I recommend to all my clients that before they attempt any new motivational programs, they at least begin to "search and destroy" the most serious demotivators.

No motivational program can ever be successfully superimposed on top of demotivators. Piling rewards on top of rewards without reducing demotivators is futile. No matter how powerful the new motivational initiatives might be, existing demotivators will eventually cancel them out. The bad taste demotivators leave remains long after the good taste of rewards is gone.

Demotivators, such as the ones discussed below, are the major enemy of any organization aspiring to SuperMotivation. Ignoring them will speak volumes about the organization's ambivalent attitudes toward employees and their concerns, whereas a strong effort by management to attack these demotivators will send a powerfully positive message to all employees.

Major Demotivators

Demotivators come in hundreds of different varieties. Each organization has its own ways of demotivating employees. The major demotivators that follow have been identified from surveys of hundreds of organizations and from interviews with thousands of employees around the world. Chances are you will recognize many, if not most, of these demotivators. (If you don't recognize them, others in your organization certainly will!)

Politics

There is a political side to almost every organization. This is the largely informal aspect of organizational life involving the competition for power, influence, resources, favor, and scarce promotions. Politics generally operates according to unwritten rules of success that send subtle, ambiguous, and anxiety-producing messages to employees about "politically correct" behaviors (such as who to fear, who to appease, who to avoid, and who to blame) if they want to keep their jobs, advance in the organization, and acquire coveted resources.

Although political savvy may be perceived as important by some employees, "politicking" is viewed with derision by *most* employees, who perceive it to be a wasteful management game that almost always affects them negatively. Whenever decisions are not clearly performance-based, they are typically attributed to politics. This perception is supported by first-hand accounts or rumors about people who didn't seem to deserve advancement, but who used politics to get ahead in their careers, and other stories about those who deserved advancement, but didn't get it because they failed to play the political game well enough.

In many organizations, it does seem as if politicians advance faster than good workers, and as if being liked (especially by those in authority) is more important than being effective. To make matters worse, the best technical performers are often among the worst politicians.

Dysfunctional organizational politics can be reduced by making every effort to eliminate secret "unwritten rules" for granting rewards, promotions, and resource allocations. All decision making should be done in the open, based on well-documented, objective decision-making criteria. Moreover, frank discussions of past instances of political decision making, coupled with a commitment to avoid these practices in the future, will go a long way toward establishing a work environment in which corporate politicians are no longer rewarded for their negative and demoralizing political behaviors.

Unclear Expectations

Without realizing it, management often sends a bewildering array of mixed messages that confuse, rather than guide, employees. "Maximize production!" "Quality is job one!" "Give customers your complete attention!" "Reduce customer contact time!" "Increase long-term profits!" "Reduce costs immediately!" "Work faster!" "Work safer!" "Be innovative!" "Keep machines operating at maximum output!" After a while, workers realize that when everything is a priority, nothing is a priority. Employees also figure out that management is confused about what it really wants. Furthermore, many organizations tell employees to do one thing and then reward another.

When expectations are unclear, employees feel anxious and sometimes behave erratically. They waste enormous amounts of energy working on the wrong tasks, accomplishing the wrong results, and becoming extremely frustrated in the process. In such an environment, few employees dare to take risks or exercise creativity, because one misstep could detonate a land mine.

Unclear expectations can be addressed through a conscious effort to reduce mixed messages, especially those pertaining to organizational goals and priorities. Management should regularly review all expectations for internal consistency. Employees should also be asked regularly about their understanding of organizational expectations and priorities. Most managers are actually shocked when they discover how little is *really* understood. The understanding of expectations should never be taken for granted.

Unnecessary Rules

Some parameters are necessary to establish the "rules of the game" in any organization. However, unless checked, rules tend to proliferate far beyond what is necessary to achieve an acceptable level of organizational control. Most rules are negative and tell employees only what *not* to do. When employees are too focused on avoiding the negatives, they don't make many positive contributions.

One entrepreneurial company started innocently enough by developing a few behavioral guidelines for employees, but these "helpful hints" eventually evolved into a two-hundred-page policies manual backed by rigid disciplinary procedures. Unnecessary rules began smothering the life out of this previously dynamic and innovative business.

To avoid this type of situation, new rules should be adopted only if they are absolutely necessary. And all existing rules should be reviewed at least once a year. Those that no longer serve a useful purpose should be promptly eliminated. In addition, policy manuals should be rigorously edited to remove unnecessary rules and to clarify those that remain.

Poorly Designed Work

Just as rules expand beyond what is really needed, work also has expansive tendencies. Organizations can become locked into activities and procedures that are perpetuated long after they have become obsolete.

Many work tasks have become hopelessly cluttered with unnecessary steps, excessive paperwork, unjustified approvals, frequent bottlenecks, avoidable delays, enormous waste, duplication of effort, and bureaucratic reporting requirements. Tasks that should take minutes often take hours, and tasks that should take hours require days or weeks to complete.[7] Furthermore, many work tasks are so unsafely designed that they inflict great harm on employees' bodies and cost American industry billions of dollars in lost time, medical costs, and workers' compensation benefits—not to mention the devastating impact on employee morale.

As we see in Chapter 7, the work reengineering movement is a noble attempt to address work design problems. There is no doubt that work tasks should be regularly reassessed for their efficiency and effectiveness, with special attention to eliminating unnecessary actions, delays, inspections, approvals, rework, and unsafe conditions. However, as we also see, technical work redesign is not enough.

Unproductive Meetings

While we're discussing unproductive work, we would be remiss not to mention unproductive meetings. Have you ever noticed how often employees leave meetings looking exhausted, battered, and bored? It has been said that "nothing saps the spirit like watching, powerless, as a meeting wanders into oblivion."[8]

Meetings tend to create negative expectations in most people. The next time a meeting is announced, you can just hear them groan: "Oh, no, not another meeting!" For most employees, meetings are an unwelcome interruption in their work schedules.

According to Gary English, "When people say they went to a meeting and 'nothing happened,' they are usually saying, 'something happened, and it was bad.' Their time was trivialized and so were they."[9] Furthermore, many meetings are often accompanied by hidden agendas, manipulation, and domination by a few so that everything *except* collaboration is encouraged.

Given the strong human desire for affiliation, it is somewhat surprising that meetings elicit such a negative reaction from employees. There is nothing wrong with meetings per se, just with meetings that are unnecessary, disorganized, passive, lengthy, political, and unproductive—which most are. Too often, meeting participants feel as if they are engaged in an exercise in futility, wasting valuable time that could be spent in more productive ways, and few employees expect much follow-up. In fact, it has been determined that excessive and unproductive meetings drive more talented employees out of companies than any other single cause.[10]

The productivity of meetings can be greatly enhanced by providing training for meeting leaders and establishing guidelines for running meetings most effectively. Also, use meeting formats that encourage everyone to participate. Furthermore, when appropriate, more cost-effective alternatives to in-person meetings (such as conference calls, computer-mediated communications, and video teleconferencing) should be considered.

In Chapter 8, you will find many practical and highly motivating suggestions for improving the quality of meetings in your organization.

Lack of Follow-Up

Meetings are not the only aspect of corporate life plagued by lack of follow-up. Have you ever experienced the all-too-common organizational disease of "program-itis"? Many well-intentioned but isolated initiatives aren't sustained long enough to make a difference. A new program is set in motion, and employees' hopes are raised ("Maybe this time it will be different"), only to be dashed. What often happens is that the sponsor loses focus, interest, or authority, or another "crisis" comes along to derail the program. So, another promising program dies—and along with it, employees' hopes for long-term improvement.

Employees in one company use a colorful acronym that clearly expresses their frustration with lack of follow-up: BOHICA (*Bend Over, Here It Comes Again!*). And a manager I once interviewed proclaimed with mock pride the dubious distinction that he had attended "several hundred management training seminars *without the slightest bit of follow-up!*"

To counteract this, a "process mentality" must replace the all-too-prevalent program mentality in American business. In addition, approval for all new projects should be withheld until there is a sufficient long-term commitment to their continuation. Then once that commitment is made, the new initiative should receive adequate resources and staffing so that it has a good chance to be successful.

Constant Change

Change is vital for organizational success, but some organizations simply like to shake things up by changing things for the sake of change. Other organizations change excessively because of lack of clear management focus or poor planning. Today's workplace is turbulent enough without workers having to worry about *unnecessary* changes—especially last-minute changes.

One employee described her frustration in the following way: "We are like pawns forced to go in whatever direction management is being pressured to go." A senior manager described his experience with change in his organization like this: "One day we'd be learning how to do business the Japanese way; six months later we'd be on to something entirely different."[11] This is precisely what Deming meant when he referred to "lack of constancy of purpose" as one of the "deadly diseases" of management.[12]

Change is actually highly motivating when it is results-oriented and well communicated. Few employees resist change when they perceive it as clearly instrumental to organizational goals. When changes are essential, the rationale for change should be promptly and precisely communicated to employees. Managers should also be encouraged to take more time to plan their activities. As we see in Chapter 6, better planning is critical in reducing the problem of excessive change.

Internal Competition

Demotivation can also result when a great motivational concept is distorted from its original purpose. For example, competition can be extremely motivating when it is against the real competitors or vis-à-vis one's own previous performance. However, too many organizations allow, and even encourage, internal competition, wherein one department or group is pitted against another. This is generally done to stimulate increased productivity.

Although internal competition may appear to have short-term benefits, in the long run it undermines trust, reduces cooperation, and generates negative emotions. So-called "healthy competition" frequently turns adversarial and transforms functions into factions, creating a sense of "us" versus "them." After a while, units stop sharing information, hoard resources, view tasks as independent, criticize and blame one another, and regard workers in the next work process as "the enemy"!

In one organization, production contests between shifts became so heated they led to sabotage by one shift against the other. In another company, a sales group declared "open season" on the customers of another sales unit. In both cases, the results were ultimately counterproductive and demotivating for all concerned.

I have found that conflicts between sales and production areas are particularly common. For example, in many organizations, salespeople are rewarded for maximizing sales volume without regard for those who are expected to produce the products. In Chapter 7, we see how the use of cross-functional improvement teams and closer internal customer-supplier relationships can dramatically reduce this kind of dysfunctional internal competitiveness.

If your organization is inherently competitive, this competitive spirit should be refocused on *external* opportunities for competition, rather than directed inward.

Dishonesty

People resent being lied to, particularly so when the falsehood comes from someone they have come to trust. That is why it is so demoralizing for employees to discover that their employer is not telling the truth.

Whether it takes the form of making a false claim, covering up a mistake, or failing to reveal an important fact, organizational dishonesty hurts employees deeply. In many companies, however, it is not considered "lying." It is rationalized as "public relations," "selective communication," or "putting a spin on the truth." Some overzealous managers even break the law to achieve corporate goals.

It is motivating for employees to trust their organization. Employees should be proud to tell the world, "I work for XYZ Corporation!" Trust is like a liquid filling up a bucket drop by drop. It takes a long time to fill the bucket. However, a single act of dishonesty can overturn the entire "trust bucket" and spill out all the trust that has been so painstakingly accumulated through the years. This is why it has been said that "trust is the most difficult thing to develop, and the easiest thing to destroy." Even minor dishonesty can have truly disastrous organization-wide repercussions.

Therefore, a strong policy addressing dishonesty should be adopted and enforced. There can be no ambiguity or equivocation about the fact that dishonesty, in any form, will not be tolerated. And whatever you do, don't compromise on ethics.

Hypocrisy

Hypocrisy is a behavioral form of dishonesty, usually involving lofty comments or promises followed by contradictory behaviors. For example, how many times have you heard: "Thanks for the feedback" (but your input was never acted upon); "We value you" (but there was no tangible display of value); "We trust you" (but you'd better ask permission before doing anything); "We believe in employee involvement" (anytime between the hours of 4:00 and 4:45 on Fridays); "We care" (as long as it's convenient and doesn't cost anything); "We are 100 percent committed to quality" (but you'd better get the product out on time, or else); or "Be innovative" (but God help you if it doesn't work)? Many organizations talk a good game, saying one thing but doing another.

Ethics is a "politically correct" business theme today, but it is also a common source of hypocrisy. Companies preach to their employees about ethical behavior and fiscal responsibility, then behave unethically and irresponsibly themselves. In a particularly deplorable example of hypocrisy, a manager told me how, after upper management preached to employees about the importance of severe belt-tightening, one senior executive submitted a monthly entertainment bill for $27,000! In a manufacturing facility I recently visited, where flammable chemicals were widely used and "No Smoking" signs were posted everywhere, the manager in charge who showed me around was smoking, and then discarded his cigarette butt on the shop floor. What do you think this kind of hypocrisy does to employee motivation?

The surest way to reduce the HQ (hypocrisy quotient) in your organization is by closely monitoring the consistency between words and actions. Above all, avoid using exaggerated claims, exhortations, and slogans that invite hypocrisy. Senior management must model "walking the talk." Managers at all levels should also become much more sensitive to employees' perception of their behavior.

Withholding Information

Withholding information (or management secretiveness) is yet another form of dishonesty that frequently demotivates employees. When I visit organizations, some of the most common complaints I hear are: "My supervisor doesn't keep me informed." "I sure wish they had told me sooner." "The company never tells us what's happening." In addition, when employees ask questions, they often get evasive answers, which makes them feel distrusted and stupid, and feeds the fear and ignorance that are already so prevalent in many organizations.

Many companies still maintain a highly paternalistic attitude toward employee communication ("We'll tell them what they need to know when they need to know it"). Organizations today are eager to call employees "partners" or "associates" or "colleagues," but few of the employees feel like real partners when management fails to share comprehensive business information.

Therefore, it is essential for organizations to move from withholding information to revealing as much as possible. "New breed" employees want to know more, much more, than employees of previous generations. As is discussed in Chapter 8, some organizations have wisely adopted an "open book" policy, through which most corporate information (including detailed financial information) is shared with employees. If a company has anything to hide from its employees, perhaps it should ask why.

Unfairness

Unfairness ranks very high among the most demotivating aspects of organizational life. Many organizations are teeming with what employees perceive as unfair practices. These practices generate more than their share of negative emotions.

Unfair compensation is probably the number-one complaint I hear from employees. Workers inevitably will compare their compensation packages (salary, wages, commissions, bonuses, benefits, etc.) with those of others, both inside and outside their organization. If they find discrepancies, this can be extremely discouraging.

Fairness is a comparative concept. This is why a professional athlete making $3 million might suddenly become dissatisfied with his salary when he finds out that another athlete is making $5 million! Furthermore, many employees are offended by existing compensation arrangements that pay CEOs millions of dollars a year for managing a company with mediocre performance, while excellent employees are paid only a few dollars more than those who just get by.[13]

Other practices that employees perceive as unfair include preferential treatment, special favors, and management perks. Virtually every employee in America is offended by reserved parking spaces and other privileges given to some employees and not to others. Few organizations recognize just how demotivating unfairness is, and so these practices persist.

Unfairness can be reduced by taking a strong position against preferential treatment of any kind. Is your organization reluctant to openly share compensation information with employees? Many are, because they know there are serious inequities. In contrast, smart organizations regularly review their compensation practices, both for internal consistency and in comparison with other organizations. In these organizations, favoritism is being eliminated, and special privileges are being drastically curtailed. (Chapter 11 discusses SuperMotivating compensation practices in detail.)

Discouraging Responses

At one time or another, all employees have tried to be creative, only to find the effort met with significant resistance. Because of this resistance, many organizations are very discouraging places in which to work.

This resistance most frequently comes in the form of discouraging supervisory comments, such as: "It won't work." "We've never done it that way before." "The boss won't buy it." "I agree with you, *but* . . ." "That's just not feasible." "It will cost too much." "You just don't understand the way the system works here." "I'll get back to you later." "Keep your mind on your job." We have all seen great ideas killed by a single wisecrack or thoughtless utterance.

Resistance also comes in the form of bureaucratic and cumbersome suggestion systems that "reward" employee ideas by way of a form letter thanking the employee for the idea, but explaining that it was rejected for one reason or another. At other times, ideas are simply ignored, making employees feel put down ("They don't feel that my ideas are worthy of attention") and resentful ("If they don't care, why should I?"). In one organization, an employee told me angrily, "See those suggestion boxes? We now use them as tool boxes!" No wonder Japanese workers average over 100 suggestions per year, whereas in this country the average is less than one suggestion per employee! Although few employees expect a testimonial dinner or a large reward for their contributions, they don't want their ideas met with disrespect, discourtesy, or even outright hostility. This demotivator alone has undoubtedly killed millions of great ideas throughout the years.

It's always easier to say "no" to an idea than it is to say "yes." To paraphrase the eighteenth-century British writer and critic Samuel Johnson, it is much easier to find reasons for *rejecting* an idea than for embracing it. Saying "yes" requires additional work. The word *no* is the most demotivating word in the English language, especially when it comes without an adequate explanation.

Obviously, not every idea for improvement will revolutionize an organization, but some might. That is why, in Chapter 8, numerous practical and highly motivating suggestions for addressing this demotivator are made.

Criticism

Criticism is a type of negative communication that takes many forms, both verbal and nonverbal. It includes such interpersonal abuse as snide remarks ("zingers"), belittling, frowns, dirty looks, and a hundred other types of "put-downs." Public criticism is particularly demotivating.

Criticism is sometimes confused with feedback, but there is a huge difference between the two. The purpose of feedback is to improve *future* performance, whereas criticism involves "being dumped on" for what happened *in the past.* Contrary to the popular expression, criticism is *never* constructive.

Criticism is extremely powerful—even more powerful than praise. It has been said that "a single criticism can sometimes wipe out the effect of a hundred compliments."

Some organizations operate according to the principle of "management by exception": If you don't hear anything negative, it means you're doing OK! Then employees wait for the inevitable timebomb of criticism to explode as soon as they make a single mistake. This management practice is focused on fault-finding and blame, while ignoring assets and accomplishments. Unlike in baseball, in the "game of business," employees sometimes get criticized when they are only batting .900! One employee recently complained to me that in his company, if he did 100 things right and one thing wrong, he would be sure to hear about the one mistake.

The most common time for criticism is during the annual performance review. Some bosses save up their criticisms and "efficiently" dump them all at once at the end of the year. This is one reason why it has been observed that it takes an average employee up to six months to recover from his or her performance review![14]

The best way to overcome criticism in the workplace is by developing a no-criticism culture. Criticism has no place in any organization that aspires to achieve SuperMotivation. Companies need to educate managers and supervisors to appreciate the value of mistakes. Furthermore, much of the problem of overreaction to mistakes is due to poor measurement and feedback, a subject that is treated in depth in Chapter 10.

Capacity Underutilization

Almost every employee wants to contribute to the maximum extent possible, but most employees never get to use their full capacities at work. In fact, researchers have found that white-collar workers spend approximately 50 percent of their time on the job doing nothing, whereas blue-collar workers are idle 40 percent of the time.[15] In a similar vein, it has been discovered that personnel utilization in office settings rarely exceeds 60 percent of capacity, and that in most cases it is below 40 percent.[16]

The capacity underutilization problem in one organization was so serious that a manager admitted to me that for years he had spent most of his time in a warehouse counting nuts, bolts, and washers and writing reports on his findings!

Some organizations are compounding the problem by filling routine production jobs with college graduates (and even those with postgraduate degrees). Superficially, this might appear to be cunningly cost-effective, and initially the employees might be delighted to have a job; however, from a motivational perspective, this is rarely a good idea.

The tremendous waste of human potential that results from capacity underutilization can be substantially reduced by changing the all-too-common approach to human resources planning wherein hiring often takes precedence over effective utilization. Before asking the question, "How can we add more people?" managers should first be required to ask, "How can we make better use of the employees we already have?"

In every organization there are many great opportunities for better employee utilization. For example, an airline was convinced that it needed to hire staff from outside the company for its new corporate newsletter. However, when the jobs were posted internally, the company was amazed to discover that out of a hundred internal applicants, eighteen had journalism degrees and ten had prior broadcast or print journalism experience![17]

Tolerating Poor Performance

Have you ever had to work with a poor performer? Chances are that you, like me, have experienced it many times. Many organizations create this demotivating situation by tolerating mediocre performance in the name of "humane" treatment (which most employees know is really a sign of management weakness, indecision, or office politics).

Some companies not only tolerate poor performance, they reward it by providing across-the-board compensation increases. American managers are also prone to give subordinates higher-than-deserved performance ratings because they think this practice will make them "look good" and win employee cooperation.

One employee described his company's attitude toward performance in the following way: "In our company, if you do a really outstanding job, you get very well rewarded. And if you do a mediocre job, you *also* get very well rewarded!" When good performers see that poor performers are receiving the same treatment (and the same compensation), they eventually question the wisdom of their own performance commitments ("Why should I bother working so hard?").

Tolerating poor performance may help a few employees survive, but it will demotivate the 95 percent who are trying to do a good job. Not only that, supervisors have to spend a disproportionate amount of time with the other 5 percent, who typically are the greatest complainers, are accident-prone, cause most of the behavior problems, and lower work-group morale. Unfortunately, the squeaky wheel *does* get most of the grease.

Low standards, undeserved generosity, lax discipline, and failure to terminate are personnel practices greeted by employees with derision rather than gratitude. These practices are not good business, nor are they ultimately humane.

Most mediocre performers weren't always that way. Many of them have become stale in their jobs, and the problem has never been corrected. Many so-called "deadwood" employees *can* become significant contributors again. The performance of many of these employees can be rejuvenated by identifying their hidden strengths and encouraging them to participate more in planning their work. Organizations should also provide plenty of counseling and assistance for problem employees, up to a point. However, if all remedial efforts fail, and if poorly performing employees continue their sub-par contributions, there is no option but to terminate them *promptly*.

Being Taken for Granted

What happens to people in organizations who quietly do a good job? Generally nothing! Most workers receive little or no positive feedback or recognition, and, sadly, most supervisors and managers are genuinely unaware of how little personal attention they give employees. Surveys have found that workers report that they are seldom, if ever, commended for their work (not even their outstanding efforts), whereas supervisors say that they are giving plenty of feedback and recognition.[18] Even organizations that are extremely generous with formal awards and recognition are often quite stingy with day-to-day contact.

Employees don't require attention all the time, but nobody wants to be taken for granted. The famous Hawthorne experiments showed that, no matter how generous the big rewards, it is the little things, like management attention, that have the greatest motivational impact.[19]

Nothing shows more genuine regard than responding promptly and constructively to employee concerns. Addressing demotivators will also send powerful "we care" messages to employees, as will greater emphasis on employee safety.

Management Invisibility

The human craving for attention explains the instant acceptance that the acronym MBWA (Management By Wandering Around) received when Tom Peters and Bob Waterman introduced it in their blockbuster bestseller *In Search of Excellence*.[20] Why did such an obvious insight appear so startling to sophisticated American managers?

Compared with management in other countries, American managers are notoriously aloof from their employees. In some companies, employees don't even know the names of the top executives. In a particularly noteworthy case, a production worker told me that he wouldn't even recognize the production manager if he walked by! Another employee described management invisibility in his organization this way: "Every time we see the suggestion boxes around here, they remind us of just how out of touch management is."

Organizations that aspire to SuperMotivation must create high management visibility by communicating to managers that they should spend more time in the operating areas of the company and less time in their offices. However, although management visibility has a huge symbolic importance to employees, just wandering around aimlessly is not enough. Managers must pause long enough to talk, ask the right questions, and, most importantly, *listen.* MBWA doesn't mean just saying hello once a quarter.

Overcontrol

Overcontrol (in one company, at least, contemptuously referred to as "snoopervision") is really the opposite of the now-popular term "empowerment." It is a characteristic of organizations that place a higher priority on maintaining the status quo than on innovation and outstanding performance. In fact, in most bureaucratic organizations, a high degree of control is actually considered to be a virtue.

Overcontrol comes in many forms, from the unwillingness of supervisors to allow employees to take even the slightest initiative without prior permission to elaborate financial constraints and unnecessary upper management approvals.

The overcontrolling manager is a legendary demon among the American workforce. One observer describes an all-too-familiar character we will call the "Red Pencil Manager." In this case, he was a project manager in a large manufacturing firm who insisted on scrutinizing every design before it was sent out to vendors for bids. While this might have been perfectly appropriate behavior for his position and level of responsibility, he had one habit that had a decidedly negative effect on his subordinates. Before even *looking* at the design (which designers had agonized over for as much as a month), he would open his drawer and pull out a red pencil; then, while the horrified designer looked on, the manager would change the design until *he* was satisfied.[21] I'm sure you would agree that this scenario would be enough to demotivate even the most resilient soul.

Too much management robs employees of a sense of personal responsibility, pride, and self-esteem. In fact, recent research indicates that perceived lack of control is a primary cause of coronary heart disease.[22] In some traditional, demotivating organizations, it seems as if the only control employees have over their work is withholding effort.

As discussed in several chapters in Part Two of this book, there are many excellent opportunities for empowering employees, while still maintaining *healthy* control.

Takeaways

If you really want to demotivate employees, just take away an entitlement. I have seen this happen time and time again, especially in generous organizations with the best intentions. For example, a new compensation program might be installed to improve performance, but because it was poorly conceived, it has to be taken away or drastically changed. An employee benefit might be added in times of plenty, then taken away in times of austerity.

In one company, employees were given overtime pay to encourage them to use a new Basic Skills Learning Center. However, when management thought employees were running up too many hours, it abolished all pay for use of the learning center. The backlash, even from employees who never used the center, was extremely hostile. The prolonged anger adversely affected morale and productivity throughout the plant for a very long time. Another company instituted a new sales commission structure, but abolished it when a few salespeople started making more money than senior vice presidents!

Takeaways are not limited to pay and benefits. In another particularly demotivating case, a high-profile project was assigned to a team of employees, but after they had completed the analysis phase, the implementation was assigned to a management group. The negative fallout from the action showed that removing authority can be the greatest takeaway of all!

Losing something we already have is always going to be a major demotivator. It is much easier to do without than to give something up.

Takeaways are totally unnecessary, and are almost always symptomatic of a management planning failure. Don't commit organizational resources to any new initiative until some contingency planning has been done. Pilot projects can help out, by enabling new programs to be tested on a small scale before they are implemented organization-wide.

Being Forced to Do Poor-Quality Work

The cost of poor quality goes far beyond the cost of replacement, scrap, and dissatisfied customers. It includes the devastatingly demotivating impact on employees.

Most workers want to feel good about the quality of their work. But alas, some organizations make decisions, and design systems, that rob employees of their right to pride in workmanship, a prerogative that the late quality guru W. Edwards Deming considered one of the keys to motivation in the workplace.[23]

Time and cost constraints are two major reasons for quality compromises. Organizations often decide that they must sacrifice quality in order to meet short-term production goals. For example, an airline reservation agent, under the directive to answer a certain number of calls per hour, was forced to cut off some callers abruptly so that she could meet her production quota and retain her job. In a large telephone company, an executive order was issued to information operators to stop using the word "please"—because it was using up too much time! In another company, an employee complained, "All the employees knew the product was garbage . . . but both the company and the customer accepted it. . . . We all would go home each day feeling rotten." This is why it is said that "the quickest way to kill the human spirit is to ask someone to do mediocre work!"

Too many organizations blame poor quality on "careless employees." Blame is highly demotivating and never solves the underlying problem. Instead, management should ask: "What's wrong with our systems that cause employees to do substandard work?"

Another answer to "poor quality" pressures is to adopt a longer-term time perspective. Encourage employee involvement in production decisions. However, if your organization wants an *immediate* impact on quality, stop production as soon as quality problems are detected. Nothing sends a more dramatic message about management's commitment to quality than *not* producing poor-quality products—regardless of the cost!

Demonstrating Management Commitment

Demotivators are draining the life out of many American companies today, and consequently, there is a tragic waste of talent and energy. It is unrealistic to expect employees to operate at high performance levels if they are constantly confronted with demotivating influences such as those just cited.

This is why it is so imperative that American business commit itself to addressing the demotivation epidemic. Demotivators simply *must* be reduced if SuperMotivation is going to have any chance of becoming a reality.

At the beginning of this chapter, I explained that demotivators proliferate where there is motivational neglect. No company with a commitment to quality and excellence would ever consciously allow demotivators to exist. However, in most cases, demotivators simply sneak up when organizations are preoccupied with other concerns. That is why managers shouldn't see the presence of demotivators as necessarily indicative of poor management. But letting them *persist,* once they have been identified, is unconscionable.

Demotivators in the workplace are symptomatic of the traditional focus on the technical aspects of the organization to the exclusion of the motivational issues. And since the problem was caused by neglect, the solution is to focus more attention on motivation. Almost without exception, I have found that once organizations start focusing real attention on motivational issues, demotivation promptly decreases.

Nobody expects demotivators to be eliminated completely. Some are just too deeply entrenched. However, making a committed effort to reduce them will do wonders for the motivational climate in any organization.

If your organization is truly committed to doing something about demotivation, then you are ready for the most important motivational program your organization will ever undertake. Once top management is really determined to defeat demotivation, your organization will have taken its first major step toward creating a high-motivation workplace.

The Demotivator Reduction Process

There are two ways in which demotivators can be attacked. First, *direct action* can remove the underlying causes of a particular demotivator. Furthermore, since many demotivators are closely related, reducing one demotivator may also reduce others. Second, *adding motivators* will almost always cause an *indirect* reduction in demotivators. (Motivators are the subject of Chapter 5.)

Here are eight steps that relate to the *direct* reduction of demotivators. All will greatly facilitate demotivator reduction in your organization.

1. *Ensure sponsorship.* As indicated above, top management commitment is essential for reducing demotivators. A high-level sponsor should serve as the champion of the demotivator reduction process.

2. *Create realistic expectations.* Realistic expectations for demotivator reduction are essential. No one should expect an overnight miracle. Demotivator reduction must be presented as an ongoing process, not a "quick fix."

3. *Empower a coordinating team.* Employee involvement is an essential ingredient in any organizational improvement program, and demotivation reduction is no exception. This is why forming a team to coordinate it is so important. Although most corrective actions will have to be mandated by upper management, such a team can provide a crucial link with the workforce throughout the process. Furthermore, while an external consultant can sometimes be helpful in launching the project, expanding it, and sustaining it, without *internal* facilitators, the project will eventually die.

Any such team should be broad-based, with a diverse, cross-functional membership representing all major areas and levels of the organization. The major qualifications for membership are interest and credibility. Team members should preferably be selected by their peers to ensure rank-and-file support. (In unionized companies, union representation is crucial.) Furthermore, rotating membership will increase opportunities for employee participation.

Involvement in such a team should not require more than a few hours per week, and adequate released time must be provided. Prior to starting, the team should be thoroughly educated about demotivators and participate in some team-building activities. The team should also select a leader from its membership. (Chapter 7 provides many useful suggestions for creating a SuperMotivating team.)

4. *Identify the highest-priority demotivators.* Trying to address all demotivators at once is unrealistic. It is far better to attack demotivators one (or a few) at a time, starting with the highest-priority ones.

There are many ways to prioritize demotivators. However, the best way is to *ask the employees.* After all, employee *perception* is at the root of all demotivators, and most employees have had quite a bit of personal experience with them. Although the coordinating team, together with the sponsor, should make the ultimate decision about what demotivators to target first, I recommend that extensive employee input be solicited.

This can be done using a variety of data collection methods, such as questionnaires, interviews, or focus groups. Whichever method or combination of methods you select, the answers to the following six questions are crucial for identifying and prioritizing demotivators:

1. What demotivators exist in the organization?
2. Where does each demotivator occur? (Although most demotivators occur organization-wide, some may be localized to specific departments or functions.)
3. When does each demotivator occur? (Demotivators sometimes occur more frequently at particular times, such as during peak production periods when there is greater stress.)
4. In what forms does each demotivator manifest itself?
5. How does each demotivator affect employees?
6. What constraints might hinder demotivator reduction? (There are many factors, such as strongly held beliefs, deeply entrenched behavior patterns, or unresolved union-management issues, that can sabotage any demotivator reduction effort.)

The first four questions will reveal the *prevalence* of demotivators, the fifth question will indicate the *seriousness* of each demotivator, and the sixth question will help determine the *feasibility* of attempting to reduce a particular demotivator. The answers to these questions can be rather easily translated into a prioritized list of demotivators. You might also find it useful to look for related demotivators. Selecting clusters of demotivators will enable more than one demotivator to be addressed concurrently.

You will find a Demotivator Identifier form in Appendix A to help you in your demotivator identification efforts.

5. *Develop a demotivator reduction strategy.* Once priorities have been established, a general approach (or strategy) for demotivator reduction should be formulated. The suggestions presented in this chapter and in Chapters 6 through 11 should be quite helpful for doing this.

In drafting a strategy, you should recognize, above all, that demotivators represent an organizational expectation problem. As stated earlier in this chapter, demotivators tend to exist and proliferate because they have been allowed to. Demotivators can usually be significantly reduced, even without any other action, when management clearly and unambiguously demonstrates that particular demotivating conditions will no longer be accepted. For example, if senior management states unequivocally that dishonesty will no longer be tolerated—and sets an appropriate example to that effect—the rest of the organization will usually get the message.

It is also vital that senior management take action to remove any rewards that, often unintentionally, reinforce demotivating behaviors. A well-established psychological principle suggests that when rewards for any behavior (positive or negative) are removed, the behavior will generally extinguish.[24]

Not only do rewards for negative behaviors need to be eliminated, but support for positive behaviors must also be established. Two crucial support factors are *example* and *training*. For instance, if you want to reduce unproductive meetings in your organization, senior managers should be the first to demonstrate productive meeting leadership behaviors. This is why meeting leadership skills training should begin at the top, and then be expanded throughout the organization.

The same basic strategy holds true for addressing all demotivators: First, create positive expectations; second, remove any rewards for negative behavior; and third, provide support for positive behaviors.

6. *Develop specific plans for demotivator reduction.* In order to be successfully implemented, any strategy needs a detailed plan. Therefore, a step-by-step plan for reducing each targeted demotivator should be developed, including action steps, deadlines, required resources, and allocations of responsibility.

Although organization-wide demotivator reduction should be carefully planned, you can supplement it with more informal efforts. Creating a "demotivator busting" attitude throughout the organization will lead to greater awareness of the problem. Furthermore, managers and supervisors should be empowered to find and reduce demotivators in their own departments and work areas.

7. *Emphasize communication during implementation.* No strategy or plan is any better than how well it is implemented. And communication is a crucial aspect of implementation. This is one area where the coordinating team can be particularly valuable. Employees throughout the organization should be regularly updated about the progress of the project, and ongoing input should be solicited. Inclusion, openness, and involvement are the hallmarks of any successful demotivator reduction process.

8. *Recognize improvements.* If you want to keep any improvement process going, recognition must be given for progress. This is another area in which the coordinating team can be particularly helpful. Team members should elicit feedback from their own departments and work areas about employees' perceptions of how well the demotivator reduction process is progressing. Positive feedback can then be communicated to those responsible for making the changes. Furthermore, we all know that management generally receives much more negative feedback than positive feedback from employees. This is an excellent opportunity to improve the ratio.

Winning the War on Demotivators

For better or for worse, it is senior management that sets the motivational climate in any organization. The rest of the organization generally follows what they see at the top—and what is tolerated. Therefore, reducing demotivation must be substantially raised on the list of management priorities.

When senior management makes a strong commitment, and this is communicated to the rest of the organization, it will create the expectation that something is going to be *done*. Whatever happens, this process cannot be perceived by employees as a sham. Motivation is a very sensitive issue, and, as we have learned, demotivators are particularly emotionally charged.

There will inevitably be skepticism concerning efforts to reduce demotivators. It is normal for employees to question management's motives. After all, most demotivators have had a long history, and have proven quite resistant to change.

This natural skepticism can be overcome through *concrete demonstrations* of management commitment. Actions speak louder than words. In some companies with which I have consulted, managers are using dramatic actions to show their seriousness about demotivator reduction—for example, taking such actions as reducing their own salaries and perks, and admitting their own responsibility for the demotivation problem. One CEO showed *his* personal commitment by having lunch in each department, explaining the plan for demotivator reduction to startled employees. In an even more dramatic gesture, another CEO publicly shredded his company's twenty-two–inch policy manual and replaced it with a one-page statement of philosophy![25]

When employees perceive that the war on demotivators is credible, and is actually being fought with vigor, they will begin to see a ray of hope. Although skeptical, they will feel that something might actually be done about the nagging demotivators that have frustrated them for so long.

In Chapter 5, you learn about the second way to defeat demotivation in your organization: *adding motivators*. These powerful motivators are the other key element of the SuperMotivation approach. Adding motivators will lead your organization further down the road toward levels of motivation, productivity, and quality never before thought possible.

Notes

1. *Entropy* is a concept derived from physics that describes the tendency of all systems to inevitably proceed to a state of disorder and chaos unless something is done about it. See J. Rifkin, *Entropy* (New York: Bantam Books, 1981).
2. M. Spouse, *Sabotage in the American Workplace* (San Francisco: Pressure Drop Press, 1992).
3. M. E. McGill, *American Business and the Quick Fix* (New York: Henry Holt, 1988), p. 113.
4. R. Levering, *A Great Place to Work* (New York: Random House, 1988).
5. K. Menninger, "Work as Sublimation," in *Human Life Cycle*, ed. W. C. Sze, (New York: Jason Aronson, 1975).
6. G. Emery and P. Emery, *The Second Force* (New York: Dutton, 1990), p. 33.
7. M. Hammer and J. Champy, *Reengineering the Corporation* (New York: Harper-Business, 1993).
8. M. P. Cronin, "Meaningful Meetings," *Inc.*, September 1994.
9. G. English, personal communication, 1995. See also G. English, "How About a Good Word for Meetings?" *Management Review*, June 1990.

10. P. B. Crosby, *Quality Without Tears* (New York: McGraw-Hill, 1984).
11. E. O. Welles, "Lost in Patagonia," *Inc.*, August 1992, p. 47.
12. W. E. Deming, *Out of the Crisis* (Cambridge, Mass.: MIT Press, 1986).
13. T. F. Gilbert and M. B. Gilbert, "Performance Engineering: Making Human Productivity a Science," *Performance and Instruction*, January 1989.
14. W. E. Deming, *Out of the Crisis* (Cambridge, Mass.: MIT Press, 1986).
15. M. LeBoeuf, *GMP: The Greatest Management Principle in the World* (New York: Berkley Books, 1985).
16. J. Duncan, "Clerical Work Needs Engineering," *The Office*, July 1969.
17. R. Levering, *A Great Place to Work* (New York: Random House, 1988).
18. R. L. Hale and R. F. Maehling, *Recognition Redefined* (Minneapolis: Tennant Company, 1992).
19. W. H. Whyte, Jr., *The Organization Man* (New York: Simon & Schuster, 1956).
20. T. J. Peters and R. H. Waterman, *In Search of Excellence* (New York: Harper & Row, 1982).
21. C. F. Vough, *Tapping the Human Resource* (New York: AMACOM, 1975).
22. A. Kohn, *Punished by Rewards* (Boston: Houghton Mifflin, 1993).
23. W. E. Deming, *Out of the Crisis* (Cambridge, Mass.: MIT Press, 1986).
24. A. Daniels, *Performance Management* (Tucker, Ga.: Performance Management Press, 1989).
25. T. J. Peters and R. H. Waterman, *In Search of Excellence* (New York: Harper & Row, 1982).

5

The Power of Motivators

Motivators have the awesome power to positively transform the context of work. They motivate because they increase *desire.* Motivators make people *want* to work, *want* to get involved, *want* to learn, *want* to achieve, *want* to gain recognition, and so on.

The power of each motivator comes from its capacity to stimulate one or more of the eight human desires discussed in Chapter 2. Although a virtually infinite number of relationships are possible, the *primary* connections between motivators and desires are shown in Figure 5-1.

Major Motivators

In the following sections, each motivator will be discussed, followed by a bottom-line principle summarizing it. Later on, in Chapters 6 through 11, you will learn specifically how to *use* these motivators to create and sustain high motivation in your organization, department, or unit.

Action

Motivation is an *active* (not a passive) state. Human beings are most highly motivated when they are *actively* involved. People want to participate in life, not just be idle observers. This is why participation in sports and games is so motivating. Sports and games satisfy the human desire for activity in ways that most work does not.

The common belief that inactivity conserves energy is absolutely false. Inactivity wastes energy. When people are passive, their energy dissipates. In contrast, the use of energy in productive pursuits actually *increases* a person's energy level.

It is unfortunate that so much of contemporary work is sedentary. Human beings were never meant to be passive for most of their working

Figure 5-1. Desires and motivators.

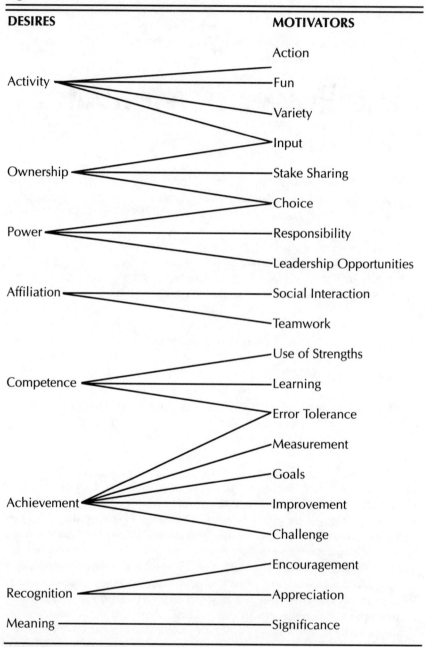

DESIRES	MOTIVATORS
	Action
Activity	Fun
	Variety
	Input
Ownership	Stake Sharing
	Choice
Power	Responsibility
	Leadership Opportunities
Affiliation	Social Interaction
	Teamwork
	Use of Strengths
Competence	Learning
	Error Tolerance
	Measurement
	Goals
Achievement	Improvement
	Challenge
	Encouragement
Recognition	Appreciation
Meaning	Significance

hours. The current trend toward increased "knowledge work" has actually led to more sedentary labor. Increased automation has reduced the need for employees to move around the office or plant.[1] Many employees spend the vast majority of their working hours sitting down, tied to a telephone, desk, computer, or some other piece of equipment.

Computerization in a paper mill, for example, has meant that machine operators, who were once accustomed to constant hands-on work, now spend most of their time sitting in an air-conditioned control booth watching a computer monitor, waiting for a problem to occur. When a problem does arise, they engage in frenetic activity to correct it, followed by more long periods of waiting. Not bad work, you say? However, when such workers are passive, inertia builds, negative thoughts and emotions creep in, and energy dissipates. Now these formerly active workers spend much of their idle time discussing "how terrible things are around this place."

To use action as a motivator means to ensure that employees have plenty of productive work (not busy work) to keep them both physically and mentally occupied. With some creativity, more active formats for work can easily be found, even within existing constraints. For example, workers can use downtime more actively and productively by learning more about the production process, improving it, preventing problems, and interacting with internal customers and suppliers.

The more active people are, the more absorbed they will be in their work, and the more likely they will be to think positively and experience positive emotions. Almost without exception, people have told me that they feel most positive and energized about work (and about life) when they are busy and highly productive.

The bottom line: *Make work more active.*

Fun

Fun at work? To many traditionalists, this may seem like a contradiction in terms. Fun is something conspicuously lacking from most workplaces. But fun energizes people. People need rejuvenation breaks in order to recharge their batteries. There is nothing more motivating than a job that is fun to do.

As we discovered in Chapter 3, although very few tasks are naturally fun, an enjoyable context can be built into virtually every job. No matter how tedious or routine a task might be, any work context can be made more fun by interspersing activities such as celebrations, humor, surprises, treats, and parties. Not only are fun activities motivating, but they

also provide welcome relief from the inevitable (and emotionally draining) pressures endemic in today's stressful workplace.

For example, when the pressure builds, one company circulates a
free beverage and snack cart. If things get too serious in another organization, managers dress up in costumes and visit various areas to inject a
little humor. Another company sponsors a "joke of the day" contest. Yet
another business selects employees to be "morale boosters" in each department. Organizations that sponsor lighthearted activities find that
these low-cost events make a big difference to employee morale.

If these examples seem a bit far out for your organization, you can
still draw upon a virtually unlimited range of other fun options. Occasional treats and surprises can go a long way toward energizing a workforce. Humor and laughter alone can release tremendous positive energy.

Right now, you might be asking what these seemingly frivolous fun
activities have to do with work. The purpose of using fun as a motivator
is *not* to amuse employees, but to make them more energetic and, consequently, more productive. These activities break the routine, stimulate
creativity, release energy, and give employees something to look forward
to.

The bottom line: *Build fun into work.*

Variety

Human beings thrive on variety. Employees need sufficient variation to
remain energetic and alert. Sameness may be comfortable, but it is also
deenergizing. (Incidentally, boredom resulting from the sameness of routine work is one of the major causes of industrial accidents.)

Variety at work can be offered in an infinite number of forms, including rearranging the physical environment, temporary changes in work
assignments, job rotation, increased customer contact (especially for employees who do not ordinarily come in contact with customers), visits to
other areas of the company, cross-training, job enrichment/enlargement,
involvement in team projects, and, as we saw in the previous section, fun
activities. Variety can be applied to any job or work area. I am not advocating constant changes (which can be demotivating), but occasional
change keeps employees revitalized, sharpens their senses, and keeps
them performing at peak levels.

Not only does variety motivate, but through it, employees develop
new skills and valuable experience, making them even more productive
contributors to the organization.

The bottom line: *Add variety to work.*

Input

One terrific way of adding variety to work is to ask employees for input on how to improve their work. Employees are full of ideas. Each worker is a priceless resource and a potential wellspring of creative input that can help improve any organization.

Unfortunately, this belief is not yet widely enough held. One employee spoke for many others in his organization when he expressed frustration with the company's traditional approach to management: "In all my years on this job, I have never known of anyone in management ever asking any one of us how we felt about the way things are done around here."

Employees *want* to be involved. They *want* to be asked for their ideas. They *want* to contribute their suggestions. They *want* to help solve problems and make decisions. When management is sincerely interested in employees' input, it taps enormous creative energy.

When employees are asked for their input, they will work much longer and harder to achieve organizational goals, carry out plans, implement ideas, and follow through on decisions. They will work much more energetically when they know it is *their* idea (at least partially), rather than management's alone.

The bottom line: *Ask for employees' input in every area about which they have expertise.*

Stake Sharing

It is very frustrating for most employees that they work each day to enrich other people—business owners, shareholders, and investors. Although not everybody can own a business, every worker can share in the ownership of the organization.

Increasingly, organizations are "stake sharing" with their employees. Although most stake-sharing efforts tend to be financially oriented, stake sharing can take many other forms, such as sharing decision-making and sharing leadership. The most common formal stake-sharing programs include employee stock ownership plans (ESOPs), stock purchase plans, profit sharing, and gainsharing.

These initiatives (some of which are discussed further in Chapter 11) are contributing significantly to employees' new sense of being part owners of their companies. Employees who used to be completely uninterested in, or even contemptuous of, management decisions are beginning to pay close attention to them. Many who previously had little concern for the financial affairs of their employer are becoming intensely interested in them. In fact, in one company at least, hourly workers meet in the break room to chart their company's stock price!

Research has shown conclusively that employees with a stake in the ownership of their organization tend to have much stronger motivation to perform in virtually everything they do.[2]

The bottom line: *Give all employees a stake in the success of the organization.*

Choice

Probably the most distinctive characteristic of human beings is their capability and inclination to make choices. This is one of the major reasons why leisure activities are so motivating—they are so full of choices! Just having a choice can make an individual feel better about doing even the most routine task.

Too often supervisors and managers treat adult workers as if they were children, and dictate to them precisely what they can and cannot do. Since life outside of work is so full of choices, workers frequently ask why they can't make more of them at work.

In a remarkable experiment, a button was installed on an assembly line, and workers were told that they could push the button to stop production whenever they encountered a quality or safety problem. Productivity and quality both increased dramatically, even though the button was never pushed.

Choice releases incredible motivational energy by enhancing employees' sense of autonomy, self-determination, and control over their lives. People are always likely to care more about doing the things they choose than about doing those that are imposed upon them. High motivation starts happening when employees start working on issues *they* really care about.

The bottom line: *Let employees make choices more often.*

Responsibility

Many traditional managers believe that workers shirk responsibility. However, what employees actually avoid is getting more work dumped on them under the guise of increased responsibility. If the responsibility is genuine, employees will eagerly embrace it.

This brings to mind the story of a janitor who surprised his supervisor by complaining, "All I ever do is clean the sinks and the floors. Why don't I ever get to clean the toilets?" This shocked the supervisor, who thought she was sparing her favorite janitor from what she considered the most unpleasant part of the job! She didn't appreciate the importance of total responsibility to employees. Even a dirty job like cleaning rest rooms loses its integrity when the responsibility gets sliced up.

Today, many organizations are beginning to realize that "new breed" employees want *more* responsibility, not less. Employees should have the opportunity to experience the satisfaction of planning and carrying out a piece of work on their own, from start to finish, without constantly having to ask permission. When workers are given greater responsibility for the work they perform, there is much higher motivation to achieve. It is *their* work, not just management's!

The bottom line: *Let employees have as much responsibility as possible for the work they do.*

Leadership Opportunities

A major myth accepted by many managers is that only a small proportion of the workforce is capable of leadership. However, leadership isn't just a privilege reserved for a chosen few; it should be shared widely.

Most supervisors and managers take leadership for granted. They don't realize how excited employees become when they are entrusted with authority. Practically everyone enjoys being a leader sometimes. Most employees don't aspire to be CEO or president, but they would like to be "top dog" at something.

Since most people have assumed leadership responsibilities at one time or another in their personal lives (whether as a parent, a teacher, a coach, or a civic leader), why shouldn't they be afforded this opportunity at work?

Organizations are full of diverse activities just crying out for leadership. With the increasing emphasis on teamwork and employee involvement, there should be abundant leadership opportunities for everyone. Such an opportunity might involve chairing an improvement team, directing a pilot project, or simply organizing a social event. Leadership, however modest, increases employees' motivation and enhances their commitment to both the task and the organization. Highly motivating organizations create an environment in which employees are eager to take the lead, not just follow the leader.

The bottom line: *Provide appropriate leadership opportunities for all employees.*

Social Interaction

Despite all the difficulties of commuting and the frustrations inherent in the traditional workplace, when given a choice of working there or at home, an overwhelming majority, as cited in Chapter 2, still choose the plant or the office. Human beings thrive on social contact, and most work settings are full of rich and varied opportunities for social interaction.

Social interaction doesn't just mean chatting in the break room or around the water cooler. *Productive* social interaction includes such diverse activities as small-group discussions, cooperative work assignments, peer tutoring, expertise sharing, collaborative problem solving, internal customer-supplier relationships, and interfacing with external customers.

Most human beings want to help others, and some organizations harness this desire by deliberately establishing networks of helping relationships and support groups in which there is a lot of sharing of information, resources, and experience. In such an environment, workers spend most of their spare time not in unproductive socializing, but talking with other workers about how improvements can be made.

Whether formal or ad hoc, social interaction is a very powerful motivator.

The bottom line: *Provide plenty of opportunities for employees to socialize productively.*

Teamwork

The most powerful form of social interaction is teamwork. Teamwork is truly revolutionizing the American workplace. In fact, it is widely predicted that work teams will soon dominate the American workplace.

All those who have participated in well-managed team activities have experienced this potent motivational impact first-hand. It has been said, "If you ask people about their richest experiences in life, they'll usually come up with something they did as part of a team."[3]

However, simply putting people together in groups does not ensure teamwork. For example, teams should never be confused with committees. In contrast to ongoing committees, a team is task-specific. Teamwork also breaks down traditional functional boundaries by uniting people in a common mission.

The hallmark of true teamwork is *synergy*, which means that the team's performance is more than the sum of the individual members' separate efforts. In sports, teams with much less talented individual players often defeat much more talented teams. When teams are working synergistically, 2 + 2 can actually equal 7! The positive and productive energy released by teamwork is truly astonishing.

In one company, a team of secretaries worked long hours *without extra pay*, taking work home for the first time in their careers. In another organization, the team spirit on some work teams was so powerful that members had difficulty returning to their regular *nonteam* assignments and remaining motivated.

Even at Harvard Business School, the traditional bastion of business individualism, the M.B.A. curriculum has recently been revamped to emphasize teamwork. People everywhere are coming to the same conclusion: "None of us is as smart as *all* of us are!"

The bottom line: *Use the power of teamwork whenever possible.*

Using Strengths

"One of the key determinants of an employee's motivation and commitment to a company is his feeling about how he is being utilized."[4] Most workers have a great many strengths that they rarely get to use.

Strengths can be job skills and knowledge (such as machine operation), general abilities (such as communicating), or personality characteristics (such as persistence). Research has found that every person can do at least one thing better than any other 10,000 people![5] There are, in fact, a great many hidden talents in every employee.

When employees are hired, they bring with them a vast array of strengths developed through previous education and work experiences, many of them apparently unrelated to their principal job duties. The intellectual abilities of American workers are particularly underutilized. This hidden talent bank is largely ignored in most organizations because it doesn't fit neatly into employees' job descriptions.

Employees find it extremely motivating to be recognized as excellent performers. When employees have worked in a particular job for years, they are bound to get very good at it. Organizations should make more effective use of these accumulated skills and knowledge. After all, they have paid dearly over the years for employees to develop this expertise.

Some organizations are realizing the value of letting employees share their strengths by using them as trainers, coaches, peer tutors, and mentors. They realize how much more effective and highly motivated employees will be when they are allowed to use *and share* the skills they already possess. In one company, a computerized "skill directory" has been established to identify employees' hidden skills, and supervisors are evaluated on how well they make use of it.

The bottom line: *Use more of employees' hidden strengths.*

Learning

In addition to wanting to use their existing strengths, employees have a strong inner desire to enhance their competence. All human beings are born with an insatiable curiosity and desire to learn.

In theory at least, the workplace is a great place for learning. Most organizations are richly endowed with learning opportunities, and there are an enormous number of new skills to master and an enormous amount of new knowledge to acquire. Organizations routinely sponsor extensive education and training programs, but the results of this training have tended to be disappointing. Learning is motivating only if, as a result, employees feel more competent—but unfortunately, too many employees do not. Sadly, many employees find company-sponsored training programs uninteresting, irrelevant, and even threatening to their self-esteem.

Formal training is only one of the many ways in which employees can acquire and develop skills. Other methods include mentoring, delegation, job rotation, job enlargement, job enrichment, working on project teams, and participating in problem solving.

The bottom line: *Provide employees with plenty of high-quality learning opportunities.*

Error Tolerance

Babe Ruth struck out more times than any other major-league baseball player in history. Albert Einstein admitted that over 90 percent of his ideas were wrong. Thomas Alva Edison boasted that he failed to invent the electric light bulb over 1,000 times. Gertrude Stein went twenty years before her first poem was accepted for publication. Vincent Van Gogh sold only one painting during his lifetime. Igor Stravinsky was literally run out of town by angry music lovers when he first presented his most famous musical composition. In fact, most innovators have found that their greatest successes have usually come on the heels of failure.

If the most successful people in history "failed" so often, then why is the average worker made to feel like such a failure when he or she makes a mistake?

If employees know that they can make errors without being unduly criticized or punished, they will be much more likely to work energetically for success—to strive for improvement, to set challenging goals, to attain goals, and to use more of their creative abilities along the way.

The bottom line: *Let "failure" become a creative force in your organization.*

Measurement

Many employees wince at the mere thought of being measured at work. It isn't measurement itself that employees dislike, but the manner in which it is frequently done. These same employees would be horrified at the prospect of bowling or playing golf, tennis, baseball, or football without keeping score!

Keeping score is probably the single most motivating aspect of sports and games, and it is no less important at work. Without scorekeeping, there is no way of winning. People actually *love* being measured, as long as the measurement is *fair and nonthreatening.*

It is a well-known fact that "the things that are measured get done." When statistics are maintained on quality (as in statistical process control), employees take quality more seriously. When safety is being measured, workers exhibit more safe behaviors. When costs are being tracked, employees watch their expenses more closely. The mere act of keeping score provides strong impetus for improved performance.

The bottom line: *Provide frequent, objective, and nonthreatening performance measures.*

Goals

Human beings are goal-oriented creatures, and consequently, goals are very powerful motivators. Goals can create great excitement, focus attention, concentrate energy, and increase persistence. Despite the value of goals, unbelievably, *only about 3 percent* of all adult Americans have any formal goals for their lives.

The one common characteristic of all successful people is that they set goals for themselves. These highly self-motivated people are able to concentrate their energies on the specific outcomes they truly desire to attain.

In contrast, when people are doing a hundred different things, their energy is split up in a hundred different ways.

Increasingly, organizations are recognizing the motivational importance of individual and team (as well as organization-wide) goals. They know that striving to achieve a valued goal is one of the most energizing experiences a person can have in life. Nothing motivates like goals people care about.

The bottom line: *Encourage employees to set goals that matter to them.*

Improvement

When goals are too large, they are overwhelming. In fact, it is *continuous improvements,* rather than great breakthroughs, that provide people with their most enduring source of motivation. Most people feel quite good when they attain a small victory in some aspect of their life. And once people experience improvement, they want more.

Improvement does not mean achieving a big overnight success. It involves a series of *little* successes en route to ever-larger successes. In fact, gradual improvement is the most reliable way to achieve any end result.

This same continuous improvement process is the force that transformed Japan from defeat to victory in the world economy. Recently, many American companies have woken up to the real power of continuous improvement.

The CEO of a major airline showed his understanding of continuous improvement when he asked each employee to "Get me one more passenger." Adding one passenger to each flight added millions of dollars to the airline's annual revenue.

The bottom line: *Create an environment in which all employees want to improve everything—including themselves.*

Challenge

After a while, any activity can become boring, unless it is challenging enough. Most healthy people seek some challenge in their lives. Some climb mountains; others skydive, windsurf, ski, wager, or engage in competitive sports. The peak experiences in life usually occur when a person's mind or body is being stretched to its limits. Challenges have an extraordinary capacity to bring out the best in people.

The same is true at work. Almost every employee will respond energetically to appropriate challenges. Although employees may initially put up resistance to new challenges, most of them actually thrive on situations that force them beyond their "comfort zones."

When work is too easy, employees become complacent and tend to rely on habits. However, as I have witnessed time and again, when challenged to attain a valued goal, previously bored and lethargic workers attain truly spectacular levels of performance. One notoriously unsafe department in a large manufacturing plant mobilized sufficient employee motivation to reduce injuries to almost zero in a matter of months (rather than the years management thought it might take).

Competition is also a major source of challenge—especially when it is against other companies or against a standard of excellence. (As discussed in Chapter 4, internal competition may motivate temporarily, but it will eventually cause demotivating conflict.)

Employees want challenge, but they don't want to be punished if they fail to attain an ambitious goal. When employees don't feel threatened, they will *always* prefer challenging tasks to easy ones.

The bottom line: *Challenge employees to stretch their limits.*

Encouragement

Measurement and encouragement should go hand in hand. Measurement tells people where they stand, and encouragement tells them that no matter where they stand, they still can win. Even when people appear to be losing, encouragement tells them, "You *can* do it, you *can* win." Encouragement releases enormous motivational energy, and sustains it even when times get tough.

Good coaches understand the importance of encouragement better than anyone. They know that even star performers need encouragement from time to time. Before the game, the coach expresses confidence in the team's ability to win. At halftime, the coach gives helpful feedback. Throughout the game, the coach is the chief cheerleader. Then toward the end of the game, the coach's encouragement helps the team release extra energy for the final quarter, the last inning, or the sprint to the finish line.

Encouragement is equally important at work. As employees strive to attain goals and to improve their performance, they want to feel that significant others have confidence in them. No matter how good your employees are, it helps them enormously to be encouraged by a manager or supervisor who wants them to score a "performance touchdown."

The bottom line: *Provide your employees with plenty of encouragement.*

Appreciation

In a survey of business motivation, workers and supervisors were asked to rank a list of motivators from 1 to 10 in order of their importance to workers.[6] The workers rated "appreciation for a job well done" as their number-one motivator. In contrast, supervisors rated it number eight! *This difference in perception is one of the major reasons why most workers feel unappreciated at work.* Few supervisors and managers realize just how important appreciation is to the average worker. After all, they reason, "Isn't good work what employees are being paid for?"

And yet appreciation is one of the most powerful, least expensive, and most "portable" motivators available. A sincere "thank you" can be delivered at any place and at any time, costs absolutely nothing, and can be more motivationally powerful than a substantial monetary bonus.

Appreciation is the psychological compensation employees desire most. William James, the father of modern psychology, considered the craving for appreciation to be "the deepest principle in human nature."[7]

How many employees do excellent work and never get any special recognition? We often fail to tell employees how much we appreciate them *until they retire.* In his farewell speech, a retiring school custodian said, "It's at times like the last day of work that you realize how much your contribution was appreciated . . . and how much you will be missed." Why do we often wait until the last minute to show employees how much we appreciate them?

The most highly motivating organizations appreciate the importance of appreciation. They make workers feel special. They make employees feel like VIPs. These organizations make sure that employees at all levels *continually* know how much they are appreciated.

The bottom line: *Create a "climate of appreciation" in your organization.*

Significance

If an organization wants its employees to give it their best efforts, the employees must believe in the *importance* of what they are doing. Today's employees want more than routine work. They want to feel that they are accomplishing something worthwhile. They want to be involved in "missions that matter."[8]

Many people who barely put in their time at work enthusiastically spend hundreds of hours *without pay* for charitable or political causes in which they strongly believe. For example, a sales representative for a major company, who had difficulty meeting her quota almost every month, was always the number-one producer in selling raffle tickets for her church.

In some organizations, employees with routine jobs perceive them as drudgery, whereas other employees in virtually identical organizations perceive them as "a calling." I have met many employees who devote extraordinary time and effort to projects they really believe in. These employees are energized by a compelling personal sense of mission. When people are truly committed, nothing will stop them. One CEO boasted that he could get his employees "to work ninety hours a week . . . and love it!" Other organizations must learn how to tap this deep desire for meaning that all employees bring to work.

Employees in all jobs and at all levels should understand precisely how their contributions fit into the big picture of the organization, and how they add value to the product or service ultimately delivered to the customer.

The bottom line: *Instill in employees a deep sense of appreciation for the significance of their efforts.*

Building Motivators Into the Context of Work

By now you should have a good idea of just how powerful motivators can be. And be assured, since desires always exist, motivators will *always* work!

Although motivators are almost universally motivating, individuals may respond differently to particular motivators, depending on the intensity of their personal desires and their past experiences. For example, what positively energizes one person may cause another discomfort. Furthermore, if any motivator is used too frequently, people can become habituated to it, and cause it to, at least temporarily, lose some of its motivating potential. Some organizations may become fixated on a particular motivator and overuse it. A common example is when teamwork becomes "a team for *every* occasion." For this reason, it is dangerous to rely too heavily on any one motivator and why one of the key principles of the SuperMotivation approach is to use a *variety* of motivators.

(Incidentally, a Motivator Planner is provided in Appendix A to help you select motivators for use in your organization.)

In addition, there must be continued vigilance concerning the impact of unaddressed demotivators. Demotivators can radically change the way employees perceive motivators. Many well-intentioned rewards have been misconstrued by employees as being insincere and manipulative when they were given in a demotivating environment.

Even now, you could probably use many of the bottom-line principles presented in this chapter to increase motivation in your organization. If you implement a select few of these, you should see a rather dramatic motivational improvement in your organization.

But SuperMotivation will not result from the occasional and haphazard use of motivators. That is why motivators need to be "systematized"—that is, *actually built into the organization itself.* In Part Two of this book, you will learn how you can, by using a variety of motivators, *motivationally transform the systems* that make up your organization.

Notes

1. S. Zuboff, *In the Age of the Smart Machine* (New York: Basic Books, 1988).
2. J. R. Schuster and P. K. Zingheim, *The New Pay* (New York: Lexington Books, 1992).
3. A. Robbins, *Unlimited Power* (New York: Fawcett Columbine, 1986), p. 408.
4. D. Sirota and A. D. Wolfson, "Pragmatic Approach to People Problems," in *People: Managing Your Most Important Asset* (Cambridge, Mass.: Harvard Business Review, 1983), p. 15.
5. D. O. Clifton and P. Nelson, *Soar With Your Strengths* (New York: Delacorte Press, 1992).
6. R. L. Hale and R. F. Maehling, *Recognition Redefined* (Minneapolis: Tennant Company, 1992).
7. W. James, *The Principles of Psychology, Vol. 1* (New York: Henry Holt, 1890).
8. C. Garfield, *Peak Performers* (New York: Avon, 1986).

Part Two
Putting SuperMotivation Into Action

Motivationally Transforming Organizational Systems

From Context to Systems

In Chapter 3, we discussed how the work context, rather than the work itself, determines the quality of an employee's experience in his or her job. The focus of Chapter 3 was on how to make work more motivating by changing its context. In the following chapters, the focus will be expanded to include the motivational transformation of the organization as a whole.

In any large company, there are literally tens of thousands of work tasks being performed. Therefore, it would be impossible to motivationally transform an entire organization by changing the context of every individual task, one by one. This is why Chapters 6 through 11 will deal with the larger context in which all work is embedded: *organizational systems*.

The Power of Organizational Systems

All organizations are composed of a great many interrelated systems. These powerful systems are, in turn, composed of procedures, policies, methods, and practices, all of which have a significant impact on employees' behaviors, attitudes, *and motivation*. Systems are extremely crucial to organizational functioning: They determine what gets done, how much gets done, when it gets done, and how well it gets done. More than any other aspect of an organization, systems determine how employees perform on a day-to-day basis, as well as how employees feel about their work.

No organization is any better than its component systems. When systems are working well, they provide organizations with tremendous leverage. They can increase individual human capabilities by furnishing the means through which many people can work together *synergistically* to achieve ambitious goals that would be impossible for isolated individuals to achieve. Effective systems not only help people achieve better results—they help achieve them *consistently*. In contrast, ineffective systems reduce the positive contributions that individual employees can make.

Developing SuperMotivating Systems

In order to achieve world-class excellence, organizations need to have systems that are both technically *and* motivationally excellent.

American organizational systems have almost always been designed exclusively from a technical perspective. Rarely, if ever, have these systems been designed with motivation in mind. Planning systems have generally been designed by planners, production systems by production experts, communication systems by communication experts, training systems by trainers, evaluation systems by evaluators, and reward systems by compensation experts. Because these technical specialists don't usually have a specific background in motivation, most American organizations aren't particularly motivating for employees. *After all, they weren't designed to be!*

Do you remember those idealistic employees described in Chapter 2 who came to work on that memorable first day expecting to set the world on fire? Although they didn't realize it at the time, they were up against systems that were much stronger than their first-day enthusiasm. These unsuspecting new hires confronted immensely powerful, demotivating organizational systems.

Many of these employees became battered and bruised trying to fight "the system," until they finally gave up and fought no more. Gradually, or not so gradually, the demotivating systems prevailed. When any highly self-motivated individual is pitted against a demotivating system, the system will win virtually every time!

The problem with most systems is that they are *in direct opposition to self-motivation*, and therefore to SuperMotivation. As we learned in Chapter 2, eight desires drive self-motivation. Although all people possess them, these powerful desires frequently encounter strong resistance. And nothing puts up more resistance to self-motivation than poorly designed and inflexible systems.

The good news is that organizational systems, when appropriately designed or redesigned, can create an environment capable of releasing enormous motivational energy that will revitalize any organization. That's what Chapters 6 through 11 are all about.

A Look Ahead

The chapters that follow focus on the six organizational systems I believe are preeminent *from a motivational perspective:* the planning system, the production system, the communication system, the training system, the evaluation system, and the reward system.

Hundreds of ideas are presented and suggestions made to help you develop SuperMotivating *systems* in your organization. All of these ideas and suggestions reflect the motivators discussed in Chapter 5. In fact, if you were to analyze the suggestions, you would find that most of them incorporate (implicitly or explicitly) *more than one* motivator, and in some cases as many as five or six.

The majority of the suggestions presented in Part Two are drawn from my twenty years of consulting experience working with hundreds of organizations around the world. However, in this book, these organizations are identified by name, size, or industry only if I felt this information was relevant to the ideas presented. Otherwise, organizational descriptions are withheld to avoid violating confidences and distracting from the *essential* content.

How to Read Part Two

Part Two is not intended for the casual reader. To get the most out of these chapters, read them *actively,* with pen and paper in hand.

As you read each chapter, I suggest you make a list of demotivators that you can reduce and motivators you can add to each system in your own organization, department, or unit. Brainstorm ideas for making your organization more motivating.

However, although you may find some ideas you will want to implement immediately, I urge you to resist the temptation until you have read the whole book (including Chapter 12). It is vital that you understand the big picture, as well as the component parts. Remember, SuperMotivation is not another isolated "quick fix"; it is a *long-term, integrated* approach to motivational improvement.

You will notice that each of the next six chapters ends with summary lists of Action Points. These points are intended to help you review the content of each chapter and share it with others in your organization.

6

SuperMotivating Planning

Motivationally transforming the planning system in any organization will contribute enormously toward fostering SuperMotivation in that organization. Despite the tremendous potential of planning systems for increasing employee motivation, no organizational system has been more consistently demotivating. Because of the importance of planning to organizational success, this situation clearly must be changed. This chapter presents a great many ideas to help you transform the planning system in your organization from *de*motivating to *Super*Motivating.

The Importance of Planning

Planning is the thinking process individuals and organizations use to prepare for more effective action. It is an investment of time that people can make *in the present* to improve their performance *in the future*. Planning is a highly creative activity that provides a blueprint for action.

There is no doubt about it: Whether mapping out a vacation trip, designing a house, preparing for an athletic contest, or creating a business plan, effective *planning* almost always leads to more effective *doing*.

An effective plan can help anyone get more value out of his or her efforts and resources. In fact, every hour spent effectively planning saves many hours of execution—and yields much better results. Some organizations have saved hundreds of hours by investing a relatively few hours in effective planning.

As work becomes more complex and competition grows keener, organizations must become increasingly skillful at planning. It is becoming more and more apparent that "those who fail to plan, plan to fail."

One of the major reasons why so many employees leave work exhausted and frustrated at the end of the day is that their work was, for one reason or another, poorly planned. Managers who do not plan effectively tend to overreact to "urgent" circumstances, making life miserable for themselves and everyone else, not to mention wasting time and resources. Lack of planning inevitably leads to unnecessary effort, unproductive work, poor results, dissipated energy, and enormous frustration for all involved.

Almost every study has shown that the best managers are those who plan most conscientiously. In fact, a recent survey of the fifty most effective CEOs in America concluded that a strong commitment to planning was an essential defining attribute of this group.[1] It has been proven over and over again in business: Planning is the smart thing to do.

Why Planning Is Resisted

If planning is so smart, then why do so many smart people and organizations fail to plan? And why does the prospect of planning generate so little enthusiasm? Given its undisputed value, it is curious how often we avoid planning or perform it in a perfunctory manner.

The reason is twofold: Most of us don't know how to plan, and we are not motivated to do so.

Although most action requires some prior thought, few of us are naturally attracted to formal planning. In fact, it may surprise you to find out that *fewer than 3 percent* of all adult Americans engage in any kind of formal planning in their own personal lives (although some people procrastinate and call it planning).

Formal planning requires time, discipline, procedures, paperwork, and commitment. It also requires people to adopt new behaviors that often lie outside their comfort zones. Given the widespread *low motivation to plan*, it should not be surprising that most of us find it much easier to take immediate action and worry about the consequences later.

The same is true for many organizations, where "putting out today's fires is given priority over planning for tomorrow."[2] This example comes directly from the top, where a majority of corporate CEOs report that they do not have enough time to plan.[3] In fact, some organizations even make heroes out of those who are able to fix the problems they created themselves through their *own* poor planning!

Even organizations committed to planning find that no matter how elaborate their planning methods are, plans still must be developed and executed by people. This is why so many sophisticated planning structures break down. Like many organizational activities, the success of planning depends *less* on technique and *more* on employee motivation.

For all too many managers, organizational planning connotes little more than fulfilling their annual "planning obligation" by sitting in lengthy and poorly led meetings, dutifully generating paper that promptly gets filed away, never to be seen again. In one organization, managers have adopted a disdainful acronym for the plans they are expected to generate: SPOTS (*Strategic Plans On The Shelf*)!

Even the best-intentioned planning efforts are often viewed by participants as cumbersome, time-consuming, and counterproductive formalities. One manager even confided to me that he'd rather attend a funeral than a planning meeting in his organization!

While many managers view planning as an undesirable interruption of their operational duties, other employees frequently see it as yet another unproductive management ritual. One employee told me that in his organization, planning is perceived as "that time when managers, who are out of touch with what is really going on, make more work for everyone else."

Furthermore, nothing seems to separate management from the rest of the workforce like planning. It keeps reminding most workers of their low status in the organization. Employees generally perceive that the most important decisions in the organization are made by others—usually behind closed doors. For many employees, planning is just another vestige of organizational politics, accompanied by secretiveness, hidden agendas, hypocritical promises, and high-sounding rhetoric.

You can easily see why planning has become associated with negative emotions and unpleasant previous experiences. Current planning systems incorporate a great many demotivators and very few motivators. You might remember that in Chapter 4, we referred to the derogatory acronym BOHICA (*Bend Over, Here It Comes Again!*). It is with just such anticipation that the workforce often greets the announcement of a new round of planning meetings.

But planning doesn't have to be that way.

Employee Involvement in Planning

Although managers who are engaged in regular planning activities may yawn at the prospect of yet another planning meeting, nonmanagement employees (who spend most of their time on the front lines) are increasingly looking to involvement in planning as a stimulating change of pace from their mind-deadening routines. For employees who are unaccustomed to planning, such involvement can add an exciting new dimension to their work. It provides them with the chance to participate in decisions that will affect current operations, and affect the future of the organization as well.

Those who complain about "mindless work" are really complaining about their lack of a significant role in planning that work. As we will see, involvement in planning can become a very special, highly motivating opportunity—a privilege, not an onerous task. In fact, employee involvement in planning has the potential for becoming one of the most motivating aspects of organizational life.

Overcoming Resistance to Planning

However, before real enthusiasm for planning can manifest itself, organizations must respond to the skepticism and cynicism left over from the past. Although planning has tremendous motivational potential, it currently is a troublesome organizational activity from a motivational perspective. In many organizations it has been perceived as demotivating, and so there may well be a deeply ingrained resistance to planning.

If your organization is truly serious about involving employees in planning, here are some powerful strategies for overcoming pent-up resistance to planning:

• *Respond openly and honestly to employee concerns.* The importance of employee concerns about planning should never be underestimated. Just because the concerns have not been openly expressed doesn't mean they don't exist. These concerns, if ignored, will exacerbate already existing negative emotions, and ultimately sabotage even the best-designed planning process.

Before they commit themselves to enthusiastic involvement in planning, skeptical employees will want candid answers to such common questions as: "Why should we do this?" "What will result from it?" "Is there genuine commitment to planning this time?" "Are the plans actually going to be used, or are they just going to be filed away?" And, most importantly, "How does this relate to my regular job responsibilities?"

Bringing these and other hidden concerns and anxieties into the open will allow them to be addressed, rather than be left to fester beneath the surface. Open and honest communication is absolutely critical to overcoming planning resistance.

• *Ensure that employees understand the importance of planning.* Because planning is one of the most misunderstood activities in any organization, a substantial educational effort may be required. When participative planning has failed in the past, this failure has commonly been due to inadequate understanding of the importance of planning, as well as of its methods.

You might consider offering *planning orientation sessions* to whet employees' appetites for planning. It is particularly important for employees to realize that they have a personal stake in the success of planning. Not only is planning a key to better business results, but it will also be reflected in future compensation, promotional opportunities, and stability of employment. Employees need to know that planning is not just an abstract concept; it is at the very heart of the success of the organization. You will be surprised at how excited many employees will get when they know what planning really is and what it can do for them.

• *Demonstrate organizational commitment to planning.* Employees must believe that planning is truly valued by the organization. This should be demonstrated through deeds, not just through words.

One of the best ways to show the value of planning is to allocate sufficient time for it. Unfortunately, few organizations schedule enough planning time. They tell their employees that planning is important, and then they try to squeeze it in between other priorities. The message this sends is loud, clear, *and negative.*

Another way to demonstrate commitment to planning is to offer time off from regular job duties to participate. Better yet, build planning responsibilities into employees' job descriptions. Whatever you do, never make planning an overload or an afterthought.

• *Make involvement in planning voluntary.* The Japanese have been extremely successful in using volunteerism in their organizational improvement efforts. This is also usually the most effective approach for employee involvement in planning. Especially in its early stages, it is much better to start off with employees who really *want* to be involved.

Let employees choose to participate, rather than feel they are being forced to do so. Sadly, in the past, too much energy has been wasted trying to get recalcitrant employees to come along for the ride—and they just ended up dragging everyone else down with their negative attitudes.

• *Show that the organization is serious about reducing planning-related demotivators.* Let employees know that efforts have been made, or at least are being made, to reduce the demotivators that have for so long taken the pleasure out of planning. Target the most deadly planning-related demotivators—most notably excessive politics, internal competition for resources, unproductive meetings, withholding information, and management overcontrol—that will surely kill any participative planning effort.

It is also crucial to reduce any planning bureaucracy that exists in the organization. Planning procedures should be streamlined by eliminating unnecessary meetings, paperwork, approvals, and delays.

How to Achieve High-Involvement Planning

Once negative attitudes toward planning have been addressed, real enthusiasm for planning can be generated by adding appropriate motivators to the context of planning. In this section, you will discover how to motivationally transform the planning system in your organization.

The key to SuperMotivating planning is *involvement.* More and more companies are finding that getting employees involved in planning not only produces better results, but also yields enormous motivational benefits. SuperMotivating organizations of the future will make it a high priority to achieve *maximum employee involvement* in planning. They will involve *all* employees, from the executive suite to the shop floor, in both strategic and operational planning.

In this section, I share a number of useful strategies for making employees more eager to *participate enthusiastically* in your organization's planning activities. This enthusiasm will also create greater desire on their part to successfully implement these plans.

• *Integrate planning and doing.* Traditionally, *planning* and *doing* have been treated as two distinct activities: first management planned the work, and then operational personnel did it. Today, many organizations are waking up to the wisdom of a more integrated approach.

According to this new, more motivating paradigm, employees *plan* what they are going to do, then they *do* it. Then, based on what they learned from their experience, they plan again, and so on. This plan–do–plan–do cycle represents a radical departure from traditional, one-shot planning efforts. Today, planning should be a *continuous process,* not just something that is done at the beginning of a performance period. Not only is this a more effective way to plan, but it also adds variety, and many other motivators, to the context of work.

• *Maximize opportunities for employee input into planning.* Although many organizations may survive without their employees' technical input, they will never thrive *motivationally* without soliciting substantial employee input into planning. Employees crave the opportunity to contribute their ideas about what should be done and how it should be done, especially in their own areas of responsibility.

In almost every organization, there are abundant opportunities for employee involvement in planning, including product planning, budgeting, scheduling, manpower planning, contingency planning, planning for quality, planning for safety, and planning for training, to name but a few. However, one study showed that although over 70 percent of the top 1,000 American companies had an employee involvement program in place, less than 15 percent of their employees participated in it.[4]

Planning is a great way to tap employees' wealth of knowledge about the work they do. Not only are workers far more knowledgeable about many of the technical aspects of their own work processes than most supervisors or managers, but, particularly in customer service jobs, they are also closer to the customer. Employees get excited about being treated like the experts they are.

• *Start small; ensure success.* Nothing is more vital to employee motivation than *initial success.* Start involving employees in planning on a small scale at first.

One CEO explained to me that his organization's successful participative planning effort was based on phasing in employee involvement *gradually.* Before employees were included as full-fledged members of planning teams, they were used as technical consultants or advisers to existing planning teams.

Another company starts by involving employees in planning tasks; it then involves them in planning projects, then in departmental planning, and finally in organizational planning.

I have seen organizations make a serious error by throwing employees into "deep water" planning teams before they have even learned to swim—sometimes leaving them traumatized and demotivated. It is important to maximize the probability of early success by giving employees planning tasks that they can succeed in, such as planning improvements in their own job or work area, before moving them on to more difficult planning duties. If a large planning task is selected, breaking it down into subtasks will make the challenge more achievable.

Planning responsibilities can be increased as employees develop their capabilities. Before long, employees will be ready to participate in extremely complex and challenging strategic and operational planning activities.

• *Involve employees in goal setting.* Goal setting is an ideal place to start participative planning, because everyone needs goals. Goal setting has been found to be particularly powerful when employees set goals for themselves.

When employees set goals for themselves, individually or as part of planning teams, they tend to be much more committed to these goals than if the goals were imposed upon them. And surprisingly, self-set goals tend to be more ambitious than those that management would have set.

When employees are encouraged (but not forced) to set ambitious goals that make them stretch beyond their comfort zones, they tend to be much more energetic. In fact, the ideal challenge was once described as "within reach, but outside of your grasp." Easy goals release little energy, whereas ambitious goals often release extraordinary amounts of energy.[5]

When employees are allowed to participate in setting corporate goals, they also tend to be much more committed to achieving them. This is what happened when a large electronics company selected "six sigma" (no more than 3.4 defects per million products) as its primary quality goal, when an airline established a 98 percent on-time departure goal, when an insurance company committed itself to reducing claims processing time from thirty days to three, and when a hotel committed itself to "100 percent customer satisfaction or your money back." In each case, the goal was highly motivating because it was extremely challenging *and* because employees were instrumental in setting it.

• *Involve employees in strategic planning.* Strategic planning may be the best opportunity in the entire organization for employee input. Unfortunately, it is frequently overlooked because strategic planning has too often been viewed as an "exclusive club" reserved for top managers only.

Strategic planning at its best is a highly creative process that tends to clarify purpose and identify options. It answers such questions as: Who are we? Why do we exist? Who are our customers? What do they need and want? What are our strengths and weaknesses? How can we improve our long-term performance? Employees *at all levels* can benefit enormously from answering questions like these.

Most employees operate in a very limited domain and lack an overall perspective on the organization as a whole. Therefore, meaningful involvement in strategic planning tends to be both informative and highly motivating.

Some organizations are involving all employees in *top-down* strategic planning. For example, according to one model, once the senior management group has developed its strategic goals, divisions, and departments, other units then become involved in developing their own. Other companies, which are not yet ready for this approach, are still involving employees in strategic discussions about crucial strategic issues, such as quality, safety, and the acquisition of new technologies.

Although traditional planning has always been top-down, more and more companies are instituting *bottom-up* planning as well. These companies realize that because low-level employees are often closest to customers, markets, and technologies, they are likely to notice business opportunities that may not be apparent to those at higher levels.[6]

One company is even implementing strategic planning at the *job* level. Employees in each area of the organization are being asked to write job mission statements, identifying their internal customers, determining customer requirements, and listing critical job success factors. Employees who had previously been quite ambivalent about their jobs are now becoming extremely excited about them.

Visioning can be a particularly powerful aspect of strategic planning from a motivational perspective. A vision is a description of the *desired future state* of the organization. In one company, employees are involved in developing visions for their own departments and work groups; these visions are then incorporated into a master organizational vision.

Another company sponsored a contest in which teams of employees were encouraged to build creative models depicting the future of their company. This contest generated enormous enthusiasm and helped employees better understand the company's vision. The models were then displayed in the lobby of the main building for employees and visitors to see.

Although visions that are perceived to be public relations exercises are extremely demotivating, visions that are well conceived, employee-involved, and widely communicated can actually create enormous excitement. Many motivating visions make employees feel: "I want to pitch in and help build that kind of organization!" (The motivating value of visions is discussed further in Chapter 8.)

• *Encourage learning through planning.* Regardless of any documents that are produced, planning should be appreciated as a tremendously important *learning process* in itself.

Involvement in planning is one of the most cost-effective, and most motivating, training opportunities an organization can offer its employees. In addition to increasing technical knowledge, involvement in planning can also greatly enhance employees' intellectual skills (such as creative thinking, problem solving, and decision making) and interpersonal skills (such as communication, teamwork, and group facilitation).

Involvement in planning activities will change your employees forever, and make them much more skillful and knowledgeable contributors to your organization.

• *Create an "error-tolerant" environment for planning.* Some organizations believe that they can't afford to let employees make mistakes. In truth, organizations can't afford *not* to. If employee involvement in planning is to be successful, employees must feel that they can be creative, or else planning will yield only the most mundane results.

Therefore, it is important to create "no criticism" expectations. Supervisors, managers, and peers should withhold premature evaluations of employees' planning contributions. Nobody wants to look foolish, and it is imperative that participants in any planning process do not feel that they are being harshly judged. Otherwise, employees will be extremely reluctant to participate. The key is to be *open* to employee input, not necessarily to *agree* with it.

Enlightened companies treat employees' contributions with the utmost respect. They are careful not to allow the insidious influence of negativity to pollute the atmosphere. They realize that negative responses can destroy any participative planning effort.

• *Build cross-functional planning teams.* Organizational effectiveness depends on teamwork (especially cross-functional teamwork), and planning is the ideal opportunity for developing it. As a predominantly group activity, planning has unparalleled potential for enhancing productive social interaction and cooperation throughout the organization.

Cooperative planning also tends to lead to more cooperative doing. As employees from different work areas and job classifications are brought together in planning teams, great opportunities are opened up for improved communication and even for the elimination of long-standing interdepartmental barriers. These collaborative planning alliances often translate into improved working relationships throughout the organization.

Give employees from different areas of the organization a common focus and a common stake in success, and nothing will be impossible!

• *Make planning meetings brief, interactive, and enjoyable.* Meetings are where planning gets done. Ultimately, the quality of the experience employees have with planning will reflect the quality of the meetings they attend. Sadly, most people report negative experiences in planning meetings.

Disorganized, unfocused, boring meetings will undermine virtually any planning effort.

Some very successful planning groups use highly interactive warm-up activities to help bridge the gap from operational work to planning, prior to getting down to business. For example, one outstanding team facilitator encourages all planning teams in his organization to start off each meeting with some humor, such as sharing a "joke of the day," a relevant cartoon, or some other light touch. Another company jump-starts its planning efforts with a Planning Kick-Off Day, complete with appropriate dignitaries and hoopla.

Make sure that each meeting has a clear purpose, and that all participants agree on it. Meetings should also be highly interactive. In order to motivate through action, get employees involved in what I call "planning *active*-ities"—techniques that maximize group involvement. Ensure that your planning meetings involve "participants," not just "attendees."

There are literally hundreds of tools and techniques for making planning meetings more active, enjoyable, and effective. My favorite group method is the Nominal Group Technique (NGT), a modified brainstorming method that I have found particularly applicable to planning. It uses "structured involvement" to get everyone contributing. The steps in the NGT are as follows:

1. Group members individually and silently generate a list of ideas.
2. Ideas are recorded in round-robin fashion (with no group discussion permitted).
3. Ideas are discussed, clarified, and edited.
4. Group members vote to rank-order ideas.[7]

There are also many other effective group process methods available.[8]

An abundance of planning tools and techniques are available to help focus and energize planning meetings, including Pareto charts, fishbone diagrams, affinity diagrams, and decision charts.[9] Participants can use flip charts, index cards, Post-it Notes, and brightly colored markers to make their work more hands-on, visual, and exciting.

Encourage employees to plaster the walls with their planning products. It is highly motivating for employees to see how much progress they are making in their planning efforts. Also, allowing some debriefing time at the end of each planning meeting will provide an excellent opportunity for feedback and collaborative learning. Meetings can be further enlivened by *occasionally* surprising participants with refreshments or even catered meals (but don't make such treats into entitlements).

No meeting is any better than the quality of its follow-up. In fact, it is the expectation of follow-up that makes a meeting "feel" productive. Therefore, make sure that employees are always given feedback concerning actions taken and results achieved as a result of each meeting.

• *Keep track of the progress of planning.* One of the most frequently asked questions about planning is, "How will we know if planning efforts are successful?" Everybody wants to know the score, but planning is, unfortunately, one of those organizational activities that is rarely measured—except by bottom-line results at the end of a performance period, when it is often too late to correct the problem.

Although planning is not the easiest thing to measure, its progress can be tracked using such methods as Gantt and PERT charts. The quality of planning products can also be appraised using *evaluation checklists*. And the quality of planning meetings can be assessed using *meeting evaluation forms*.

Planning teams should be encouraged to give periodic progress reports to management. This will increase the sense of accountability, give team members the chance to practice their presentation skills, and provide managers with an opportunity to show their interest in employees' planning efforts.

• *Provide recognition for planning.* It is highly motivating for employees to receive special acknowledgment for their planning efforts. Unfortunately, in most organizations, planning evokes no positive reinforcement whatsoever. In SuperMotivating companies of the future, planning will be widely acknowledged as a major contribution to the organization, and employee-planners will receive plenty of praise and other forms of recognition.

In one company, a cross-functional planning team was assigned the responsibility of preparing a plan for its division. At the completion of its task, the team itself invited senior management to a combined presentation and celebration at a local hotel. It was very positively reinforcing when the entire Executive Committee showed up. The managers who attended were so astonished by the thoroughness and sophistication of the plan that they asked the team to lead its implementation. You can just imagine how excited these employees were to receive such a vote of confidence! Any organization contemplating high-involvement planning should consider doing something similar.

One final note: Before you commence any planning effort, I strongly recommend that you review some of the excellent published materials on team building and participatory planning methods currently available. I have personally found *Successful Team Building, The Team Handbook, The Memory Jogger Plus,* and *Tips for Teams*[10] particularly helpful. Many other relevant information sources are listed in the References section at the end of the book.

Progress Check

Now that you have read the recommendations for creating a more motivating planning system, how many of these ideas do you think could actually be applied in your company? Has something in this chapter captured your imagination and prompted a surge of desire to take action?

You might find it useful at this point to take some time to see how many planning system *demotivators* would be reduced and how many *motivators* would be added if you used the ideas suggested in this chapter to revitalize the planning system in your organization. (In Appendix A, you will find reference checklists listing both demotivators and motivators to help refresh your memory.)

If you do so, I am certain that you will find that adopting the ideas in this chapter will significantly reduce, if not eliminate, most planning system demotivators. Furthermore, I am also certain that you will find that *almost every motivator* is used at least once in the suggestions presented.

Action Points

The following Action Points provide a snapshot summary of the major suggestions made in this chapter. They will help your organization achieve high-involvement planning and get greater value out of your planning efforts and resources.

How to Overcome Resistance to Planning

- Respond openly and honestly to employee concerns.
- Ensure that employees understand the importance of planning.
- Demonstrate organizational commitment to planning.
- Make involvement in planning voluntary.
- Show that the organization is serious about reducing planning-related demotivators.

How to Achieve High-Involvement Planning

- Integrate planning and doing.
- Maximize opportunities for employee input into planning.
- Start small; ensure success.
- Involve employees in goal setting.
- Involve employees in strategic planning.
- Encourage learning through planning.
- Create an "error-tolerant" environment for planning.
- Build cross-functional planning teams.
- Make planning meetings brief, interactive, and enjoyable.

- Keep track of the progress of planning.
- Provide recognition for planning.

Notes

1. W. J. Pelton, S. Sackman, and R. Boguslaw, *Tough Choices: The Decision-Making Styles of America's Top 50 CEOs* (Homewood, Ill.: Dow Jones-Irwin, 1990).
2. R. A. Mackenzie, *The Time Trap* (New York: McGraw-Hill, 1975), p. 43.
3. Ibid.
4. P. Block, "Reassigning Responsibility," *NSPI News & Notes* (National Society for Performance & Instruction), October 1994.
5. R. H. Schaffer, *The Breakthrough Strategy* (Cambridge, Mass.: Ballinger, 1988).
6. N. Nohria and J. D. Barkley, "An Action Perspective: The Crux of the New Management," *California Management Review*, Summer 1994.
7. A. L. Delbecq, A. H. Van de Ven, and D. H. Gustafson, *Group Techniques for Program Planning* (Glenview, Ill.: Scott, Foresman, 1975).
8. See, for example, P. R. Scholtes, *The Team Handbook* (Madison, Wis.: Joiner Associates, 1990).
9. M. Brassard, *The Memory Jogger Plus* (Methuen, Mass.: GOAL/QPC, 1989).
10. T. L. Quick, *Successful Team Building* (New York: AMACOM, 1992); P. R. Scholtes, *The Team Handbook* (Madison, Wis.: Joiner Associates, 1990); M. Brassard, *The Memory Jogger Plus* (Methuen, Mass.: GOAL/QPC, 1989); K. Fisher, S. Rayner, and W. Belgard, *Tips for Teams* (New York: McGraw-Hill, 1995).

7

SuperMotivating Production

Now that you have seen how the planning system in your organization can be motivationally transformed, it's time to tackle the *production system*. Revitalizing the production system may well be the most difficult—but the most rewarding—motivational challenge facing any organization.

The Importance of Production

Production is what most employees are paid for, and what employees spend most of their time doing. Everybody, in every organization, is involved in some form of production work.

Production is the value-adding process through which something of less value is converted into something with more value.

Although production is commonly regarded as a process performed to provide an end product or service for external customers, most production activities actually benefit internal customers. In fact, as Schonberger has explained in *Building a Chain of Customers,* organizations are composed of "a chain" of internal customers and suppliers.[1] Nearly every work process in every organization produces some product or service that adds value to another work process. For example, accounting work *produces* financial data, personnel work *produces* personnel records, training work *produces* training programs, data processing work *produces* computer hardware configurations and customized software—all for *internal* customers. All of these "production" processes and many others supply added value to the production work of others so that the organization as a whole can produce the finished products and services that will ultimately satisfy external (paying) customers.

The *production system* of an organization consists of all the individual production processes within that organization. In fact, almost all the work performed in organizations—certainly well over 90 percent of it—occurs within the production system.

Traditional Production Systems

Since the advent of mass production, maximizing productivity has been the overriding goal of production systems. Frederick Taylor's "scientific management" approach to production enabled American companies to achieve extraordinary production efficiencies.[2] This was accomplished by breaking jobs down into simple, routine tasks, with each worker repetitively performing a small piece of the overall job.

Scientific management was the driving force behind the twentieth-century version of the industrial revolution. Through it, companies were able to achieve remarkable levels of production to satisfy the enormous worldwide appetite for American products. Huge factories, employing thousands of workers each, dotted the landscape and became the symbol of American manufacturing "excellence."

The scientific management factory or office took the form of an assembly line in which "mindless" workers were treated like any other factor of production. (The motivational deficiencies of this production model should be self-evident.) It is no wonder that traditional production systems have been dominated by routine behavior—and low motivation. In fact, traditional production systems were actually *designed* to accommodate low motivation!

Work Reengineering

Today, production systems are being forced to change. New customer expectations and intense competition are causing a dramatic shift from the traditional emphasis on mass production to more customization, and from an exclusive focus on productivity to a greater emphasis on quality.

Striving for both high productivity *and* high quality is requiring a whole new approach to production. The traditional mass production model is being superseded by one that is much more customer-focused. As a result, scientific management's emphasis on rigidity, uniformity, specialization, and centralization is giving way to a new production paradigm stressing flexibility, customization, decentralization, and continuous improvement.

The transition to this new paradigm has necessitated major organizational changes. This is why many organizations are "reengineering" their production systems. Work reengineering, recently popularized by Michael Hammer and James Champy in their book *Reengineering the Corporation*, is an aggressive approach to work redesign, pretty much along the same lines as that used by Japanese companies to achieve world-class quality status.[3]

Although work reengineering and many other contemporary approaches to organizational improvement clearly represent a qualitative leap forward from scientific management, they give scant attention to the vital motivational piece of the puzzle. No matter how radically production processes are technically reengineered—through such means as simplifying, automating, and eliminating unnecessary work—the *motivational* side of production still needs to be addressed. A permanent answer to low productivity and poor quality in production systems will not be achieved until the motivational aspects of work are reengineered as well.

I can assure you that if your company takes *motivational* reengineering as seriously as many organizations have taken *technical* work reengineering, the increased motivational energy in your organization's production system will knock your socks off—not to mention sending productivity and quality soaring!

How to Motivationally Transform the Production System

As we learned previously, adding motivators to the context of work has the awesome power to release enormous motivational energy. The challenge of transforming the production system is to "engineer" as many motivators as possible into the system so that employees' desires can be stimulated by a motivating context, rather than resisted by a demotivating one. This is precisely what the suggestions in this chapter will help your organization to do.

Establish an Active Work Orientation

Is a passive work orientation prevalent in your production system? Ask yourself: How much time do employees spend sitting and waiting? Do employees tend to wait for supervisory direction before taking action? Do they habitually, and unnecessarily, use the telephone as a substitute for personal visits? These are just a few of the symptoms of the vicious cycle of low motivation that afflicts many, if not most, traditional production systems.

In the most motivating organizations, employees should be *productively busy* all day, and should leave work feeling that they have really accomplished something worthwhile. During the work day, they should be physically active, moving around whenever possible, actively seeking information and direction (rather than waiting for it to come to them), regularly interacting with other employees, releasing and using plenty of productive energy.

In SuperMotivating production systems, the preferred work orientation is active.

You can begin to create a more active work orientation in your organization by reviewing the amount of time that employees spend actively versus passively, and then computing an active/passive work ratio. Discuss the active work orientation concept with employees, and solicit their ideas on how their work can become more active.

One of the major impediments to an active work orientation in production systems is that individual initiative is often discouraged. Workers feel as if they always need to ask permission before doing anything that is not strictly within the limited boundaries of their job descriptions. To overcome this problem, employees and supervisors should collaboratively generate a list of optional activities that can be added to workers' schedules (especially during downtime). These activities can include such tasks as process improvement, maintenance, decision making, problem solving, problem prevention, and discussing the needs of internal customers and suppliers.

In addition, one of the best ways of ensuring that employees are active and productive is to shift their focus toward the customer. Empower them to take initiative to satisfy their internal and external customers.

Make Work More Fun and Effective

In too many workplaces, fun is discouraged. Most employees have to leave work in order to have any fun at all.

However, *SuperMotivating production systems encourage employees to have productive fun.*

Management in some organizations is beginning to realize that fun and effectiveness are not mutually exclusive; they go hand in hand. Although many organizations do sponsor fun social activities (such as picnics, parties, and refreshment breaks), a few, rare organizations know how to do it right.

One company energized its employees to use an e-mail system they had previously resisted by sending electronic invitations to an "e-mail party." To attend, employees had to receive the invitation and send back an electronic RSVP. It was amazing how quickly employees learned to use the system effectively!

Another company empowered an employee-led "Fun and Effective Team" to initiate activities that would increase the effectiveness of work, and also make work more fun. Productivity soared, as did morale.

Yet another organization that prides itself on having a good corporate sense of humor actively encourages "controlled silliness," sponsors laughter breaks, and even airs a "joke of the day" over the PA system.

Another good way to make work more fun is to jazz up the physical environment. Factories and offices can be rather dark and dismal places. Why not let employees redecorate them? Even if the redecoration is quite modest, it can add a very personal and original touch. Alternatively, just allow employees to decorate their own work areas.

A progressive manufacturing firm invites all its employees to display their own and their children's artwork on the wall areas throughout its various buildings. This gives the spirits of both the artists and the "art appreciators" quite a lift, while also getting workers' families more involved in the business.

The SuperMotivating workplace of the future won't be metallic gray; it will be decked out in a "coat of many colors"!

Fun releases enormous positive energy, whereas too much seriousness blocks it. Organizations that know how to have fun are much more productive and have many fewer disciplinary problems, complaints, and gripes. Fun also stimulates creativity. Any organization that doesn't know how to have fun is definitely not getting the maximum energy from its workforce.

Make Variety a Way of Life

As we learned in Chapter 3, virtually any task will eventually become dull and monotonous. But one of the best ways to increase motivation in any production system is to *add variety* to the context of work.

In SuperMotivating production systems, variety is a way of life.

In some organizations, work duties are being dramatically expanded. The same employees who used to perform a single, repetitive task all day long are increasingly being asked to perform a wide variety of more stimulating and challenging *auxiliary duties.* For example, in one company, employees whose sole job used to be making 80,000 soldering connections a day are now performing minor maintenance on equipment, updating control charts, participating in problem-solving sessions, meeting regularly with internal customers and suppliers, serving on departmental committees and cross-functional task forces, participating on improvement teams, taking part in information-sharing forums with management, contributing ideas to organization-wide suggestion systems, and writing articles for an employee newsletter.

In one customer-focused hotel chain, the traditional expectation that bellhops confine themselves to carrying luggage and hailing taxi cabs is becoming obsolete. In this organization, bellhops are also trained and empowered to greet guests, check them in and out, perform concierge services, arrange for valet parking, and perform a wide range of other tasks.

In other organizations, innovative working arrangements (such as job rotation, job sharing, job switching, and temporary work assignments) are adding both variety to work and flexibility to the workforce.

Let Employees Make More Choices

The major difference between work and a hobby is that people *choose* the hobby. Everything feels better when it is chosen, rather than imposed. And yet, despite what we know about the importance of choice in motivation, employees rarely have any significant choices concerning their work.

SuperMotivating production systems encourage employees to make choices about their work.

Although some tasks must certainly be compulsory, and production schedules must be met, there are usually a great many discretionary tasks that could be performed. For example, in most production systems, there are virtually unlimited opportunities for quality improvement, problem solving, accident prevention, and training. The most motivating jobs let employees choose at least some of their own work from a "menu" of discretionary items.

A management consulting firm tries to practice what it preaches by involving employees in brainstorming a potpourri of discretionary tasks from which they actually build their own job descriptions. One delighted employee described it as "a lot like a work version of a salad bar!" These new job descriptions belong to the employees, not to management, and they are even changed from time to time. (Who said job descriptions need to be carved in stone?)

Other organizations let employees choose their own work schedules, break times, improvement teams, special projects, tools and equipment, training, etc.

In the SuperMotivating factory or office of the future, work won't be a dismal management-mandated chore; it will be an exciting adventure—co-created by workers themselves.

Maximize Employee Input

Although employees want to contribute as much as possible to their organizations, too many companies fail to use the extraordinary knowledge their employees possess. Workers are too often told in many ways (verbally and nonverbally) to mind their own business or stick to their own job. Most supervisors and managers do not appear to be interested in what employees have to say. In fact, a survey found that American managers put forward their own ideas *nine times as often* as they build on or support the ideas of their employees.[4]

In contrast, *SuperMotivating production systems maximize opportunities for employee input.* And there is no lack of opportunity for increasing productivity, improving quality, and reducing costs.

In enlightened organizations, managers and supervisors realize that *all* employees are experts in the work they do. Among the most valuable assets organizations possess are the ideas and initiative of their employees. In fact, it has been found that the most successful companies treat everyone as a source of creative input.[5]

One company tells all new supervisors during their orientation to the job: "The person doing the work knows more about that job than anyone else. So, use that knowledge!" In another company, production workers are viewed as innovators, not just operators.

In a large manufacturing firm, machine operators are not only workers; they have also been dubbed "performance improvement consultants." Their job descriptions now include many work improvement activities previously handled by staff personnel. In fact, one industrial engineer told me that "the operators [in his company] contributed ideas that no one else had even conceived of."

During my years as a supervisor and manager, I did a lot of input soliciting, and listened attentively to a great many ideas. Some of these ideas saved thousands, hundreds of thousands, or millions of dollars, but, more importantly, the employees whose ideas were solicited felt that management valued their input. And this was highly motivating. In just one case, a team of hourly and salaried employees made capital purchase recommendations that saved their company several million dollars!

Increase Employees' Responsibility (and Authority)

Most Americans dream of self-employment. This is because virtually all human beings want more control over their lives. Unfortunately, very few employees get much sense of power in their current work. Too often, management withholds authority and grants only partial responsibility.

In contrast, *SuperMotivating production systems provide employees with as much responsibility (and authority) as possible for their work.*

Every worker should have a meaningful unit of work to do, and he or she should understand the contribution that this piece of work makes to the larger whole.

Do you remember the janitor in Chapter 5 who wanted responsibility for the *whole* job? Employees want to proudly proclaim: "This is *my* job." "This is the product *I* made." As Robert Levering has stated in *A Great Place to Work,* "Good workplaces provide ways for people to assume increased responsibility for their own work."[6] However, bear in mind that as far as employees are concerned, responsibility without authority is just more work.

One organization that used to have a serious lack of cleanliness problem decided to give *full* responsibility (and authority) to the workers. When this company also initiated regular "family day" visits, the employees were extremely proud to show off their work area—and their flawless housekeeping.

Another large manufacturer has empowered problem-solving SWAT Teams to intervene when crucial production problems are encountered. These fully trained teams of volunteer problem solvers are deployed throughout the plant, like a volunteer fire department, to assist other employees in solving vexing problems and in learning from them.

Another company has attempted to turn employees' "jobs" into their own "businesses." Employees now have responsibility (and authority) for many traditional staff and supervisory functions, such as scheduling, quality, safety, hiring, training, and performance evaluation. Each work group is even given a small discretionary budget to fund employee-initiated work improvements.

Organizations that aspire to SuperMotivation are increasing the "degrees of freedom" they give their employees, rather than thinking of new ways to impose limits on them. One highly customer-focused airline authorizes employees to do "whatever is necessary" to satisfy customers. An electronics company empowers its field service representatives to immediately replace any equipment customers are dissatisfied with. A department store chain tells its employees: "Rule number one is to use your good judgment in all situations; there are no additional rules."

This is how one CEO described how he put his employees in charge of quality: "We informed line workers that from now on it would be their responsibility to make certain that only top-quality product left the plant. . . . It surprised me how readily people accepted this ownership."[7]

When management gives real responsibility *with authority,* employees start to think and act like owners. In one company, enhanced responsibility and authority increased productivity by 68 percent![8] One newly empowered employee told me: "For the first time, I feel that this is *my* work, and I am actually excited about coming to work each day."

Encourage Productive Social Interaction

As we observed in Chapter 5, most businesses view social interaction in the workplace as essentially nonproductive and tend to discourage it, at least during working hours. This is because few organizations appreciate the tremendous *synergistic potential* that exists among their employees. In contrast to the traditional view of social interaction, research has found that workers' relationships with one another make a huge motivational difference.[9]

Unfortunately, in too many traditional production systems, employees experience adversarial relationships. Internal customers and suppliers, especially those in different units, rarely get to meet or talk, except to blame each other for problems they encounter.

For example, in a prominent paper products manufacturing company, workers in one department had to accept incompatible paper rolls from another department, and then try to convert them into first-quality tissue and toweling. No wonder these employees felt frustrated, resentful, and apathetic. If only the workers in the two departments had had the opportunity to discuss the paper incompatibility problem with each other, it could have easily been solved. But because the system didn't allow any constructive interdepartmental interaction, the relationship between the units continued steadily downhill, and along with it went morale.

In contrast, internal suppliers should be encouraged to ask their internal customers such questions as: "What do you want from us?" "Are you having any problems with the products or services we are providing?" "How can we serve you better?" When they do so, they also find and build "win-win" connections between departments, focusing more on the commonalities and less on the differences. One organization encourages the use of "individual initiative networks," ad hoc, cross-functional groups that provide employees with the opportunity to interact, solve problems, and support each other's improvement efforts.[10] This organization has found that when employees are encouraged to *synergistically interact*—to engage in helping, rather than adversarial, relationships—the positive energy released is truly impressive.

SuperMotivating production systems encourage employees to interact with others who have crucial roles in the success of what they are doing.

Build SuperMotivating Production Teams

There is no better way to use the talent of your workforce than in teams. Nothing is more motivating than being part of a winning team—and any production system provides unlimited opportunities for winning teamwork.

There are many different kinds of production teams, such as quality improvement teams, work reengineering teams, problem-solving teams, teams to address specific projects, self-directed work teams, and so on. In fact, there is virtually nothing an *effective team* can't do. However, the value of any team depends on how well team members work together—that is, the quality of the teamwork. Powerful teams don't just happen; they must be deliberately built.

Here are some practical suggestions for how to build *SuperMotivating production teams:*

• *Seek volunteers.* Although it is not possible to rely on volunteers to staff all teams, a team will certainly be at an advantage when employees *want* to be part of it.

• *Clarify the team's mission.* There is only one reason for a team to exist: to accomplish some purpose. When the purpose (mission) of the team is clear, then all members are better able to focus their energies on attaining it.

• *Ensure sponsorship.* Teams should be backed by someone with the authority to provide the necessary resources and facilitate the implementation of the team's recommendations.

• *Make sure the team reflects appropriate diversity.* In order to maximize synergy, the best teams are composed of people with diverse backgrounds. In contrast, the least effective teams are those composed of people from similar jobs and backgrounds.[11] "Likeness" tends to perpetuate more of the same, whereas diversity stimulates both creativity and motivation.

• *Clarify ground rules.* The most effective teams reach early consensus on ground rules (or housekeeping items), such as meeting times, attendance, punctuality, participation, breaks, and homework, and on behaviors that will facilitate or inhibit team success, so that these issues will not cause disruptive conflict later on.

• *Make meetings brief, interactive, and fun.* People hate long, passive, boring meetings. As discussed in the last chapter, the best meetings are fast-paced and highly involving.

• *Equip the team with conflict management capabilities.* Disagreement is inevitable in any team. An *effective* team is not just a group of "yes-people." When teams encounter conflict, team members should have the internal capacity to resolve it promptly and productively.

• *Select facilitative leadership.* The number-one problem for most teams is lack of effective leadership. The most productive teams are not led by controlling leaders but by facilitators who know how to use group dynamics to bring out the best in others.

• *Allow sufficient time for team building.* It takes time for any group to become a genuine team. Severe time constraints early on can be extremely detrimental to team building. The most effective teams need time to progress through the normal stages of team development.[12] One company has demonstrated its commitment to team building in a highly motivating way: by sponsoring facilitated, off-site "team initiation" sessions to ensure that *every* improvement team gets off to the best possible start.

• *Promote a strong team identity.* Under the right conditions, team members can develop extremely strong, healthy, and mutually energizing bonds with one another. Some teams increase this sense of affiliation by using a variety of identity enhancers, such as team names, slogans, banners, logos, T-shirts, caps, and coffee mugs.

• *Define when the team's work will be done.* Unlike committees, teams do not exist in perpetuity. When a team's mission has been accomplished, it should be disbanded so that team members can redeploy their energies to other productive projects. Therefore, every team should know up front when to cease operations.

• *Celebrate the team's successes.* Give all teams a sense of completion, closure, and accomplishment. Regardless of the size, every victory is worth celebrating.

SuperMotivating teams should not just be formed, they need to be *set up for success.* When they are, the power of synergy is truly awesome!

Encourage Self-Measurement

In Chapter 5, we established the enormous motivational power of measurement, as long as it is used positively to encourage, facilitate, and guide, *not to control, find fault, or punish.* Measurement is never a problem;

the problem is the negative consequences that too often follow measurement. Unfortunately, too many traditional production systems are associated with negative measurement practices.

I have found that the secret of motivating measurement is *self*-measurement. *SuperMotivating production systems encourage employees to measure their own performance.*

In contrast to the normally negative employee reaction to external measurement, self-measurement tends to produce immensely positive and motivating responses. When workers are in charge of measurement, they know the system is there to help them, not to "get" them.

Almost any performance (individual or group) can be self-measured. SuperMotivating organizations of the future will let their employees devise their own measures, monitor them, and then take appropriate corrective action. Whether the measures pertain to quantity, quality, timeliness, cost, or safety, employees are fully capable of identifying appropriate performance measures and keeping track of their own score.

I advocate the use of "performance scorecards," an exciting self-measurement tool, to be discussed in more depth in Chapter 10. Like a scorecard in golf, this work version tells employees in a nonjudgmental way how well they are doing. When they are winning, the scorecard encourages them to keep it up. When they are losing, the scorecard prompts them to mobilize additional motivational resources in order to improve their performance.

Furthermore, you would be amazed to see how tough workers can be on themselves and others when they are in charge of measurement. In fact, in one company, a significant drop on their safety-related performance scorecard led employees to pledge never to let that happen again.

Self-measurement also facilitates personal goal setting and stimulates self-improvement. One hourly textile worker raised her performance from 35 percent efficiency to 120 percent efficiency based on the feedback supplied by a self-monitored performance efficiency graph.[13] And a data entry technician improved her performance from 550,000 strokes per month to over 3,500,000 through self-measurement![14]

Create a "Climate of Appreciation"

Virtually every employee wants more appreciation, and nowhere is the organizational "appreciation gap" larger than in the production system. Most traditional production systems provide a low level of positive recognition.

One employee summed up his frustration in the following way: "What happens when I bust my butt? Absolutely nothing!"

In contrast, in SuperMotivating production systems, employees are regularly told, both verbally and nonverbally, how much they are appreciated, and they are reminded of the significance of their contributions.

Realizing that little, but thoughtful, recognition means so much to people, some organizations show their appreciation for employees in a large number of diverse, creative, but not necessarily costly, ways.

A well-thought-out expression of appreciation is much more powerful motivationally than a large monetary bonus just dumped on workers by a wealthy company. To illustrate this point, consider the following two real-life situations: In one company, a bonus amounting to several thousand dollars each was added to the last paycheck of all employees before Christmas. In another company, a catered dinner (costing only ten dollars per person) was served to each work unit or crew by managers and supervisors during the week before Christmas, along with sincere verbal appreciation for a job well done. You probably won't be surprised to hear that the dinner was far more positively received than the monetary bonus!

Other organizations use little treats (such as distributing popcorn or surprising employees with a pizza party) to celebrate small but significant accomplishments or milestones. These initiatives create a "party atmosphere" and highlight achievements in a relaxed manner. As we discover in Chapter 11, opportunities for showing appreciation are limited only by our imaginations.

Action Points

The following Action Points review the ways suggested in this chapter that the production system in your organization can be motivationally reengineered.

How to Motivationally Transform the Production System

- Establish an active work orientation.
- Make work more fun and effective.
- Make variety a way of life.
- Let employees make more choices.
- Maximize employee input.
- Increase employees' responsibility (and authority).
- Encourage productive social interaction.
- Empower SuperMotivating production teams.

- Encourage self-measurement.
- Create a "climate of appreciation."

How to Build SuperMotivating Production Teams

- Seek volunteers.
- Clarify the team's mission.
- Ensure sponsorship.
- Make sure the team reflects appropriate diversity.
- Clarify ground rules.
- Make meetings brief, interactive, and fun.
- Equip the team with conflict management capabilities.
- Select facilitative leadership.
- Allow sufficient time for team building.
- Promote a strong team identity.
- Define when the team's work will be done.
- Celebrate the team's successes.

Notes

1. R. J. Schonberger, *Building a Chain of Customers* (New York: The Free Press, 1990).
2. F. W. Taylor, *Principles of Scientific Management* (New York: Harper, 1912).
3. M. Hammer and J. Champy, *Reengineering the Corporation* (New York: Harper-Business, 1993).
4. M. Imai, *Kaizen* (New York: McGraw-Hill, 1986).
5. R. H. Waterman, Jr., *Adhocracy* (New York: Norton, 1990).
6. R. Levering, *A Great Place to Work* (New York: Random House, 1988).
7. R. Stayer, "How I Learned to Let My Workers Lead," *Harvard Business Review,* November–December 1990.
8. J. DeVille, *The Psychology of Leadership* (New York: New American Library, 1984).
9. E. H. Schein, *Organizational Psychology* (Englewood Cliffs, N.J.: Prentice-Hall, 1980).
10. S. M. Herman, *A Force of Ones* (San Francisco: Jossey-Bass, 1994).
11. R. J. Schonberger, *Building a Chain of Customers* (New York: The Free Press, 1990).
12. T. L. Quick, *Successful Team Building* (New York: AMACOM, 1992).
13. L. M. Miller, *American Spirit* (New York: Warner Books, 1984).
14. D. O. Clifton and P. Nelson, *Soar with Your Strengths* (New York: Delacorte Press, 1992).

8
SuperMotivating Communication

The Power of Communication

It is impossible for people to work together, or for companies to be successful, without effective communication. Approximately 80 percent of our waking hours are spent in some form of communication. When communication is good, relationships tend to be positive; when it is poor, relationships are also. Nothing dramatizes the incredible power of communication like the Biblical story of the Tower of Babel.[1] In that story, the people were communicating so effectively in building a tower toward heaven that God exclaimed, "Nothing which they purpose to do will be impossible for them."

It is true: *When people are communicating effectively, nothing is impossible!*

Communication Entropy

All of us take communication for granted, like breathing, and tend to give it little conscious notice. Similarly, few companies give adequate attention to communication.

According to the law of entropy, anything that is neglected will tend to deteriorate over time.[2] Like a road that is never repaved, the "information superhighway" can become full of potholes.

While communication is the most powerful of management technologies, the words used in communication are also profoundly error-prone. There is a tendency in all communication toward misunderstanding, conflict, and confusion. In fact, it has been found that as many as 75 percent of all mistakes made in the workplace are due to ineffective communication.[3] Even in small companies, it is amazing how little *real* communication takes place.

Furthermore, although there is a tremendous amount of information disseminated, much of it is useless. For example, virtually every company generates numbers and reports that don't even need to exist.

Whether we are communicating one-on-one, in a group, or throughout an entire organization, communication failures are inevitable unless we work diligently to avoid them. Effective communication requires hard work and consistent effort.

Demotivating Communication

When organizations administer employee attitude surveys, the most prominent concerns identified by employees invariably pertain to poor communication. In my own research, I have found that at least 90 percent of American companies have serious communication deficiencies.

At least half of the demotivators discussed in Chapter 4 are *directly* related to communication, and the other half are *indirectly* related to it. Communication-related demotivators can pervade an entire organization, generating dangerously contagious negative emotions, which in turn create an overall climate of negativity within the organization. How employees perceive, and feel about, communication in their organization is a key determinant of the motivational climate.

The challenge for us in the remainder of this chapter is to create a SuperMotivating communication system from one that is, most likely, currently demotivating.

The Communication System

The *communication system* in an organization is made up of all the *direct* methods of information sharing, such as announcements, meetings, face-to-face discussions, telephone conversations, electronic messaging, reports, manuals, memos, bulletin boards, technical documentation, newsletters, and posters. Most of us are quite familiar with these communication methods. However, these methods are just the tip of the iceberg.

Each day, literally thousands of messages are being sent to employees *indirectly*. Even without saying a word, organizations speak volumes through such indirect means as architecture, working arrangements, organizational charts, titles, status symbols, rewards, punishments, evaluation criteria, and budget priorities. These and many other indirect messages convey a tremendous amount of information to employees about "the way things really are around here." Every aspect of your organization communicates some message to employees. (In fact, as we will see later, indirect communication is actually much more powerful than direct communication, because, as every employee knows, the truthfulness of words is always suspect, but actions rarely lie.)

Through both direct and indirect communication channels, employees receive a vast amount of information, from which they are usually able to piece together a fairly comprehensive sense of what is going on in the organization. Interestingly, although this information is, at best, subjective, incomplete, and fragmentary, it is surprising how consistent this perception is among employees within the same organization, and how consistently *negative* it often is.

How to Motivationally Transform Organizational Communication

As Saul Gellerman stated in *Motivation in the Real World*, "If you want to motivate, you have to communicate. Communication is indispensable to motivation."[4]

The ideas and recommendations presented in the rest of this chapter will show you how to reduce deadly communication demotivators, while simultaneously adding a great many positive motivators. The result will be a communication system that will both communicate *and* motivate. As we will see, SuperMotivating communication systems are *open, powerful,* and *interactive.*

Communicate Openly

Is your organization telling employees enough? If yours is like most companies, the answer is no.

Lack of information is a major cause of employee anxiety. What people don't know makes them nervous. For example, if I am on an airplane and it encounters turbulence, or if the flight is delayed, I want to know why. Not knowing the whole story makes me nervous. Employees also want to know what is causing the "bumpy rides" in their organizations. What people don't understand is often perceived as a threat.

When people don't know something they think they should know, they will try to acquire that knowledge somewhere else. That's why almost every organization has a grapevine or a rumor mill to compensate for the sparse information available through regular channels. This source of generally distorted and erroneous information is yet another example of communication entropy.

Most organizations are satisfied with minimal communication. They communicate only when they think employees need to know. Few managers realize how interested employees are in learning more about the organization—its plans, its successes, and even its failures.

Although they often claim to be protecting employees from information overload, managements' frequently paternalistic and protective attitudes toward information have resulted in unnecessary secretiveness, which is extremely demotivating. In contrast, being "in the know" makes employees feel valued and appreciated, and increases commitment.

SuperMotivating communication is open communication. Here are some of the things any organization can do to increase the openness of its communication:

• *Share everything.* The traditional approach to communication has been to tell employees as little as possible. The new, SuperMotivating approach is to tell employees as much as possible. There is really nothing that needs to be held back. Employees want to know everything: about strategy, goals, sales, costs, profit and loss, etc. Organizations should establish much more expansive guidelines for what information should and should not be shared. Here's an important principle of SuperMotivating communication: When in doubt, overcommunicate!

• *Communicate frequently.* Some organizations have been known to communicate openly once in a while. This is not adequate. An important quality of SuperMotivating communication is its frequency. Regularly scheduled communication should be the norm. Employees should receive weekly, monthly, or quarterly business briefings. One large organization schedules monthly "State of the Company" meetings to keep employees informed. Although the exact frequency of corporate communication might depend on many practical considerations, as a general rule of thumb: The more frequent, the better.

• *Communicate promptly.* When something noteworthy happens, it should be communicated promptly—not a week or a month later. Any time lag between event and announcement undermines the sense of trust. When something important happens, employees should be informed *immediately.*

• *Discuss the undiscussables.* The "secrets" almost everyone knows about (but won't discuss) have been called "undiscussables."[5] They are undiscussable only because management has chosen to suppress the discussion of a particularly sensitive issue (such as a controversial termination). Unfortunately, the failure to acknowledge and discuss this common knowledge simply adds to its mystique and contributes to fear within the organization. Bringing the undiscussables into the open is a major step toward defeating politics (and fear) in the workplace.

• *Share "inside information."* It has been said that "Confidentiality is the enemy of trust." Nothing will do more to usher in a new era of open communication in your organization than sharing information that has previously been considered confidential.

One company lets employees attend senior management meetings. Another organization invites employees to "Spend a Day with the President" (or another senior executive). Yet another sponsors lunches for employees to meet with top management to discuss key business issues. These initiatives send a powerful message to employees: "We trust you and consider you to be business partners; therefore, there is no longer any reason to withhold information from you."

• *Discuss failures.* Every individual and organization makes mistakes. Open communication is not possible in an environment in which failures cannot be discussed. One CEO even widely publicizes *his own* mistakes to remind all employees that everyone makes them. Employees appreciate a willingness on the part of managers to share their failures, as well as their successes. This type of revelation is a major signal that openness is for real.

• *Discuss ethical lapses.* Nothing reflects a more open communication climate than an admission of guilt. I don't know of any individual or organization "without sin." Surveys have shown that when organizations promptly 'fess up and come clean, it greatly enhances their credibility, both internally and externally. Admitting these ethical lapses makes a powerful statement to employees that they can *also* be open in their own communication.

Communicate Powerfully

In order to have the desired impact, SuperMotivating communication must get employees *excited* about the information presented. It must stimulate *desire,* and get employees to want to *take action* on the information they receive. Given the tremendous competition for employees' attention, both within and outside the organization, this is a tall order indeed.

The following suggestions will help you dramatically increase the power of communication in your organization:

• *Communicate vividly.* Most of the time, we communicate with words. Words are particularly powerful when they are vivid—when they create mental images that are stimulating, compelling, dramatic, realistic, and well defined.

Probably the best examples of vivid communication are corporate vision and mission statements. As mentioned in Chapter 6, a powerful vision can excite employees about a desired future state for the organization. This excitement can get them to rally around the vision, and make it come to pass. Most founders of successful organizations developed compelling visions for their companies, often long before others thought their ideas were feasible. For example, Ray Kroc *envisioned* brightly colored McDonald's restaurants in every neighborhood. Steve Jobs *envisioned* a user-friendly personal computer in every home. Fred Smith *envisioned* a super-efficient overnight mail business in direct competition with the U.S. Postal Service. Edwin Land *envisioned* instant photography for the average person. Ted Turner *envisioned* a cable television network that would provide all-news programming twenty-four hours a day.

Most of these founders' visions were greeted with laughter and derision, rather than applause, when they first formulated them. But their personal vision propelled them and their organizations forward. And when they achieved success, the critics stopped laughing!

It doesn't take an entrepreneurial founder to formulate a compelling vision. Every organization can, and should, have one. For instance, Scandinavian Airlines System (SAS) was a struggling, run-of-the-mill European airline until Jan Carlzon formulated a vision "to become the world's best airline for the business traveler." This brief, but vivid, statement was able to energize 20,000 employees to strive together to attain it.

Everybody wants to be "the best" at something. Striving to be the best is a highly motivating challenge that can instill great significance into ordinary jobs. As Peter Senge stated in *The Fifth Discipline*, "People truly want to be part of something larger than themselves. They want to contribute to something important."[6] Every organization is capable of becoming the best at something.

Other organizations have also been successful at energizing their employees through the use of vivid language. For example, IBM was able to build a powerful company around the slogan "The system is the solution." Ford Motor Company was able to get the entire organization to rally around "Quality is job one." Xerox revitalized itself by creating a new internal image as "Team Xerox." Stew Leonard's Dairy inculcates in each employee that the mission of his or her job is "to make the customer say 'Wow!'" Now, that's vivid communication! Vivid communications have the power to release enormous energy.

• *Communicate visually.* Whereas visions and missions can create powerful "word pictures," something more visual is often called for. We all know how effective visual depictions can be in advertising to external customers. Some organizations have used a similar strategy to increase the power of internal communication.

One company uses a "daily scoreboard" to send the message to employees that work is like a game—albeit a serious one.[7] The scoreboard, which looks a lot like a sports scoreboard, keeps a running tally of such business indicators as sales, production, costs (both capital and operating), and profit and loss. Once employees understand "the score," they follow it as closely as they would the score in their favorite sport or game.

One of the most powerful forms of visual communication is the *symbol*. A symbol is usually a simple visual representation of something more complex. For example, a logo attempts to distill the essence of an organization in a single figure.

In a particularly effective use of symbolism, one Fortune 500 company began displaying blue check marks *everywhere:* on posters, coffee mugs, hats, scratch pads, etc. The purpose was to build interest in and excitement about the new corporate commitment: "Consider it done!" This symbol—representing the check-offs on a to-do list—was extremely successful in conveying a new sense of urgency throughout the company.[8]

The CEO of another company made his rounds in a Superman-like costume as a visible symbol of the strength of the company's new product line. A medical equipment manufacturer arranged for all interested employees to visit local hospitals to view the company's medical products *in action.* And yet another manufacturing company requires all office employees to visit the plant so that they will have a greater appreciation for the manufacturing process they support.

In another company, videotapes are used to share success stories with the rest of the workforce. When an individual or team has achieved something notable, a camera crew is sent out to videotape the team explaining its accomplishment so that other employees can, at least vicariously, learn from the experience. A prominent Fortune 100 company has found video so effective that it has set up its own corporate television network.

• *Explain why.* Employees not only want to know *what* has happened, they also want to know *why.* Unfortunately, of all the five W's (what, who, where, when, and why), "why" is the most commonly ignored.

Often management makes excellent decisions, but fails to communicate the reasons behind them to employees. And as we discovered in Chapter 1, the new breed of employee is not eager to follow blindly.

Employees want to know *why* policies have been adopted, *why* sales have increased or decreased, *why* a personnel change was made, and *why* another company was acquired. Although this understanding might not be essential for doing a particular job, it is instrumental to creating a SuperMotivating context for communication, and it's also a vital part of employee education.

SuperMotivating organizations realize how important it is to communicate "whys-ly"!

• *Communicate personally.* Too much corporate communication tends to be impersonal. As we saw in Chapter 4, it is all too easy for key managers to remain comfortably cloistered in their offices, away from where the work is being done.

Very few companies appreciate the important role that *personal attention* plays in motivating communication. Most companies don't realize that "slick" presentations often have the opposite effect as intended. Employees typically view them as less credible (and less motivating) than more informal—and much less costly—presentations. It is fine to hear a riveting speech, read a vivid mission statement, attend an informative briefing, or view a well-produced videotape, but there is no substitute for personal one-on-one communication.

Here's what a few organizations are doing to personalize communication:

One medium-sized manufacturing company expects all managers to spend at least three hours each week visiting the operating areas of the company. Their responsibility is to talk one-on-one with employees about their jobs. They are encouraged to ask such questions as: "How is your job?" "Is anything bothering you?" "How can I make things better for you?" But, most importantly, they are expected to *listen* and *take action.* This powerful social interaction is evaluated, and managers are rated on the quality, as well as the quantity, of this regular communication.

It has been predicted that the most successful companies of the future "will be run by managers who walk the shop floor day in and day out."[9] What is your organization doing to personalize communication?

• *Communicate positively.* Too much organizational communication is negative. When this is combined with all the other negativity in employees' lives, the consequences can be extremely demotivating.

Management should make a point of sharing more *good news* with employees. When something good happens in a particular area, share it with the organization as a whole. One company shares the Top Ten employee accomplishments of the week. Employees are excited about working in a company where so many positive things are happening, and it energizes employees to accomplish more.

So much of what people say in organizations conveys *implied criticism*. For example, supervisors have been known to ask questions like "Why are you behind schedule?" "What's wrong with you?" It is much more motivating when those questions are reframed more positively, such as: "What is the status of your production?" "What can I do to help?"

Furthermore, instead of using the discouraging phrases listed in Chapter 4, try using encouraging phrases, such as "Thanks for the feedback." "Let's give it a try." "Keep up the good work." "I'm glad you're on my team." "It's good to work with you." "Well done." "Thanks for the effort."

I am not advocating "Pollyanna management," but I am suggesting a more consciously positive approach to corporate communication. Certainly, you shouldn't ignore the negatives, but be sure to focus most of your attention on the positives.

Creating such a positive communication environment will generate much more interest, excitement, and desire, and release enormous positive motivational energy.

• *Communicate indirectly.* Earlier in this chapter, indirect communication was briefly mentioned as a crucial element of an organization's communication system. No matter what organizations *say*, employees will perceive more truth in what they *do*. For example, regardless of what is said during a new-employee orientation or in public relations material, the reality of an organization ultimately manifests itself in how the organization does business.

A company can talk as much as it wants to about teamwork, but unless there are rewards for team effort, few employees will take the verbal statements seriously. An organization might swear it is committed to excellence, but if it retains and promotes mediocre performers, employees will immediately see the truth. A company might proclaim its commitment to safety, but then hide or rationalize accidents.

In fact, after a while, if actions do not match words, employees will often begin to take direct verbal communications with the proverbial grain of salt. In many surveys I have done in a variety of organizations, employees always emphasize that the nonverbal aspects of communication are much more credible to them than the words that are spoken.

Indirect communication can be a particularly powerful motivational force when it is used to reinforce important verbal messages. The most motivating companies send *intentional* indirect messages to their employees. Some are showing their trust in employees by breaking down traditional barriers, such as removing time clocks. One company demonstrates its trust in employees in a subtle, but powerful, way: by establishing an honor system for vending machines and in the company cafeteria. Employees keep track of their own debts and pay for food and drink by placing their money in an "honor box." When there is a shortfall, the employees themselves voluntarily make up the difference. Another company eliminated the need for management approval for all purchases under $100 (previously, even a $1 purchase required management approval).

When excessive paperwork was overwhelming another company, management sent a powerful message by removing half of the company's photocopying machines! (However, if it were not for the collaborative process used to arrive at the decision, this might have been construed as a demotivating takeaway.)

The CEO of a company positioning itself to be the low-cost leader in its industry unequivocally refuses to fly first class. In fact, his policy is to buy the lowest-fare "super saver" ticket available, despite any inconvenience it might cause him. Do you think this sends a powerful message throughout the organization? You bet it does!

Most companies send some of their most powerful indirect messages through evaluation criteria and rewards. In Chapters 10 and 11, we see how to transform evaluation and rewards into the most positive indirect communication tools that any organization has at its disposal.

Too many companies still do not realize that what they *do* communicates much more powerfully than what they *say*. That is why every organization should look closely at the indirect messages it sends.

• *Communicate honestly.* Although trust is the foundation of effective communication, it has been found that 72 percent of the American working population believe that basic trust in management is disappearing,[10] and 80 percent of employees say that they don't trust top management.[11] These findings should be disconcerting to anyone concerned with communication or motivation in the American workplace.

Remember that in Chapter 4 we talked about the "trust bucket"? It requires a lot of truth to fill the bucket, but only one lie to upset it. Suffice it to say that any organization hoping to build a climate of trust must take honesty very seriously.

When a large electronics company discovered a product defect, it immediately held information meetings to explain the problem *in full* to employees, so that they wouldn't get partial information through the grapevine or the morning newspaper. Management turned what could have been an extremely demotivating situation into a highly motivating one.

• *Communicate consistently.* If you keep saying the same thing long enough, employees will eventually understand what you are saying and realize that you are serious about it. Consistent communication sends a powerful message to employees that the organization is really *committed* to a particular approach. In contrast, when organizations flit from theme to theme, employees become confused about what is really important.

If your organization is really serious about quality, quality should be a constant topic of discussion. If safety is a high priority, it should be discussed continuously in a variety of forums and through the use of a variety of media.

One company president kept asking his direct reports *at each meeting* what positive actions they were taking to reduce accidents. This same question (along with the implied expectations) cascaded down through the organization, sending a clear message to everyone that safety really *was* a high priority. The result was a dramatic reduction in accidents, and this safety improvement program didn't cost the company a dime!

Keep reinforcing the same key themes and messages over and over again. And check your organizational communications regularly for possible inconsistencies. Then, if you find inconsistencies, eliminate them promptly.

Communicate Interactively

In traditional organizations, communication channels are almost all directed *downward.* Much of corporate communication is not really communication at all, but talking, telling, lecturing, informing, and exhorting.

One-way communication sends extremely demotivating messages to employees. It tells them, among other things, that their input isn't valued.

It is vital for management to hear from employees, because employees have information that management needs to hear. For example, it has been estimated that only 4 percent of all problems are known to senior management, only 9 percent to middle management, but nearly 100 percent to rank-and-file employees.[12]

Some managers justify one-way communication by blaming it on lack of employee initiative. After all, they say, "My door is always open." One employee only half-facetiously commented about the "open-door policy" in his organization by proclaiming, "Of course this company has an open-door policy. If anyone doesn't like the way things are done, management shows them to the open door!" Another employee explained his version of why there is so little interactive communication in his department: "It is hard to talk to a boss who is standing on a pulpit."

When done well, interactive communication can be among the most motivating aspects of organizational life. The three most visible components of interactive communication (discussions, meetings, and suggestion systems) are the focus of the rest of this chapter.

SuperMotivating Discussions

The dictionary defines discussion as "an earnest conversation." This means that all parties in the discussion *earnestly desire* to understand what the others are saying. Is this the case in your organization? Do employees earnestly desire to hear from management, and does management earnestly desire to hear from employees? Creating a climate conducive to interactive discussion is not as difficult as one might think.

One company schedules regular "rap sessions," in which senior executives sit down with employees in all areas of the company to discuss employees' ideas and concerns. These discussions work because management is serious about obtaining the feedback. It isn't just a token gesture. Even the CEO joins in the discussions from time to time.

Another company schedules quarterly "town meetings" to discuss key issues and answer employee questions. Still another company uses a similar approach to interactive communication which it calls "The Sounding Board." These organizations are finding that such meetings not only motivate, but also help to prevent employees' storing up gripes that can eventually explode into "bitch sessions" or other negative behavior.

Other organizations increase employees' sense of responsibility for communication by letting them organize their own meetings. A division of a Fortune 500 company has empowered a Communication Improvement Team to coordinate all communication improvement efforts throughout the division. Another company asked employees to select "communication coordinators" to facilitate interactive communication between senior management and each department. Organizations such as these are finding that employee-sponsored communication creates a greater sense of employee ownership in the communication system.

Some organizations are using "electronic discussions" to enable employees to communicate with managers by electronic mail and receive prompt replies. One high-tech company has an e-mail hotline directly to the CEO, and has found that when employees are given such an opportunity, they rarely abuse it.

In another company, computer conferencing allows employees to carry on highly flexible computer-mediated discussions day or night, without having to be on-line at the same time. And yet another company uses audio- and videoconferencing to link employees with one another and with senior managers. With new communication technologies becoming so readily available, interactive communication is no longer hindered by distance or work schedules. Interactive audio, video, and computer hookups can be established *anywhere* and *at any time.*

Interactive communication with senior management does not have to be formal, although formality is generally more likely to ensure that it happens. One airline chief executive set an excellent example of informal discussions by arriving at work each morning by 7:15 A.M., then spending the next hour in the flight operations area conversing with pilots and flight attendants before heading back to his office.[13]

SuperMotivating Meetings

Meetings are typically one of the most problematical areas of organizational communication. In fact, in Chapter 4, we listed "unproductive meetings" as a major organizational demotivator. Many people fail to realize that, including preparation and follow-up, a two-hour meeting for five people can consume twenty to thirty total hours and cost several thousand dollars.

However, despite current practice, meetings have the potential to be highly interactive and extremely motivating. Here are some keys to SuperMotivating meetings:

- *Determine whether the meeting is required.* Too many meetings are called because there was a previous need or because it has become a habit to meet. Other meetings take place to avoid personal accountability or to temporarily escape from "real work." Ask yourself: Could the information be shared or the decisions made in a more cost-effective way, such as polling people by telephone?

- *Ensure that the right people are invited to attend.* Do they have the knowledge and the authority to make the required decisions? Consider letting employees decide for themselves whether their attendance at a particular meeting is necessary.

- *Provide for effective leadership.* A good leader is an essential ingredient for a productive and successful meeting.

- *Keep the meeting brief.* Energy dissipates quickly. Make good use of participants' limited attention spans while you can.

- *Prepare an agenda.* Your agenda is like a script for the meeting. A well-crafted agenda can go a long way toward keeping a meeting focused and productive.

• *Determine what information needs to be shared and what decisions need to be made.* The agenda should be carefully designed to accomplish these key meeting goals.

• *Focus on one or a few key items.* Don't try to accomplish too much.

• *Set limits for each item.* Remember Parkinson's law: Activity expands to fill the time allotted to it. If there are no time limits, then, by default, an unlimited amount of time has been allotted for each item.

• *Solicit input from the meeting participants regarding the draft agenda.* Participants will feel much more ownership in the meeting if they have been given an opportunity to provide input.

• *Expect preparation.* Keep meetings short by assigning "homework." In fact, in the best meetings, much of the work is done outside of the meeting—before and after.

• *Design the meeting to be interactive.* Make sure that there are plenty of opportunities in the planned meeting for participants to actively participate.

• *Distribute the agenda in advance.* Encourage participants to prepare in advance for the meeting. Participant preparation will reduce wasted meeting time.

• *Start and end on time.* Late meetings are a demotivator for those who come on time. Long meetings are a demotivator for everyone! Manage meeting time well.

• *Create a climate conducive to open communication.* Establish norms favorable to open communication, such as "no premature evaluation of ideas." Don't let a few participants dominate. Everyone should have an opportunity to contribute.

• *Minimize criticism.* Too many meetings are "shooting galleries," in which participants' ideas get shot down. One innovative company came up with a very creative way to reduce criticism in meetings. At the beginning of each meeting, a single M&M candy was distributed to each participant. When a negative comment was made, the person had to eat his or her M&M. When the piece of candy was gone, the person was not allowed to make another negative comment! This technique alone made meetings a more positive and enjoyable experience for everyone.[14]

• *Resolve conflict promptly.* When conflict does arise, it is important neither to "fight it out" nor suppress it. Focus on areas of agreement. If there is a conflict among a small number of the meeting participants, the best way to resolve it is privately, outside of the group context. You might also want to consider tabling the issue or postponing the meeting until the conflict is resolved. Sometimes an outside mediator can be useful in such a situation.

• *Invite active participation.* Meetings should be active, not passive, experiences. Take advantage of every opportunity to solicit input from participants. Give *everyone* a chance to participate in some way. You might even consider giving a treat (such as a candy bar), like one meeting leader successfully did, when participants contributed ideas.

• *Use visual aids.* As discussed earlier, visuals can be extremely powerful communication tools. I wouldn't think of calling a meeting without at least one flip chart in the room. Tape flip-chart pages all over the walls. Participants love to see their ideas posted. Seeing one's ideas in print generates a lot of enthusiasm and a much greater sense of ownership.

• *Evaluate meetings.* Find out what participants liked best or least about the meeting. Solicit suggestions for how meetings can be improved (and participation increased) in the future. Such evaluation provides a great opportunity to obtain participants' input.

• *Ensure follow-up.* Most meeting participants are accustomed to "dead-end" meetings; they rarely hear a word about the issues discussed once the meeting is finished. Nothing will send a more powerful message that something different is occurring than providing for follow-up after the meeting.

SuperMotivating Suggestion Systems

One of the outstanding features of Japanese companies is that they are able to generate an amazing number of suggestions from workers. In fact, one Japanese company generated *over six million ideas* from its employees in a single year!

On the other side of the Pacific, the unfortunate stereotype of the American suggestion system is a black box on the factory floor into which employees deposit ideas—never to hear about them again. Although this is not always the case, suggestion systems are nonetheless greeted with cynicism by most employees.

I recently read about one employee who made a suggestion for improving a manufacturing process that saved his company hundreds of thousands of dollars. Sadly, the employee reported that he had been thinking about sharing the idea for thirty-two years, but his supervisor had never shown any interest in what he had to say![15]

This situation provides a particularly compelling argument for systematizing motivation. Employees' contributions should never be dependent on the reaction of a single individual.

While nothing is more demotivating than making a suggestion that gets stuck in a "black box" (or a "black hole") or gets criticized, nothing is more motivating to employees than making a suggestion and having it implemented. When properly designed, suggestion systems can be among the most motivating aspects of any company. As Edelston and Buhagiar explain in *I-Power,* "Having ideas on how to make work more productive is fun . . . exciting . . . [and] invigorating."[16] In fact, a good suggestion system can keep workers interested in their jobs, even when other factors might not be optimal.

Here's how you can SuperMotivate the suggestion system in your organization:

- *Create a positive environment in which all ideas are welcomed, respected, and appreciated.* Employees need to feel that their input is really welcome, and that no idea is too small or too trivial for consideration.

- *Establish a system that is free of all unnecessary bureaucracy.* Keep the procedures for submitting, evaluating, and acting on ideas as simple, straightforward, and user-friendly as possible. Reduce barriers. Do a "demotivator check," and remove any demotivators that might sabotage the system.

- *Solicit only constructive ideas.* A suggestion system is no place for negativity, and it should never be allowed to become a forum for complaining. A suggestion system should be a positive force for personal and organizational improvement. One company encourages more positive and focused suggestions by using "suggestion stimulators." Each week, a new "What can we do to improve . . . ?" question is posed to employees.

- *Make "making suggestions" an integral part of everyone's job.* Add it to every job description. Include it in every performance evaluation.

- *Implement as many employee suggestions as possible.* The purpose of any suggestion system should be to implement improvements, not just to collect suggestions. Therefore, as many implementable suggestions as possible should be solicited. One company does this by including an evaluation checklist on each suggestion form, so that employees can do a preliminary "implementability check" before submitting their ideas. Another company uses teams of employees to investigate and select suggestions for implementation.

An innovative idea is to give each employee one "trump card" per year. Employees can use this card to get at least one pet idea implemented immediately—within certain cost limits, of course. The "trump card" gives employees a tremendous sense of empowerment, even if they never use it!

• *Help employees improve their suggestions.* Too often the response to suggestions is yes or no. When this is the case, an idea that is 90 percent doable is often rejected because of the 10 percent that isn't. A better approach is to work with employees to improve their suggestions rather than rejecting them completely.

• *All ideas should receive a prompt and positive response.* Avoid the black box/black hole mentality. Employees should be convinced that, whether accepted or not, their ideas are at least going to be given careful consideration. To guarantee this, in one company, all suggestions are reviewed *daily* by an evaluation committee.

• *Give positive recognition for all suggestions submitted.* Although the most important recognition any employee can receive is to see his or her suggestion implemented, the most successful suggestion systems also provide some external positive reinforcement for *all* ideas submitted, whether they are implemented or not. One company publishes the names of all those who make suggestions in a weekly "Idea Power" newsletter. Other companies send thank-you notes or give employees a small payment (perhaps $1 or $2) when they submit an idea. Some companies give more substantial monetary and nonmonetary rewards when suggestions are implemented (particularly for those resulting in significant productivity or quality improvements). Other organizations sustain excitement by awarding employees "points" for each suggestion submitted. When the points reach a certain level, they are redeemable for gifts from a gift catalogue.

Action Points

The Action Points below provide a summary of the recommendations made in this chapter for motivationally transforming the communication system in your organization:

How to Communicate Openly

• Share everything.
• Communicate frequently.
• Communicate promptly.
• Discuss the undiscussables.
• Share inside information.
• Discuss failures.
• Discuss ethical lapses.

How to Communicate Powerfully

- Communicate vividly.
- Communicate visually.
- Explain why.
- Communicate personally.
- Communicate positively.
- Communicate indirectly.
- Communicate honestly.
- Communicate consistently.

How to Communicate Interactively

- Facilitate SuperMotivating discussions:
  —Implement regular question-and-answer sessions with employees.
  —Give employees more responsibility for organizational communication.
  —Sponsor "electronic discussions."
  —Encourage informal senior management visits.

- Run SuperMotivating meetings:
  —Determine whether the meeting is required.
  —Make sure the right people are invited to attend.
  —Ensure effective leadership.
  —Keep the meeting brief.
  —Prepare an agenda.
  —Determine what information needs to be shared and what decisions need to be made.
  —Focus on one or a few key issues.
  —Set time limits for each item.
  —Solicit input from meeting partcipants regarding the draft agenda.
  —Design the meeting to be interactive.
  —Distribute the agenda in advance.
  —Start and end on time.
  —Create a climate conducive to open communication.
  —Minimize criticism.
  —Resolve conflict promptly.
  —Invite active participation.
  —Use visual aids.
  —Evaluate meetings.

- Create a SuperMotivating suggestion system:
  —Create a positive environment in which all ideas are welcomed, respected, and appreciated.
  —Establish a system that is free of all unnecessary bureaucracy.
  —Solicit only constructive ideas.
  —Make "making suggestions" an integral part of everyone's job.
  —Implement as many employee suggestions as possible.
  —Help employees improve their suggestions.
  —All ideas should receive a prompt and positive response.
  —Give positive recognition for all suggestions submitted.

Notes

1. Genesis 11:1–9.
2. J. Rifkin, *Entropy* (New York: Bantam Books, 1981).
3. F. Pryor, *The Energetic Manager* (Englewood Cliffs, N.J.: Prentice-Hall, 1987).
4. S. W. Gellerman, *Motivation in the Real World* (New York: Dutton, 1992), p. 71.
5. K. D. Ryan and D. K. Ostreich, *Driving Fear Out of the Workplace* (San Francisco: Jossey-Bass, 1991).
6. P. Senge, *The Fifth Discipline* (New York: Doubleday, 1990), pp. 274–275.
7. C. Caggiano, "The Profit-Promoting Daily Scoreboard," *Inc.*, May 1994.
8. D. Armstrong, *Managing by Storying Around* (New York: Doubleday, 1992).
9. E. O. Welles, "Lost in Patagonia," *Inc.*, August 1992.
10. R. C. Huseman and J. D. Hatfield, *Managing the Equity Factor* (Boston: Houghton Mifflin, 1989).
11. R. H. Rosen, *The Healthy Company* (Los Angeles: Tarcher, 1991).
12. R. C. Whiteley, *The Customer-Driven Company* (Reading, Mass.: Addison-Wesley, 1991).
13. H. D. Putnam, *The Winds of Turbulence* (New York: HarperBusiness, 1991).
14. D. Armstrong, *Managing by Storying Around* (New York: Doubleday, 1992).
15. R. M. Kanter, *The Change Masters* (New York: Simon & Schuster, 1983).
16. M. Edelston and M. Buhagiar, *I-Power* (Fort Lee, N.J.: Barricade Books, 1992).

9

SuperMotivating Training

Nothing differentiates outstanding companies from mediocre ones like a commitment to training. The most successful companies in the world are the ones that make the largest investment in training their employees.[1]

It has been estimated that American industry spends over $50 billion each year on direct training costs, and over $200 billion when indirect costs are added. High-performing companies typically spend between 2 and 4 percent of their payroll on training. Although training can be one of the most costly support systems in any business, one CEO told me, "We've found that in our organization at least, ignorance is much more expensive than training." It has been said that "training is at the top of winning companies' agendas these days."[2]

The Training System

Training systems in large organizations generally offer a wide range of developmental activities, including new employee orientation, job-skills training, continuing professional education, supervisory and management development, interpersonal skills (communication and teamwork) training, conceptual skills (problem-solving, decision-making, and creativity) training, and even basic skills (literacy and numeracy) training.

In larger organizations, most of these training activities are administered by full-time, in-house training staffs. Smaller companies tend to sponsor fewer training activities, and those offered are more likely to be delivered using external resources (such as colleges, universities, professional associations, and consultants).[3]

Regardless of the methods used, the training system in any organization is aimed at enhancing the collective competence of the workforce.[4] This system will become increasingly important to companies over the next decade and beyond, since, while it is true that organizations try to hire the most qualified employees they can find, it has been estimated that by the year 2000, the skills of more than 25 million Americans will have to be significantly upgraded.[5]

In recent years, the technical aspects of training have advanced significantly. With today's sophisticated instructional design and training technology, courses can be designed to teach virtually any skill quickly and effectively. But as with the other organizational systems, the motivational aspects of training have been largely ignored. *Motivation is the weak link in almost every training system.*

Demotivating Aspects of Training

A successful training system should stimulate employees' desire to learn and create an environment conducive to applying, on the job, what is learned during training. Unfortunately, training (especially management development) is often treated as just "another favorite panacea" for solving business problems.[6] Untold billions have been wasted on unfocused, impractical, and inappropriate training over the years.

Most organizations tend to grossly underestimate the difficulty of new learning, and the energy required. Too many organizations simply drop their employees into brief training sessions and plop them back on the job, unrealistically expecting fully functioning skills to develop.[7]

Learning any new skill—whether technical or managerial—requires some habit change, and it is difficult for people to change their habits. One frustrated trainer dejectedly confided in me: "We gave them eight hours of our very best training, but it really didn't seem to accomplish much. After the training was over, they just went back and did things the same old way they had before."

In addition, it is not unusual for employees to have experienced frustration, anxiety, discomfort, embarrassment, failure, disappointment, and other negative emotions in previous learning experiences. Learning carries with it the constant threat of failure. Mistakes are an inevitable part of learning. There are times when almost all learners feel they are making little or no progress, or even moving backwards. These and other powerful countermotivational forces combine to create substantial barriers to learning.

But impediments to learning are only part of the demotivation associated with most training systems. Very few employees ever leave a training course, no matter how well designed, with much skill proficiency. To make matters worse, many supervisors, and jobs, do not allow sufficient time for the development of these still-awkward skills.

In addition, trainees often find that while they were away, work stacked up and productivity pressures increased, and that there is little or no support for the use of new skills on the job. In fact, supervisors are notoriously ambivalent about training, and sometimes even hostile toward it. Many employees report that on completion of a training program, their supervisor says something like, "O.K., you've had your training; now get back to work!" Under these conditions, learning, which should be a pleasure, becomes a constant struggle, and training becomes increasingly viewed by employees as yet another demotivating aspect of work.

How to Motivationally Transform the Training System

If the tremendous investment companies make in training is really going to pay off, they will have to direct more attention to the motivational side of training. Enhancing competence in the workplace requires a training system that will send positive, motivating messages to all employees.

The following sections offer numerous suggestions for *motivationally transforming* the training system in any organization. These suggestions incorporate virtually every motivator discussed in Chapter 5 in one form or another. In the process of adding these motivators, you will find that most of the currently demotivating aspects of training will also be substantially reduced.

Create an Outstanding Orientation Process

During the first few weeks and months of employment, the tone for an entire career is often established. Too often, employees are oriented to their new jobs in the manner described in the following narrative: "Usually when I start on a new job, the first thing that happens is the person who hired me takes a minute to describe what I'm supposed to do, and then throws me out there to do it."[8]

In order to be most effective, a new employee orientation should be a continuing process of enculturation that occurs over a prolonged period of time. During this orientation period, employees should learn about the organization (its history, philosophy, strategy, values, objectives, organizational structure, products, customers, policies, etc.), career development opportunities, compensation and benefits, health and safety, internal communications, training, and performance expectations. New employees should also have a chance to tour company facilities, review company documentation, and interact with key managers and a wide range of other employees.

One company has designed a particularly powerful, and spectacularly successful, four-week orientation process for its new hires. A checklist is used to guide new employees through the orientation activities, which include numerous lectures, tours, interviews, seminars, films, and discussions. Employees sign off on the checklist when each activity has been completed. In addition, each new hire is assigned an experienced employee to "mentor" him or her during the process. Supervisors and managers of each new employee are held accountable for the success of the orientation process, which is rigorously evaluated upon completion.

Make Training a Privilege

In some organizations, training is perceived to be a form of punishment. Employees feel they are being trained because there is something wrong with them. For these employees, training is about as exciting as a trip to the dentist!

In contrast, SuperMotivating organizations should tell employees, through both words and behavior, that training is being provided because they are so valuable to the organization.

In one company I have worked closely with, regular education and training is required for *everyone*, from the CEO to the janitorial staff. In fact, the CEO sits in on some classes to demonstrate his own commitment to training. Moreover, the top employees are rewarded with additional education and training *of their choice*. There is no doubt about the prevailing attitude toward training in this company, and this attitude is contagious.

Schedule Adequate Time for Training

One of the best ways to send positive messages about training is to schedule adequate time for it. Too many organizations spend huge amounts on training, but undermine their investment by trying to squeeze it in between other activities. If training is really important, adequate time must be reserved for it. *Training that is rushed is demotivating.*

Organizations must begin to consider training a top priority, not an afterthought. For example, one company shows how much it values training by adjusting work schedules for training up front, not after the fact.

Provide Training Just-in-Time

If you want your employees to invest significant energy in learning, they must perceive a personal need for it. No matter how much people might resist learning, when faced with a genuine, pressing need, everyone will become an avid learner.

An engineer I know resisted learning a particular computer software program for months, until he was assigned a project for which it was essential. Within a week, he had become the project team's in-house expert on the software! Based on this and other similar experiences, some organizations have adopted "just-in-time training." They schedule training when employees are most motivated to learn: when there is an urgent need to use the new skills (for example, right before a change in responsibilities or when a new technology is about to be installed). This "just-in-time" approach (in contrast to the traditional "store-it-up-now-and-use-it-later-maybe" approach to training[9]) gives more of a sense of purpose to training and stimulates much greater desire to learn.

Focus Training on Core Competencies

Training can also deteriorate into little more than information dumping provided to employees "just in case" they ever have to know. This "include-everything-but-the-kitchen-sink" approach to training wastes time and dissipates employees' energies that could be better spent on performance improvement activities more relevant to their particular jobs or functions.

Smart organizations are now basing their training on one or a few *core competencies* in each job that are most instrumental to the employee's success. These critical success skills, identified through in-depth needs analysis and pretesting, form the foundation of their job-skills training curriculum.

Involve Employees in Making Training Decisions

Training is a fertile territory for choice, but most companies impose training requirements on employees: "This is the training you need." "This is the course we are sending you to." These overcontrolling messages are demotivating, and often lead to negative (and rebellious) attitudes on the part of trainees.

Let's look at one company's alternative approach: At the beginning of each year, employees rate their *own* skills on a self-assessment questionnaire (incidentally, when validated against actual performance measures, the self-ratings turned out to be quite accurate). Based on this self-assessment, an annual training plan is developed collaboratively between each employee and his or her supervisor. With this new sense of owner-ship, employees participate in training courses with extraordinary enthu-siasm.

In another company, interested employees are invited to participate on training design teams. In addition, all employees get a chance to make suggestions for future training by completing a questionnaire or partici-pating in a focus group. Some companies let employees choose their own training from a "menu" of course options, as well as select session times most convenient for them.

Another approach that is gaining in popularity is called self-paced learning, which is based on the observation that everyone learns at a dif-ferent speed. As long as performance standards are not compromised, some organizations allow employees to take as much time as they need to pass proficiency tests. Computer-assisted instruction is particularly ap-propriate for managing self-paced learning.

Establish a Supportive Environment for Learning

As discussed above, for many employees, learning has been an anxiety-producing experience. If we expect employees to adopt new habits and venture outside their comfort zones, a safe place must be created where they can both learn and try out their new skills. A supportive learning environment is characterized by strong interpersonal support, lack of crit-icism, and trust in the learning process itself.

One company begins each of its training programs by asking trainees to list and agree on the rules they will follow during the training course. These norms generally include such items as "come on time to each train-ing session," "no criticism allowed," "no interruptions," and "everything said is confidential." Because employees develop these norms them-selves, they almost always abide by them. Furthermore, these self-im-posed rules ensure a much less threatening climate for learning and far less learning-related anxiety on the part of employees.

Provide Adequate Practice

Acquiring proficiency at any task requires a significant investment of time. No matter how outstanding the instruction, there is simply no sub-stitute for practice.

How much practice would you like the pilot of your flight to have had before entering the cockpit? Probably quite a lot. Then why do we give operational and customer service employees so little time to prepare for *their* trade before they are sent out on the firing line? Is it because we really don't think their jobs are very important? At any rate, this is often the demotivating message being sent to them.

A growing number of smart companies are making sure that employees keep practicing their new skills until they are able to pass competency tests and become certified to use the skills in the field. Employees in these competency-based organizations have no doubts about their company's commitment to training, and to excellent performance.

Ensure Early Success

Interestingly enough, practically all the training we receive in life, whether on the job or outside of it, begins with the same basic premise: The best way to learn the components is in the order in which they will be performed. In tennis, this means first learning to hit shots from the back court. In golf, this means first learning to make long drives off the tee. On the job, this may mean learning a very difficult skill before easier ones.

Although this sequential approach may seem the most logical, it is not necessarily the best way to design training *from a motivational perspective.*

Let's go back to the golf analogy. The poor initial drives off the tee most fledgling golfers experience are practically guaranteed to frustrate new learners, and, for some at least, also reduce their motivation to take up the game.

From a *motivational* point of view, it would be preferable for neophyte golfers to begin with short putts. When a new learner is able to consistently master a hole-in-one from one foot away, say five consecutive times, overall confidence and self-esteem will be high, and the individual will be ready to move on to higher achievements, like an eighteen-inch putt, then to putts from three, four, and five feet away from the hole. This strategy can also be used for virtually any complex task on the job, where motivation may be considerably lower than it is on the golf course.

This approach, which *almost guarantees* success, is based on the well-established motivational principle that "failure at first is apt to dampen the energy for all future attempts."[10] Designing training so that the simple tasks may be mastered before going on to the more difficult ones will provide every learner with consistently successful, and much more highly motivating, learning experiences.

Build Variety Into Learning

Training should never be boring. The antidote to boredom is *variety.* There is an abundance of training resources available. There is no reason why industrial training is still dominated by the old-fashioned lecture method.

With just a little creativity, organizations can design training programs that will keep trainees attentive and interested in learning. Offering employees individualized training plans, including a wide variety of training options and developmental assignments, is an excellent way of achieving this.

Organizations that want to stimulate and sustain enthusiasm for learning use a variety of media (such as overhead transparencies, flip charts, films, videotapes, CD-ROMs, and computers), rather than traditional, demotivating "chalk and talk" lectures. A wide range of instructional activities are also being used, including hands-on practice, simulations, games, role playing, small-group discussions, participation presentations, action planning, expert panels, and guest speakers, to name but a few. In these organizations, employees tend to look forward to training, rather than dread it.

For many other practical suggestions on how to add variety to your training, see my book *Improving Individual Performance.*[11]

Make Learning Fun

One corporate CEO advocates what he calls the "kindergarten principle" to increase motivation to learn.[12] This principle is based on the observation that most kids enjoy kindergarten, but after that, their enjoyment of learning goes steadily downhill. SuperMotivating organizations of the future will put the fun back into learning.

One innovative company uses a simulation to teach employees about how the company operates—complete with play money. Another company uses a variety of game show formats (such as "Jeopardy" or "Family Feud") to enliven some of its training sessions. Each "show" (training session) "stars" an "M.C." (trainer), and features two teams of trainees competing against each other by answering questions or demonstrating skills. Teams receive points for each correct response. Team members are free to help one another, which adds to building a cooperative, supportive environment for learning. At the end of each game, both teams receive humorous prizes. There is a lot of applause, laughter, and good-natured competition. Not only is this approach fun, but these training sessions have resulted in outstanding learning results. Yet another company enters

employees in a prize drawing each time they pass the quiz at the end of
a self-instructional training module (as a result, test scores increased 50
percent).

The only drawback of "fun learning" is that some employees have so
much fun learning they sometimes don't want to get back to work!

Concentrate on Developing Employees' Strengths

Believe it or not, it has been found that 90 percent of our nation's training
resources have been aimed at eliminating weaknesses, and only 10 percent at building strengths. This is unfortunate, because it has been found
that competence begins with the discovery of strengths,[13] and is developed into excellence through the repeated use of these strengths.[14]
Strengths, like muscles, will atrophy when they're not used.

When employees are operating in areas of weakness, they feel incompetent, and all the training in the world won't do much to correct the
deficiency. A prime example is customer service. There are some people
who are simply temperamentally unsuited for interacting with the public.
How much of our training resources have been spent trying to put square
pegs in round holes?

In *The Conative Connection*, Kathy Kolbe has identified four "work
preferences": "Fact Finders" are better at performing information tasks;
"Follow Through" people are systematic, cautious, and dependable;
"Quick Starters" are innovative and risk-oriented; and "Implementors"
prefer technical, hands-on tasks.[15] Rather than denying these individual
differences, organizations should assess these strengths and make use of
them.

SuperMotivating organizations of the future will devote substantial
effort to identifying and strengthening competencies. These organizations
will be careful to select the right people for the right jobs in the first place,
and then enhance their strengths through appropriate, powerful, and
highly motivating training interventions.

Use Peer Tutoring and Mentoring

Some organizations have found that peer tutoring and mentoring are
great ways to use employees' existing strengths, and simultaneously to
leverage scarce training resources.

As we saw in Chapter 1, every organization has highly motivated
individuals who, over the years, have "self-learned" amazing shortcuts
and improved work methods. Sadly, these exemplary performers have
too often been taken for granted. Fortunately, things are beginning to

change. Organizations are increasingly asking their star performers to share their expertise with other employees. You might think that the employees who had to learn their exemplary skills on their own would be reluctant to share the secrets of their success with other employees, but just the opposite is true. Most are delighted to have finally been recognized for their virtuoso performance.

Peer tutoring occurs when employees are called upon to share their expertise with others in *short-term*, on-the-job, one-on-one training sessions. Mentoring, on the other hand, tends to involve a *longer-term* relationship between an expert employee and a less expert one. Some organizations have adopted innovative arrangements such as "learning exchanges" and "idea fairs" to give employees the opportunity of sharing their expertise with each other.

One company has increased the flexibility of its workforce by adopting an organization-wide "buddy system," pairing employees in complementary jobs so that they can share knowledge. For example, a machine operator might be paired with a maintenance technician, and a customer service agent with an order processing clerk. Each employee learns valuable lessons about the other's job, and develops considerable empathy in the process. For the organization, this innovative arrangement has led to significantly improved productivity, quality, and cooperative working relationships, while simultaneously reducing training costs.

Facilitate On-the-Job Transfer

For training to be effective, the new knowledge and skills must be sustained through use on the job. At the end of a typical training course, newly acquired skills are often quite tenuous, and proficiency has rarely reached a self-sustaining level. What happens *after* training is actually more important than what happens *during* it. Sadly, too many companies abandon their trainees once the course is over.

While learning a new skill is motivating, *not* using it on the job is downright demotivating. Organizations that care about learning, and about motivation, realize that transfer of training must be a high-priority issue.

Some companies are facilitating on-the-job application of skills by training *intact groups* of employees who work together so that they are able to provide motivational support to one another when they return to the job. Organizations are also increasingly using "job aids," step-by-step performance guides that direct employees in the proper use of their new skills.[16] Job aids reduce the need for employees to memorize every step in a new work procedure before using it. This tends to enhance trainee confidence and increases employees' initial success in applying new skills on the job.

To further improve on-the-job application, a large consumer products company mandates *follow-up meetings* after almost every training course. These meetings reinforce the importance of training, while giving employees an opportunity to discuss on-the-job application experiences with other trainees and to receive encouragement from their peers. Employees find that when their company puts greater emphasis on learning, and especially on on-the-job application, so do they.

Many other highly motivating ways of providing post-training follow-up are discussed in my article "But Will They Use Training on the Job?" (which appeared in the September 1982 issue of *Training* magazine).

Increase Supervisory Support for Training

The supervisor may well be the most critical link between training and on-the-job performance. And yet, despite the crucial role supervisors play in employee performance, they generally have little formal responsibility (or accountability) for the success of employees' training. Remember the manager in Chapter 4 who boasted of attending several hundred management training seminars without "the slightest bit of follow-up"?

One company decided it was time to turn this situation around by getting supervisors (and managers) more actively involved in the training of each of their direct reports. All managers and supervisors are expected to provide coaching sessions for each of their employees *before* and *after* each training program they attend. The focus of these discussions is on how the training content can be most effectively applied on the job. Employees report getting much more out of training than previously, and supervisors are seeing major improvements in on-the-job performance.[17]

Develop Employees' Self-Learning Skills

The ability to learn on one's own is arguably the most important skill that anyone can acquire. All employees need to become more self-directed learners.[18]

Although everybody already possesses some self-learning skills, SuperMotivating organizations of the future will be systematically disseminating these skills throughout their workforce.

One company has established a self-directed learning process whereby employees choose learning opportunities and training resources from menus of options. In this process, trainers serve as resource persons, rather than as the primary dispensers of knowledge.

However, as important as self-learning is, team learning may soon become even more important.[19] This is why a fast-growing consulting firm requires all project teams to schedule review meetings after every project so that staff members can maximize learning from the experience. Employees lightheartedly refer to the review meetings after less successful projects as "autopsies." However, no matter what the content of the meeting, one norm is always followed: There is no criticism or blame allowed. This company knows that "In the world class company, there are no mistakes—only learning experiences."[20]

Celebrate Learning

One major reason learning has so often been associated with negative emotions is that mistakes are too often highlighted, while successes are taken for granted. Many organizations award employees with certificates of attendance, but I'm sure you'll agree that few employees find simply showing up at a mandated training session meaningful grounds for celebration.

One company I recently advised decided to give employees their training certificates *only* when they have demonstrated increased competence in the work. Employees in this organization now take training much more seriously, and are much more likely to use their incipient skills on the job. Moreover, they feel a justified sense of accomplishment when they have done so successfully. And now the delayed certificate awarding ceremony has real significance.

Toward a "Learning Organization"

The vision being depicted in this chapter is one of a "learning organization." As Peter Senge states in *The Fifth Discipline,* "The organizations that will truly excel in the future will be the organizations that discover how to tap people's commitment and capacity to learn at all levels."[21]

In learning organizations, employees will constantly be learning. And the environment will be such that employees will be active in pursuit of *their own* competence, while the organization provides resources and support. There may even be fewer formal courses offered, but informal learning will be occurring everywhere. Work and learning will be inseparable.

In these learning organizations of the future, employees will also be constantly learning from one another. There will be a lot of team learning and peer support. Furthermore, a wide range of learning resources (books, audiotapes, videotapes, computer terminals, experts, etc.) will be readily accessible to everyone, along with the time to use them. In short, *learning organizations will be SuperMotivating organizations!*

Action Points

The following Action Points summarize the recommendations presented in this chapter. They review the ways suggested for turning the training system in your organization into one that stimulates desire to learn and is conducive to applying learning on the job—that is, a SuperMotivating one.

How to Motivationally Transform the Training System

- Create an outstanding orientation process.
- Make training a privilege.
- Schedule adequate time for training.
- Provide training just-in-time.
- Focus training on core competencies.
- Involve employees in making training decisions.
- Establish a supportive environment for learning.
- Provide adequate practice.
- Ensure early success.
- Build variety into learning.
- Make learning fun.
- Concentrate on developing employees' strengths.
- Use peer tutoring and mentoring.
- Facilitate on-the-job transfer.
- Increase supervisory support for training.
- Develop employees' self-learning skills.
- Celebrate learning.

Notes

1. T. Peters, *Thriving on Chaos* (New York: Knopf, 1987).
2. J. M. Kouzes and B. Z. Posner, *Credibility* (San Francisco: Jossey-Bass, 1993), p. 159.
3. Many state and federal training grants are available to assist companies in enhancing their training efforts.
4. J. Hall, *The Competence Process* (The Woodlands, Tex.: Teleometrics International, 1980).

5. W. B. Johnson, *Workforce 2000* (Indianapolis: Hudson Institute, 1987).

6. R. H. Schaffer, *The Breakthrough Strategy* (Cambridge, Mass.: Ballinger, 1988), p. 46.

7. D. R. Spitzer, "Five Keys to Successful Training," *Training,* September 1986.

8. M. E. Gerber, *The E-Myth* (Cambridge, Mass.: Ballinger, 1986), pp. 119–120.

9. R. H. Schaffer, *The Breakthrough Strategy* (Cambridge, Mass.: Ballinger, 1988), p. 147.

10. W. James, *The Principles of Psychology,* Vol. 1 (New York: Henry Holt, 1890), p. 123.

11. D. R. Spitzer, *Improving Individual Performance* (Englewood Cliffs, N.J.: Educational Technology Publications, 1986).

12. H. F. Rosenbluth and D. M. Peters, *The Customer Comes Second* (New York: Morrow, 1990).

13. A. Zaleznik, *Executives Guide to Motivating People* (Chicago: Bonus Books, 1990).

14. D. O. Clifton and P. Nelson, *Soar With Your Strengths* (New York: Delacorte Press, 1992).

15. K. Kolbe, *The Conative Connection* (Reading, Mass.: Addison-Wesley, 1990).

16. T. F. Gilbert, *Human Competence* (New York: McGraw-Hill, 1978).

17. D. R. Spitzer, "Training: What It Is and How to Use It," *Performance & Instruction,* September 1991.

18. P. Senge, *The Fifth Discipline* (New York: Doubleday, 1990).

19. Ibid.

20. R. J. Schonberger, *Building a Chain of Customers* (New York: The Free Press, 1990), p. 29.

21. P. Senge, *The Fifth Discipline* (New York: Doubleday, 1990), p. 4.

10

SuperMotivating Evaluation

No aspect of work has proven more consistently demotivating than evaluation. In fact, in most organizations, the mere mention of the word *evaluation* will trigger negative emotions in employees.

Because employees are often uncertain about how well they are performing and how their performance will be evaluated, feelings of anxiety are likely to manifest themselves in varying degrees. While the actual threat to any "satisfactory" employee may be quite small, many employees still have a nagging, subconscious suspicion that a bad evaluation "could happen to me." This anxiety is further exacerbated by a host of evaluation-related demotivators (including organizational politics, unclear expectations, perceived unfairness, internal competition, criticism, and withheld information), and the ever-present, ominous threat of layoffs.

However, it is not evaluation itself that is the problem; the problem is how evaluation is used at work. In other contexts, such as in sports and games, evaluation is highly motivating. In fact, evaluation in sports is so motivating that enthusiasts spend endless hours studying evaluation statistics, even memorizing them. So why can't evaluation be motivating at work? The answer is: *It can!*

From Demotivating to Motivating Evaluation

Much of the problem with evaluation is due to the negativity with which it has traditionally been associated. Most of the evaluative messages we have received throughout our lives have been negative. And this negativity bias continues at work.

But when properly designed, evaluation has the potential to be one of the most motivating and self-esteem-boosting activities in any organization. Your organization's evaluation system can be used to generate tremendous excitement about performance, and to stimulate strong *desire* among employees for performance improvement.

There are two components of evaluation: measurement and feedback. Because measurement is the foundation of evaluation, it is discussed first.

The Power of Measurement

It is a well-known fact that people do what is measured, and employees form their perception about organizational measurement, first and foremost, by observing what happens to other employees: who gets rewarded, who gets punished, and, especially, why.

No matter what is said in an organization, *what is measured* sends a much more powerful message to the workforce.

The trouble with measurement in most organizations is that it is usually subjective, and it often doesn't measure performance that matters most. Nevertheless, human beings have become quite adept at playing the performance measurement game. According to the rules of this game, employees do whatever they think is necessary to make themselves look good.

One employee with a Fortune 500 company said that performance measurement in his organization centers on "keeping busy, not complaining, political sensitivity, and smiling at the right people." In *Conduct Expected,* William Lareau explained that in too many organizations, "technical job skills are a minor consideration compared to the image you project."[1]

In another prominent company, which is consistently rated as one of the best companies to work for in America, employees disdainfully refer to themselves as "The Get-Along Gang," reflecting what they perceive as being an overemphasis on strong interpersonal skills and team player attributes. Sadly, it does seem today as if employees are being judged more on how well housebroken they are than on how well they perform!

Since people will conform pretty much to whatever is being measured, it is vitally important that the measures be the right ones. Measures that are poorly conceived can have seriously detrimental effects.

In one highly publicized case, a pizza delivery company that closely monitored the on-time performance of its drivers was inadvertently encouraging reckless driving. An insurance agency that based its performance measurement of sales agents on the number of calls made ended up with fewer sales—and a much larger telephone bill! In another situation, maintenance mechanics at a manufacturing plant were measured on "wrench time" (the proportion of time actually spent making repairs). Unfortunately, this measure encouraged mechanics to look busy and discouraged them from carefully analyzing problems before making the repairs. Yet another company that used the number of recorded accidents as its primary measure of safety found that rather than reducing accidents, it was discouraging the *reporting* of accidents!

These instances of *mis*measurement not only negatively affect performance, they also seriously undermine motivation.

In contrast to most measurement at work, which is often subjective and misleading, measurement in sports and games has been painstakingly thought out and designed to be objective and explicit. The measurement process in most sports and games provides the score clearly—without bias or partiality—and the criteria for winning are known by all. At any point in time, individual players and their teams know precisely where they stand and in which areas they need to improve. There is no uncertainty, no anxiety. Even when subjective evaluation is used (such as in diving and figure skating), the subjectivity is minimized through the use of multiple judges and extremely precise rating criteria.

Although the thought of developing such a measurement system at work might appear to be a pipe dream, I am convinced that any organization willing to put the effort into developing more effective and responsive measurement will soon notice dramatic improvements in both employee performance *and* motivation.

SuperMotivating Measurement

The first step toward SuperMotivating measurement is to establish a more positive climate for it. This can be accomplished by taking open, visible steps to counteract the predominantly negative, demotivating preconceptions that presently exist about measurement.

For example, most employees think that measurement has a primarily negative purpose—to "check up" or to "find fault" with them. Consequently, they often resist it, look for ways around it, or even try to sabotage it.

If, on the other hand, employees become convinced that measurement exists to help them improve their performance, their attitude toward it is more likely to be positive and cooperative.

The ultimate test of performance measurement in any company occurs when organizational results are disappointing. This is when employees will pay very close attention to what happens next. They want to know whether the negative data will trigger the usual punitive responses (such as criticism, blame, the search for a scapegoat, or preemptive firings).

On the other hand, if they see that the subpar performance triggers constructive responses (such as problem solving or mobilizing a team of employees to explore what went wrong and how the situation can be improved in the future), they will know that something different is taking place!

Repositioning measurement from a process used to judge, coerce, and punish to one that is positive, facilitative, and motivating is an important challenge for any organizaton. In the following sections, four ways to make SuperMotivating measurement a reality in your organization are suggested.

Identify Objective Performance Measures

The worst form of measurement is subjective judgment. Nobody likes his or her performance to be measured solely on the basis of another person's opinion.

In contrast, *objective measurement* (such as that used in sports and games) is generally welcomed. That is why we must continually strive for greater objectivity in the workplace.

Interestingly enough, the main reason why organizations have relied on subjective measurement for so long is their reluctance to accept the increased accountability that comes with objective measurement. But the ability to measure performance objectively has always existed, through the use of "operational definitions."[2] Most performance can actually be *counted,* and, far from being anxiety-producing and threatening (as the more traditional methods are), the resulting objectivity is highly motivating for all concerned.

For example, if you want to measure quality, try giving it an operational definition, such as: "Quality equals x number of defects per thousand items." Suddenly it's measurable! Employees know what's expected; goals can be established; performance can be objectively managed; and excellent performance can be appropriately rewarded.

The same is true with safety, cost-effectiveness, or any other seemingly abstract performance dimension needing to be measured. Virtually all measures will be vague until they are precisely defined. Once performance is operationally defined, objective measurement not only becomes possible, it becomes easy!

Use Performance Scorecards

Human performance has two aspects: *results* (which are what people produce or accomplish) and *behaviors* (which are what people do to achieve results). Virtually every aspect of performance can be measured with a high degree of accuracy if both results *and* behaviors are objectively measured.

Number of sales, average order size, revenue generated, units produced, number of rejects, cost per unit, inventory level, number of accidents, and other such results, can be readily quantified and assigned a numerical value. But this is only half of performance measurement. Without behavior measurement, there is no indication of how employees are getting their results, or the lack of them. Unfortunately, few organizations do a good job of measuring behaviors.

"Performance scorecards" (first referred to in Chapter 7) are one of the most promising developments in performance measurement. Performance scorecards are essentially checklists of behaviors instrumental for achieving a particular result (such as a certain level of productivity, quality, customer service, or safety). When they are used, accurate *and motivating* behavioral measurement becomes possible.

The basic procedure for using a performance scorecard is as follows: First, a specific result must be determined and then enabling behaviors derived. These behaviors should be carefully pinpointed to ensure that they are readily observable. (If one behavior is considered to be more important than another, it can be given a higher weight.) Each time a listed behavior is observed, a notation is made on the scorecard. At the end of each measurement period, a composite numerical score is calculated, based on the number of positive observations and the behavioral weight given each item. Virtually any set of behaviors can be objectively measured in this way.

One large manufacturing company discovered what years of measurement research have clearly shown: Results-oriented measures of safety (such as "number of lost-time accidents") were not very helpful in determining how safely employees were actually working. Therefore, this company decided to use "safety scorecards" to measure safety in several of its plants. Employees accumulated points every time they were observed doing something safely. Not only did the incidence of safe behavior increase immediately, but safety results also did.

In the first three months of the program, lost-time accidents in one of the plants decreased 60 percent, and safety in other plants also improved significantly. As a side benefit, labor-management relations also improved because employees no longer felt harassed about safety. One of the most valuable lessons managers learned was that it is more powerful *simply to post the score* without all the superfluous criticism and exhortation commonly associated with performance measurement. From this humble beginning, positive measurement has became a hugely motivating force in this company, and the use of performance scorecards is expanding into other areas of plant operation, including productivity and quality.

It should be noted that *only positive behaviors* are used on performance scorecards. This positive focus provides two major benefits: It reinforces the positive behaviors, and it makes measurement a much more positive experience for employees. As a result, believe it or not, employees actually look forward to being measured!

Involve Employees in Developing Measures

Any organization that wants its employees to eagerly embrace measurement should involve them, from the outset, in identifying performance measures. For example, a major hotel chain had traditionally used two key measures of reservation agent productivity: "number of calls answered" and "number of reservations made." These measures might have looked good in reports, but they were not popular with the agents, who found that these measures did not consider the complexity of the calls, and even discouraged quality customer service.

When the agents were finally asked for their input, they suggested using "conversion rate" (the ratio of the number of reservations made to calls received) instead. They argued that this was a much better measure of the *quality* of their performance. Like a batting average, the conversion rate could be used by agents to keep track of their own performance. As a side benefit, it encouraged agents to sell reservations, not just answer calls.

By soliciting agent involvement, this company was able to overcome what has been called "the major drawback of traditional performance measures . . . that they exclude the people being measured."[3] And this company also found out that employee involvement is one of the best routes toward SuperMotivation.

Encourage Self-Measurement

In Chapter 7, the secret of motivating measurement was revealed: *self-measurement*. When employees are allowed to measure themselves, understanding, ownership, and personal commitment to the job are much greater than when the locus of measurement is external.

The ability to measure and keep track of their own performance enables all workers to maximize both performance and motivation. And this ability will become all the more important as companies continue to move toward self-managed work teams.

However, the ability to self-measure will take time to develop, since it is unfamiliar to most people. All our lives, we have depended upon other people to measure us: parents, teachers, bosses. This external dependency has contributed to the negative attitudes most people have toward measurement.

In contrast to external measurement, self-measurement is the highest and most motivating form of measurement. It incorporates many of the motivators discussed in Chapter 5, while communicating trust and respect to employees.

The objection to self-measurement that I hear most frequently is that employees might cheat. My experience is that employees will cheat only when the rewards for winning, or the penalties for losing, are too large. (This is one of the strongest arguments *against* the excessive use of external rewards, a subject to be discussed in the next chapter.) When measurement is used primarily for learning and self-improvement, there is no reason to cheat. Like self-learning, discussed in the previous chapter, self-measurement will become a crucial part of the learning organizations (and the SuperMotivating organizations) of the future.

How to Generate Further Excitement About Measurement

When you first began reading this chapter, you might have been incredulous at the notion of employees becoming *excited* about measurement. By now, I hope you see that this is a distinct possibility. Objective measurement, performance scorecards, employee involvement in selecting measures, and self-measurement will revolutionize measurement in any organization that dares to give them a try!

Here are some other ideas to try if you want to generate even *more* excitement about measurement:

- Sponsor kick-off celebrations for new measurement initiatives, with appropriate pomp and ceremony.
- Have senior managers visit areas of the company that are involved in innovative measurement activities to offer encouragement and support.
- Talk to employees about measurement whenever you get a chance.

Ask them about the measures they are using. Show a personal interest in their work and its measurement.

- Educate employees about measurement. Sponsor educational programs centering on work measurement.
- Recognize employees' contributions to measurement activities.

From Measurement to Feedback

The second component of evaluation is *feedback*. Feedback is the way performance measurement data are communicated. Although all measurement data provide some built-in feedback, few people are able to adjust their performance based on measurement data alone.

This is why so many people participate in formal feedback programs, such as weight loss classes. It isn't because they need a professional to tell them how much they weigh. The value of such programs rests primarily on the external feedback they provide: assisting people to interpret measurement data, develop action plans, receive encouragement, and stick with the program long enough to see results.

In most companies, the purpose of feedback is to provide information about an employee's past performance that will give a sense of how well or how poorly that employee is doing in the eyes of the organization. However, the key to *effective* feedback is its ability to provide information that helps employees to improve future performance. Unfortunately, feedback too often hurts rather than helps.

The quality of feedback is dependent on the quality of measurement. If there are any flaws in measurement, these flaws tend to be amplified during feedback, when the false information is communicated. Just as an inaccurate thermometer reading will distort all subsequent discussion of the weather, so faulty performance measurement will result in erroneous feedback to employees about their performance. However, if your measurement system is good (that is, objective and based on valid measures of results and behaviors), there is every reason to believe that feedback will be fair and accurate.

Unfortunately, even if the measurement data used by an organization are, for the most part, objective and accurate, there are still other potential feedback trouble spots.

The Feedback Gap

Sadly, there tends to be a large gap between the feedback that people want and the feedback they get. Employees in organizations everywhere report that they receive too little feedback, whereas supervisors repeat-edly say that they are giving plenty of it.[4] One study found that American workers get *less than half* the feedback that workers in Singapore, Taiwan, Hong Kong, and Japan receive.[5]

Here is a highly illustrative story regarding the lack of feedback given at work: A man walked into a local drug store and asked the druggist if he could use the telephone. The druggist overheard the following conver-sation: "Hello, Consolidated Foods? About six months ago, I saw an opening for a sales position. Is it still available?" After a pause, the man continued, "Oh, you filled it five months ago. How is he working out?" After another pause, the man said, "Thank you. Bye."

Following the call, the druggist expressed his sympathy to the man for not being able to obtain the position he inquired about. The man re-plied, "Oh, I *am* the one who got that job. I was just calling to find out how I am doing!"[6]

Although few would go to such an extreme to obtain feedback, most employees are just as starved for information about their performance. Few employees get comprehensive feedback more than once a year, and, even then it is of doubtful quality.

Not only does feedback at work tend to be infrequent, it also tends to be predominantly negative. On average, negative feedback is given five times more often than positive feedback. And on occasions when con-structive feedback does come, it is often too late for employees to use it to improve their performance. Clearly, the feedback gap in most American companies needs to be bridged.

SuperMotivating Feedback

Like measurement, feedback within the context of sports and games can be highly motivating. Players routinely receive a great deal of encourag-ing feedback, such as coaching, cheerleading, praise, applause, and recog-nition—all of which are integral aspects of virtually every sport. This is a far cry from the feedback employees receive in most work settings.

As one employee told me, the only time his company ever gives mo-tivating feedback is during the annual blood donation drive. During that campaign, progress is communicated daily, displayed on signs and graphs, posted on bulletin boards, and discussed in staff meetings. Em-ployees actually become excited about giving blood, and the goal is ex-ceeded—every year! I have often wondered why more organizations haven't learned the obvious lessons from examples like this.

One company that *has* learned achieved extremely promising results when it started posting a huge scoreboard updating operational results daily. The production manager told me, "All we have to do is post the score each day; the employees do the rest. Work has become more like a game!"

It should be clear that feedback is of great importance for improving human performance, and for increasing motivation. Let's look at some of the ways organizational feedback can become SuperMotivating.

Improve Supervisor Feedback

Although it has been my purpose throughout this book to *systematize* motivation whenever possible, the vast majority of employees will, for the foreseeable future, continue to receive most feedback about their performance directly from their immediate supervisor. Because individual supervisors approach feedback differently, it is extremely important that the role of the supervisor as the primary feedback giver be made as effective, and as motivating, as possible.

Here are some suggestions for improving the *quality* and *consistency* of supervisor feedback:

• *Create explicit feedback expectations.* One of the best ways to systematize feedback is to let feedback givers know precisely *when* and *how* feedback is to be given. Therefore, organization-wide feedback expectations and guidelines should be established as part of any evaluation system.

Studies have found that the best supervisors provide the most frequent feedback: daily, weekly, and monthly—they don't wait for the annual performance review. Organizations need to *require* frequent feedback.

• *Provide feedback training.* As indicated in Chapter 9, we cannot expect anyone to perform effectively without appropriate training and adequate practice. Therefore, no supervisor should be expected to provide effective, and motivating, feedback without intensive training. There is already a great deal of knowledge available about the best ways to provide feedback. This knowledge should be more widely disseminated. Supervisors, and others, will feel much more comfortable giving feedback when they have real competence in doing so.

• *Increase positive feedback.* All human beings crave positive feedback. It is the good news about performance that tells us that we are on the right track. Positive feedback keeps people striving toward their goals.

Unfortunately, positive performance feedback is not as common as employees would like. One employee sadly told me that in her organization, "one perceived weakness often masks a hundred strengths." This innate human tendency toward negativity must be checked. This is why supervisors should regularly "calibrate" their perceptions of others.

To accomplish this one company requires supervisors to submit monthly "F+" (positive feedback) forms showing the positive feedback they have given during the previous month. It has been estimated that positive feedback in this company has increased by over 500 percent, and morale has soared.

If you want to have a SuperMotivated workforce, make sure someone recognizes what all employees are doing right.

Supervisors and managers need positive feedback, too. That is why some companies make sure they also receive it—from *their* bosses.

• *Make negative feedback more positive.* Negative feedback (also referred to as "corrective feedback") is information that tells people something is wrong, and what they can do to improve their performance. There are times when all employees, even the best performers, need to receive this kind of feedback.

The major problem with negative feedback is that it usually feels like criticism. It also tends to provoke a defensive reaction because people are so accustomed to being punished when they make mistakes.

Here are some suggestions for how supervisors can turn negative feedback into positive, helpful, SuperMotivating feedback:

- Correct employees only when it will help improve their future performance.
- Correct an employee's mistake when it happens, not days, weeks, or months later.
- Don't deal with more than one performance issue at a time.
- Give negative feedback in private.
- Focus on the solution, not the problem.
- Close the discussion on a positive note.
- Always follow up with the employee.
- Recognize progress whenever it occurs.

One final point: Watch your nonverbal behavior. No matter what one says, the most powerful messages are often sent nonverbally, such as by facial expressions and body language. A misplaced frown or a scornful look can turn a potential learning opportunity into a devastating blow to an employee's self-esteem.

Elicit Positive Feedback From Customers

One of the most valuable forms of feedback any employee can receive is *feedback from customers* (both internal and external). Unfortunately, because of the human tendency to take positives for granted, when customer feedback is given, it is generally negative.

Smart organizations solicit proactive feedback from customers, rather than waiting for negative feedback to explode in their faces. In this way, employees can keep score of their performance "home runs," rather than just hearing about their "strikeouts."

This is why, from time to time, one airline distributes certificates to passengers when they board each flight. Passengers are asked to complete the certificates and present one to any employee who provides them with exceptional service. Employees can redeem the certificates for prizes from a gift catalogue. Employees have found this feedback method to be a refreshing change from the irate-customer feedback they so often receive when passengers experience delays or flight cancellations (for which they are usually not to blame).

A manufacturing company uses a similar approach to elicit feedback from *internal* customers. Certificates are distributed to each employee. They are to be given to other employees who provide excellent internal customer service. This has helped to make internal customer-supplier linkages more visible and has created more positive, motivating relationships throughout the company.

Use Performance Graphs

One of the best ways to systematize feedback is through the use of performance graphs. Graphs provide vivid pictures of performance trends so that employees can monitor their own performance. When graphs are well designed and frequently updated, feedback is virtually automatic. Although it is nice to get occasional personal approval, graphs usually provide sufficient feedback all by themselves.

In one plant where product quality was being graphed, workers eagerly followed their performance, monitoring trends as the graph followed its jagged, but upward, path. When they reached a "goal line" on their graph, there were congratulations all around. There was no need for a supervisor to tell them they had done well; they already knew they had! (In fact, supervisory feedback at that point might have even appeared condescending.) When the graph showed a temporary decline, there was no criticism or blame. The workers simply discovered the problem themselves, and corrected it. Under other circumstances, the workers probably would have received negative external feedback.

Graphs provide the following advantages over interpersonal feedback alone:

- Graphs are not dependent on people.
- Graphs make progress visible.
- Graphs stimulate positive emotions.
- Graphs trigger action.

Toward SuperMotivating Performance Appraisal

Earlier, we spoke of motivating feedback in sports and games and of the popularity of formal feedback programs renowned for helping people improve their lives. These ongoing, informative, constructive, encouraging, and success-oriented programs are precisely what performance appraisal should be like. Needless to say, this is not the case today in most organizations.

In fact, performance appraisal is one of the most generally despised aspects of organizational life. Around performance review time many employees experience their emotional nadir. Some employees are so anxious that they can't sleep the night before. One prominent observer has gone so far as to identify traditional performance appraisal as the most powerful inhibitor of quality and productivity in the Western world![7]

One of the reasons that performance appraisal has been so demotivating is its close relationship to promotion, compensation, and discipline. When employees perceive that their performance review will culminate in a compensation or disciplinary judgment, they are bound to be defensive about *any* negative feedback they receive.[8]

Therefore, the first step to take in the direction of SuperMotivating performance appraisal is to *change the focus.* The real purpose of performance appraisal should be on development—on improving future performance—not on compensation, promotion, or discipline.

When employees begin to realize that performance appraisal is going to help them to grow and to be more successful in their jobs, not only will they be much more receptive to both positive *and* negative feedback, they will actually welcome it.

When one company recognized its performance appraisal problems, it decided to change its entire approach. The first step it took was symbolic; it gave it a more appropriate name: "Performance Development Process." This certainly did a much better job of communicating to employees that the major focus was on development. It also accomplished another important function: It emphasized that performance development was going to be an *ongoing activity,* not merely the one-shot, end-of-the-year, thoroughly demotivating "data dump" that so many employees in this organization had grown accustomed to.

A performance development process, such as the one used by this company, should have four phases:

1. *Performance planning.* As a first step, employees and their supervisors meet at the beginning of each performance period to discuss expectations. Subsequent appraisal activities are then focused on providing feedback on the employee's progress in meeting these expectations.

2. *Regular feedback.* Employees receive ongoing, if informal, feedback—preferably on a daily basis, but certainly no less regularly than once a week. Supervisors are trained in how to give positive, constructive feedback, pointing out and reinforcing strengths, improvement, and progress. When negative (corrective) feedback is called for, supervisors are expected to use a positive approach (such as the one suggested earlier in this chapter).

3. *Interim reviews.* Employees shouldn't have to wait until the end of the year to get comprehensive feedback. The purpose of an interim review is to summarize the feedback given up to that time, and to discuss the employee's development thus far. Interim reviews (weekly, monthly, or quarterly) will remove many of the negatives currently associated with the traditional one-shot annual review.

4. *Annual review.* In an ongoing feedback process, the annual performance review tends to be deemphasized. In such a process, the performance review becomes a summary (a review) of the feedback previously given. It should *never* introduce any new information. If supervisors have done their job throughout the performance period, there should be no surprises at all. The annual review should be a time of celebration, not one of fear and trepidation, and a time of looking forward to the next period with confidence and positive anticipation.

Although managers and supervisors in the above company initially resisted the new approach because of the additional effort they thought it would entail, it has worked out extremely well for all concerned. Employees now get much more timely and less intimidating feedback. Furthermore, the in-depth training that accompanied the program has turned the supervisors into virtuoso feedback providers! Both employees and supervisors are now enthusiastic about the Performance Development Process. In fact, one corporate vice president told me, "I wouldn't have believed it if I hadn't seen it with my own eyes: The major demotivator in this company has become a major motivator!"

Here are some other important caveats for transforming performance appraisal from a dreaded experience into a positive, useful, and motivating one:

- *Avoid quantitative ratings.* Quantitative performance ratings should not be confused with the objective quantification methods described in the measurement section. By attempting to find *quantifiable measures,* organizations can reduce subjective judgments. *Quantitative ratings* are usually a crude attempt to create an artificial "common denominator" so that employees can be ranked for merit pay and other compensation and personnel decisions.

    For example, the use of numerical performance categories such as (5) outstanding, (4) exceeds expectations, (3) meets expectations, (2) below expectations, and (1) far below expectations causes most employees to feel like *losers* because even when they are doing their jobs as prescribed, they are two categories below the top rating. Indeed, no subjectivity is more insidious than subjectivity masquerading as objectivity, which is precisely what numerical rating scales are. In addition, performance ratings are extremely susceptible to many kinds of measurement errors.[9]

- *Reduce the emphasis on forms.* Not only do many organizations inappropriately rate and rank employees, they also suffer from a form fixation. In these companies, it sometimes appears as if the purpose of appraisal is to complete a form, not to provide feedback to employees. Although forms can serve as useful documentation, they too often dictate the appraisal process, rather than support it, and they also tend to needlessly increase the paperwork burden of those doing the appraising.

- *Use multiple appraisers.* Because all human beings are prone to bias (both positive and negative), interpretation of performance data is open to considerable distortion. That is why, in sports and games, when any aspect of performance cannot be easily counted, judgments are usually made by more than one rater. Why is it, then, that performance appraisal at work almost always depends on one person's judgment? Smart companies are beginning to use multiple performance appraisers, including the employee, the supervisor, peers (co-workers), team members, and internal customers and suppliers. In fact, one expert even indicated that "the only proper evaluation is group evaluation in which a person's work is looked at by all the people who interface with that person."[10]

    Combining judgments from many different vantage points will ultimately provide a much fairer, more accurate, and more comprehensive picture of an employee's performance. Furthermore, organizations that depend on a high level of teamwork are increasingly using team-based performance appraisals as the method of choice.

• *Stress honesty.* Performance appraisal has been particularly prone to dishonesty. Many managers and supervisors are simply not prepared to tell the truth about employee performance. This observation applies especially to the evaluation of poor performers. The common practice of evaluating poor performers as "satisfactory" devalues the entire performance appraisal process for everybody else.

As I was quoted as saying in an article on the problems of performance appraisal, "Managers are afraid of performance appraisals because they are afraid of their people. They are afraid to confront people, to tell them straightaway that they are doing a bad job. I've seen managers agonize for weeks over a performance review for a person everyone in the department knew to be incompetent."[11]

Honesty in performance appraisal should become a norm in any organization that is serious about performance and high motivation.

• *Encourage self-appraisal.* Probably the most important performance appraisers are employees themselves. All employees should have the opportunity to self-appraise at least once a year. Self-appraisal is an extremely valuable and motivating developmental experience in which few employees have had an opportunity to participate. In fact, it has been said that, "Regardless of how employee performance is appraised, the performance evaluation that will carry the most weight will be the evaluation that employees make of themselves."[12]

Self-appraisal serves a number of purposes: It treats employees like adults who have the ability to evaluate themselves; it develops self-evaluation skills; it encourages positively self-critical attitudes toward performance; it provides the opportunity to reconcile perceptual differences between supervisors and employees; and it shows employees that the company really *does* care about what they have to say.

• *Discuss draft reviews.* The problem with a lot of performance reviews is that they are "given to" employees, rather than being the basis for motivating, *interactive* discussions.

One excellent way to achieve a more open exchange of information is to give employees an opportunity to discuss the reviews, *in draft form,* with their supervisor, prior to their finalization. Such preliminary performance discussions also permit greater consideration of the contextual factors that are so often ignored in assessing employee performance. In fact, Deming and others have pointed out that as much as 94 percent of all performance problems are caused by factors over which employees have no control.[13]

An innovative hospital schedules *preview sessions* prior to every annual performance review. During this session, supervisors and employees discuss all the raw data received from a variety of sources, including "critical incidents" (narrative descriptions of particular events that occurred during the performance period), the employee's own self-appraisal, the supervisor's preliminary appraisal, and input from patients and internal customers and suppliers. These previews have created a much more positive atmosphere for performance appraisal throughout the organization, and have given employees a more active role in the appraisal process.

• *Encourage employees to initiate performance discussions.* Most employees have been conditioned to sit back passively and wait for their supervisor to discuss their performance with them. Instead, employees should be encouraged to initiate feedback discussions at any time. When employees begin to view performance appraisal as a positive, developmental process, they will actively seek out feedback, rather than wait for it to come to them. This also takes some of the pressure off supervisors, who are too often perceived to be the sole initiators of performance feedback.

• *Let employees appraise their supervisors.* Nothing will send a more powerful, motivating message that management is really serious about performance, development, and improvement than letting employees appraise their supervisors. Fair is fair! This feedback is also crucial to supervisor development.

New Directions in Performance Evaluation

You have probably already figured out that the area of performance evaluation is ripe for change. No organizational system needs change more! I have never met an employee who didn't want to see the evaluation system in his or her organization change dramatically. However, transforming the *system* of evaluation will require a radical change in our *thinking* about evaluation.

As alluded to throughout this chapter, there appear to be at *least* five major trends taking place in the field of performance evaluation that are beginning to change the motivational climate of performance evaluation:

1. The trend away from subjective measurement toward more objective measurement
2. The trend away from one-shot performance reviews toward ongoing performance appraisal processes
3. The trend away from the focus of evaluation on compensation decision making toward a focus on development

4. The trend away from supervisor evaluation toward multiple-source evaluation

5. The trend away from external evaluation toward self-evaluation

I am confident that the ideas presented in this chapter will open up many new and exciting opportunities for improving the evaluation system in your organization.

Action Points

The prospects are very positive for organizational evaluation. The Action Points presented below summarize ways in which the evaluation system in any organization can be motivationally transformed into a process characterized by objectivity, self-measurement, and interactive performance communication.

How to Create SuperMotivating Measurement

- Establish a positive climate for measurement.
- Identify objective performance measures.
- Objectively measure behaviors, as well as results.
- Use performance scorecards.
- Involve employees in developing measures.
- Encourage self-measurement.
- Generate excitement about measurement.

How to Achieve SuperMotivating Feedback

- Improve supervisor feedback:
  —Create explicit feedback expectations.
  —Provide feedback training.
  —Increase positive feedback.
  —Make negative feedback more positive.
- Elicit positive feedback from customers.
- Use performance graphs.

How to Attain SuperMotivating Performance Appraisal

- Focus on development.
- Establish a performance development process, including:
  —Performance planning.
  —Regular feedback.

—Interim reviews.
—Annual review.
• Avoid quantitative ratings.
• Reduce the emphasis on forms.
• Use multiple appraisers.
• Stress honesty.
• Encourage self-appraisal.
• Discuss draft reviews.
• Encourage employees to initiate performance discussions.
• Let employees appraise their supervisors.

Notes

1. W. Lareau, *Conduct Expected* (Piscataway, N.J.: New Century, 1985), p. 16.
2. W. E. Deming, *Out of the Crisis* (Cambridge, Mass.: MIT Press, 1986).
3. M. L. Srikanth, "For Performance, Think Nontraditional," *Industry Week,* July 6, 1992, p. 52.
4. R. C. Huseman and J. D. Hatfield, *Managing the Equity Factor* (Cambridge, Mass.: Houghton Mifflin, 1989).
5. M. Imai, *Kaizen* (New York; McGraw-Hill, 1986).
6. Story adapted from J. Clemmer, *Firing on All Cylinders* (London: Piatkus, 1991).
7. W. E. Deming, *Out of the Crisis* (Cambridge, Mass.: MIT Press, 1986).
8. D. L. Kirkpatrick, "Performance Appraisal: When Two Jobs Are Too Many," *Training,* March 1986.
9. See, for example, C. E. Schneider, R. W. Beatty, and L. S. Baird, *The Performance Management Sourcebook* (Amherst, Mass.: Human Resource Development Press, 1987).
10. P. B. Crosby, *Running Things* (New York: Mentor, 1989), p. 243.
11. R. Zemke, "Is Performance Appraisal a Paper Tiger?" *Training,* December 1985, p. 25.
12. C. C. Manz and H. P. Sims, *SuperLeadership* (New York: Berkley, 1989), p. 7.
13. W. E. Deming, *Out of the Crisis* (Cambridge, Mass.: MIT Press, 1986).

11

SuperMotivating Rewards

One of the major themes of this book is that rewards are only one part of the overall motivation puzzle. Nevertheless, they are a very important part. When handled adroitly, rewards can be a pivotal element in a unified, strategic approach to organizational motivation. However, before proceeding, it is important to note that rewards don't motivate; it is the anticipation of rewards that does. When rewards are given, their role as powerful *incentives* to motivate is reinforced.

Many organizations are increasingly discovering that not only are traditional rewards becoming extremely limited in their ability to motivate today's workforce, but they are also extremely costly. In too many companies, the reward system has become a bottomless hole into which millions, even billions, of dollars are thrown away annually, while employees complain that they don't find the reward system very rewarding, and frequently consider it to be one of the most *de*motivating aspects of their company.

Just as with other organizational systems, motivationally transforming the reward system requires looking at it with a fresh, new perspective. The most important question to ask in evaluating the reward system in your organization is, "Do the rewards elicit the kind of *performance* management desires?" In this chapter, you will learn how to make rewards both a more *powerful* and a more *cost-effective* part of your motivational arsenal.

Reward Systems

The reward system in any organization is made up of all the methods and mechanisms, both formal and informal, used to identify and allocate rewards. It includes base pay (wages or salary), incentive pay (such as bonuses and commissions), nonmonetary rewards (such as gifts, celebrations, and personal recognition), promotions, and benefits.

The key to the effectiveness of any reward system is the *motivational impact* of the rewards included in the system. All rewards have two components: the *intrinsic value* (the actual monetary worth of the reward) and the *recognition value* (the emotional effect of the reward on the recipient). The recognition value is by far the most important component from a motivational perspective.

Most companies simply don't know how to manage their reward system so that it becomes a strategic motivational weapon. In the next section, we will see why most companies do not get nearly enough value out of their reward systems.

Why Some Rewards Aren't Rewarding

From the average employee's viewpoint, the major irritant in almost every reward system is the perception of unfairness. Very few employees feel that they are being paid fairly. They are constantly comparing the rewards they receive with those of others. People tend to be more sensitive to what they are *not* receiving than to what they *are*. It has been found that no matter how much they are being paid, employees want, on average, 25 percent more.[1] In addition 83 percent of all hourly employees and 53 percent of management employees in a national survey reported feeling underrewarded.[2]

The most important component in any reward system is the relationship that exists between *rewards* and *performance*. While a few employees are rewarded generously for their performance, most employees receive few, if any, performance-based rewards—not even for exceptional performance. Employees are more likely to be rewarded for seniority, conformity, and personality traits than for superior performance. They are rewarded for being there, rather than for being motivated or getting results.

In too many reward situations, there are more losers than winners. For example, we often fail to realize that when there is an "Employee of the Month," there are also many others who are unhappy because they were not selected. Another example of this occurred when one organization awarded the managers responsible for a successful new product introduction $1 million in bonus compensation. The impact of this bonus on the *other* employees was devastating. Often the employees who receive the rewards feel great for a while, but everybody else feels lousy for a long, long time.

Many organizations have found that rewards end up having exactly the opposite of the intended effect. Unfortunately, much of the time, organizations *reward the wrong things*—and then get them! For example, most American companies tend to use rewards that encourage short-term rather than long-term performance. These rewards foster such behaviors as playing it safe, not making waves, and getting along with others, rather than initiative, risk taking, and creativity.

As one expert explained: "Managers who complain that their workers are not motivated might do well to consider the possibility that they have installed reward systems which are paying off for behaviors other than those they are seeking."[3] For example, even though most organizations today are trying to encourage teamwork, most employees are rewarded only for individual performance. As one observer put it, "We talk about teamwork at training sessions . . . and then we destroy it in the compensation system."[4] Another particularly deplorable example of rewarding wrong behavior is the way managers are rewarded for spending their entire budgets, but if they are thrifty they get their budgets cut for the next year.

Apart from rewarding negative behavior, nothing is more demotivating than the "entitlement mentality." As we saw in Chapter 1, rewards given to everyone are not very rewarding! Entitlements have become a steady drain on most organizations' resources without increasing effectiveness.

Furthermore, no organizational system is more susceptible to the quick fix than the reward system. Management often takes the shortcut of "waving rewards around" instead of looking for lasting solutions to motivational problems. And so the company becomes saddled with another costly, time-consuming incentive program.[5]

Even when financial rewards do improve performance, they are rarely cost-effective. Employees soon become habituated to whatever level of compensation is currently being given. Consequently, one writer warns us: "Attempting to motivate workers by external means requires ever-increasing external rewards to make the same impact."[6] Another astute observer summed up the problem with financial rewards this way: "Money motivation just costs too damn much."[7]

As we will see in the next section, even when the intrinsic (or monetary) value is very small, the *recognition value* of rewards can be very large.

Recognition: The Ultimate Reward

I have never met anyone who wasn't motivated by the desire for recognition. When a Gallup survey was done of employees throughout the

United States, recognition was *by far* the number-one motivator identified.[8] In fact, Mark Twain was reputed to have said, "I can live for two months on a good compliment!" (Unfortunately, if Twain worked for the average American company, he wouldn't be able to live for two *days*.)

Recognition is the most cost-effective reward there is. While the high cost of most rewards forces us to give them sparingly, verbal recognition can be given at any time, *at no cost whatsoever.* In fact, smart companies are realizing that there is no reward more powerful than genuine appreciation.[9]

For example, a large insurance company initiated a program it called "PEET—Program to Ensure that Everybody's Thanked." Another major company thanked employees for attaining a major production milestone by offering "Breakfast with the Boss." The company president cooked breakfast and served it to all employees, even though it took him twenty-four hours! The positive motivational impact was enormous.

The same basic concept can be implemented on a much smaller scale. A supervisor I know brought a home-cooked meal to his night shift workers to express his appreciation for their extra efforts during a particularly stressful period.

One senior executive installed a special telephone in his office so that purchasing agents could call him directly to report price concessions they had won from vendors. He would thank them on the phone and follow up with a personal congratulatory note.[10]

A company that recently initiated a major organizational change program instituted weekly R & R (review and reinforcement) meetings to give middle managers a chance to share their accomplishments, so that they could receive program-relevant recognition from their peers and from top management.

Organizations can show their appreciation of their employees in many different ways. In one particularly interesting case, a corporate CEO was trying to figure out a way to recognize an employee who had just done a great job. He picked up a banana (which his wife had packed in his lunch) from his desk and spontaneously handed it to the astonished employee with hearty congratulations. Now one of the highest honors in that company has been dubbed the Golden Banana Award!

In another organization, the janitorial staff made an ad hoc decision to recognize the best performer each month—with a broom. Gradually, this has evolved into more formal recognition: The Golden Broom Award. Another company presents a stuffed koala bear to employees who contribute significantly to quality improvement. They call it the "Koala T." Bear Award.[11]

Highly motivating organizations also make "heroes" out of their employees. Some organizations use innovative celebrations to honor achievement. One sales executive went so far as to rent a football stadium to throw a big party for all his employees and their families in recognition for the achievement of a major sales goal. His sales "heroes" entered the stadium through the tunnel, and, as they were announced on the public address system, each was greeted with thunderous applause!

A small manufacturing company went all-out to celebrate its safety "heroes" when they attained a major safety milestone—one hundred days without a single accident. On the morning of day one hundred, it was announced that a catered lunch would be served the next day if they made it to the end of the 5:30 shift without an accident. At 5:15, anticipation was building. Managers took confetti and streamers to the balcony overlooking the shop. When the whistle blew, there were congratulations all around, confetti flew through the air, and banners were unfurled. It was a great moment of victory for everyone.[12]

Even small successes can be celebrated. One company gives its employee "heroes" standing ovations when they attain even minor personal performance milestones.

Other organizations sponsor "family days" at amusement parks, cook-outs, and recognition luncheons. There is no limit to the ways in which organizations can show how much they appreciate their employees.

I have found that there are six keys to effective recognition: (1) Do it often; (2) do it promptly; (3) be creative; (4) make it easy for people to do; (5) involve all employees; and (6) build it into the system.

There is an irrefutable law of behavioral psychology: If you want someone to repeat a behavior, positively recognize it.[13] One major obstacle to effective recognition has been the tendency to wait until something "significant enough" happens. The SuperMotivating approach to recognition is to look for *any* employee doing something right, *right now,* and recognize it.

Although some of the examples given above are indeed quite creative, most companies are not very imaginative when it comes to recognition. Why not use the ideas presented above as a starting point, and exercise your own powers of creativity?

Unfortunately, giving recognition is not something most people at work feel comfortable doing. That is why several companies I know of distribute preprinted pads of "R+ Notes," so that managers, supervisors, and peers can just fill in the blanks to *positively reinforce* achievement.

All employees should have the opportunity to give recognition, and to participate in selecting individuals and teams for special awards. Providing recognition should be everybody's job. In fact, peers and team members are often in a better position to see positive contributions than managers are. One company even includes recognition giving in *every* employee's job description, and it provides training in how to give recognition most effectively both to subordinate employees and to peers.

Some companies are mandating recognition giving in other ways, including adopting "R+ logs," on which supervisors and managers are expected to record each instance of positive reinforcement they give. This also enables *their* bosses to give them positive reinforcement—for giving it to others.

Establish a "recognition culture" in your company or unit. It may be difficult at first, but, after a while, it will become second nature.

Small Is Beautiful: The Power of Little Rewards

Once again, the real power of recognition lies in the message it sends, not in the price tag. In fact, some of the most effective rewards cost *absolutely nothing*!

Depending on how they are presented, very ordinary rewards can make a person feel very special. Little treats, presented appreciatively, can mean more *motivationally* than large raises. Although many employees might be reluctant to admit it, the small rewards are often more attractive than the larger ones. I am still amazed at how much positive motivational impact a 30¢ doughnut can have. That is why a company president advises all his managers: "When planning rewards for employees, use your hearts—not just your money."

A health-conscious company distributes fruit bowls to employees' work areas when key performance milestones are attained. Another company uses a more fattening approach: fresh-baked chocolate-chip cookies to say "thank you."

Whatever rewards are used, it has been found that the best low-cost rewards are job-related, specify the reasons for which they are given, and are personalized to the individual.[14]

It is great when rewards can also improve employees' work environments. One secretary received a more ergonomically designed chair as a "thank you" for working extra-long hours on a high-priority project. A retail employee wanted a rug to stand on by the cash register to cushion the hard floor, and in recognition of her hard work, she was given a gift certificate to a carpet store and allowed to pick out any rug she wanted.

I have found that one key to an effective reward, of any size, is its *symbolism*. Some very ordinary items can be imbued with extraordinary significance to people, far in excess of their monetary value. The more symbolic the item, the more likely it is to continue reminding the employee of why it was given. For instance, a T-shirt or coffee mug with a meaningful inscription will continue rewarding those who wear it, or use it, long after its initial receipt. The success of any reward (or any gift, for that matter) is in the *thoughtfulness* it reflects.

Companies all over America are using a wide range of low-cost, creative rewards to tell employees how much they are appreciated, such as the following:

- Refreshments (soft drinks, popcorn, fruit, doughnuts)
- Meals (free lunches, pizza, picnics)
- Gift certificates (for stores, restaurants, theaters)
- Magazine subscriptions
- Books, audiotapes, videotapes
- Memberships (airport lounges, health clubs)
- Personalized items (caps, T-shirts, jackets, mugs)
- Work environment (improved work equipment, better tools)
- Training (seminar of choice, conference attendance)
- Sports (rounds of golf, sports equipment)
- Transportation (taxi to work, gas, car wash)
- Commendations (certificates, letters, thank-you notes)
- Money (small, instant cash bonuses)

You might notice that many of the items on this starter list are highly personal, and wouldn't necessarily be rewarding for everyone. Some companies use a "reward survey" to find out what small rewards might be most special for individual employees, or a "reward menu" so that employees can select the items they would most enjoy receiving.

Personalizing rewards shows that a company cares enough to discover what appeals to each employee, rather than just distributing generic gifts. This kind of personal treatment also reflects the golden rule of rewards: "Give unto others what *they* would have you give unto *them.*" It also reduces the following danger: In one organization I was visiting, an employee opened a big drawer in his desk and disdainfully showed me all the "worthless trinkets" he had collected over the years.

Any thoughtful reward can be effective. But have you ever wondered how many certificates, lapel pins, coffee mugs, or T-shirts any employee can get excited about receiving? By using a variety of rewards, you can overcome the satiation effect.

Some companies are realizing that low-cost reward programs can be made *even lower-cost* by creating symbiotic linkages with local vendors. In exchange for publicizing their products and services, many businesses are willing to offer significant discounts on products and services to be used in company recognition programs.

Additionally, it might prove advantageous to tie rewards in with professional growth. Some companies offer professional association dues, journal subscriptions, training, conference attendance, and continuing education as rewards, rather than entitlements.

Too often, after a reward is given, there is a motivational let-down. This sometimes causes companies to reject the whole low-cost reward concept. Instead, try using a point system. Rather than rewarding each individual behavior or accomplishment, you can allow employees to accumulate points. When employees save up enough points, they are eligible to receive a reward from a reward menu or catalogue. This keeps the anticipation of rewards fresh for longer periods of time.

Another variation on this theme is a lottery. Employees who achieve a certain qualifying standard are entered in a company lottery for cash or gifts. Lotteries are particularly cost-effective, since only one or a few employees actually win. If they are set up correctly, lotteries can also be highly reinforcing for *all* employees, even those who don't win.

One company uses a game it calls "Safety Bingo." The game goes something like this: All employees receive weekly bingo cards. When employees are observed working safely, they are given a number. When an employee fills up his or her entire bingo card, he or she receives a safety jacket, or some other safety-related item. After their third winning card, employees get to choose their prize from a gift catalogue. This program has maintained a lot of excitement for safety, and has made routine work more fun overall. Virtually any well-known game can be used to sustain interest and enthusiasm.

Interestingly, researchers who have investigated the motivational dynamics of these workplace "games" have found that the major motivator is the playing, not the prize![15]

Whatever you give, give with sincere appreciation. No reward is any better than the way it is delivered. I have seen large cash bonuses thrown at employees with little feeling attached, and no matter how large the amount, the motivational effects have been disappointing. On the other hand, I have seen very small tokens given that had an enormously positive impact on employee motivation and performance.

Low-cost rewards can also be extremely effective when used on a group basis. When using group incentives, I strongly recommend that the rewards chosen have the greatest positive impact on the quality of work life of as many employees as possible, and that the rewards selected be items of enduring value. This way a reward will keep reminding employees of *why* it was given. For example, one company offered to place soft drink and ice machines in each area of the plant if employees would improve cleanliness to a certain standard. The standard was achieved within one month, and the machines (along with commemorative plaques) were installed with all due pomp and ceremony.

Finally, here are three important caveats:

1. *Make sure you are rewarding the right things.* For example, if you want teamwork, don't focus your recognition on individual contributions. If you want your customers to receive service *after* the sale, don't just reward the sale. If you want quality, don't primarily recognize productivity. This point cannot be stressed too strongly or repeated too often.

2. *Whatever you do, don't let rewards become entitlements.* Too many rewards have become institutionalized. When employees start routinely expecting them, rewards cease to be rewarding. The best rewards come as pleasant surprises. Remember, today's rewards can become tomorrow's entitlements!

3. *Don't let anyone who is selling a particular form of motivation advise you on how to motivate your employees.* It is not surprising that companies that sell plaques recommend plaques for every occasion. In such cases, there is a clear conflict of interest!

There is no doubt that low-cost rewards can be extremely effective in motivating the kind of behavior and results that organizations want and need. Although they are relatively inexpensive, if done properly, these rewards can generate great excitement and enthusiasm for achievement, and *this* is priceless.

Creative Promotions

Promotions have traditionally been considered the ultimate reward, since they have tended to bring with them both additional money and increased status. In fact, in the past, most employees could count on regular promotions if they performed satisfactorily for a sufficiently long period of time. It was also generally believed that most career employees would *eventually* gravitate to the upper echelons of the organization.

No aspect of the organizational reward system has changed as radically as promotions. In fact, today in most organizations nine out of ten employees fail to reach the upper levels.[16] This means that most employees are made to feel like losers in the contest "to get ahead." The traditional promotion entitlement has become a demotivating takeaway.

Almost one-third of middle management has disappeared. Those who remain are more likely to stay longer. In fact, it has been estimated that by the late 1990s, there will be more than thirty candidates for each middle management opening. As Peter Drucker observed, "Newcomers now will find that the pipelines are full. Most of the baby-boomers have gone as far as they will go in management and will stay in their present jobs another thirty years or so."[17]

For some younger workers, this is a very depressing prospect. What makes it even more frustrating is that they see how much deadwood there is above them in the management ranks. In cases in which upward movement is still possible, companies must be very careful to promote as many people as possible from within the organization. Failing to do so will become a major demotivator.

The biggest problem with promotions today is *unrealistic expectations.* Employees simply need to accept the fact that the rules of the promotion game have radically changed.

However, despite the apparently demotivating state of upward mobility, the situation is not as bleak as it might at first appear. There are many creative alternatives to the traditional upward promotion—options that can still be very motivating. These include parallel paths, lateral paths, enrichment, downward moves, part-time status, and external moves.

- *Parallel career paths* (or "dual tracks") are emerging in many organizations, reflecting both the lack of upward opportunities and the greater value being placed on technical expertise. In some companies, employees opt for a professional/technical career track. They can be promoted to more senior technical positions without ever having to become managers.

- *Lateral career paths* allow employees to move horizontally without the stigma often attached to it. In some organizations, lateral moves (to positions at the same hierarchical level) are even being treated as promotions, with the same honors that go along with upward moves.

- *Enrichment* allows employees to stay in their existing jobs, and still take on more stimulating and responsible work.

- *Downward moves* used to be called "demotions." But now, they are sometimes just a smart thing to do. In days past, employees might have been overpromoted or wrongly promoted into management. These people may choose to move downward because they feel more comfortable in a technical position, or they might be able to contribute more in another position.

• *Part-time status* can sometimes be an appealing alternative to full-time employment. Some employees, such as those who want more free time, have pressing family responsibilities, or wish to start a home business, might find part-time employment a particularly attractive option. Another variation on this theme is job sharing, whereby two or more employees can share the same job.

• *External moves* occur when employees and their companies decide there are no longer mutually beneficial opportunities within the organization. Sometimes, it is a forced termination; other times, it might be a shared decision, and, in such cases, companies usually provide extensive outplacement support.

In the future, SuperMotivating organizations will need to become more creative in learning to use the reward potential of alternative career development options such as these, and to treat them as *real* promotions.

In addition, more emphasis will need to be placed on personalized career plans, rather than generic career paths that everyone is expected to follow. Once companies educate employees about creative career options, the stigma attached to alternative career paths will diminish. And when more equitable financial arrangements are devised, the final onus will be removed.

This brings us to the next element of the organizational reward system: financial compensation.

Traditional Compensation

Money is a particularly attractive reward because it can buy anything people need or want, and it is the only reward that everybody, *without exception*, values. Money has also been called "life's report card."[18] However, it is also the most difficult reward to use effectively.[19]

When we think of compensation, we tend to think first of "base pay" (wages or salary).

Employees also typically receive annual salary increments, including a COLA (cost of living adjustment) and frequently an annual "merit increase." Although the COLA has no motivating value, it does make sense to adjust salaries for increases in the cost of living.

However, merit pay, as typically used, has little or no motivating value, and it is extremely costly to companies. Merit pay is essentially an annuity based on one year's performance. It also generally reflects a small differential between the increases given to "satisfactory" employees and those given to "outstanding" performers. In one study, it was found that, on average, the increases were 4.7 percent and 7.7 percent, respectively.[20] In other words, outstanding performers received only an additional 3 percent of their previous salary as a reward for their outstanding efforts! When this amount is added to existing base pay and adjusted for increased deductions, the difference is minuscule. Furthermore, it has been found that the positive effects of any pay raise tend to wear off in two weeks![21]

Innovative Compensation Options

Motivating compensation should be both *performance-based* and *cost-effective*. Research has shown that using performance-based pay alone can improve employee performance by as much as 40 percent![22] But to have this kind of impact, it must be done well. It is surprising that despite conclusive research affirming the efficacy of performance-based pay and the years of success in using it as a sales motivator, most companies don't offer any performance-based incentives at all to their rank-and-file employees.[23]

One of the oldest, and most misunderstood, forms of performance-based compensation is *piecework*, or piece-rate pay. In this approach, employees receive wages based on their individual productivity. Although this form of compensation has proven very effective for increasing short-term productivity, when misused, it has been criticized for having a number of negative side effects.[24] However, if production is all you want, piecework is an excellent way to get it.

(By the way, *any* change in compensation should be carefully studied for its total motivational impact prior to implementation.)

Another approach is using *performance bonuses*, which allow organizations to reward meritorious performance over a particular period of time, without having to keep paying for it for the rest of an employee's career. Companies that once gave salary increases of 4 or 5 percent are now finding that they can give much more generous financial rewards because the lump-sum bonuses aren't being added to base salary. Since these rewards permit greater differentials between various levels of performance, they tend to be much more powerful and effective motivators. When well implemented, performance bonuses are the most cost-effective way to financially reward individual achievement.

Gainsharing is a method for sharing specific organizational improvements (gains) with the employees who contributed to them. Under this plan, employees' efforts toward increased productivity, improved quality, or reduced costs can be appropriately rewarded. The company splits the increased profits or reduced costs with participating employees, according to some predetermined formula.

Gainsharing can sometimes become a more motivating substitute for a portion of base pay, if employees agree to its use. In one particularly interesting case, a grocery chain won a 25 percent wage concession from employees in certain stores in exchange for participating in a gainsharing program. According to the agreement, if employees could keep labor costs to 9.5 percent of sales, they would receive a cash payment equal to 1.5 percent of sales; they would receive 1 percent if labor costs were 10 percent and 0.5 percent if labor costs were 11 percent. Stores that participated in this program experienced a 24 percent increase in sales, while labor costs fell from above the industry average to well below it![25]

In another gainsharing program, this time in a small manufacturing company, management shared 50 percent of the $40,000 it saved from implementing 300 employee ideas. The following year, the company received over 3,000 suggestions!

Profit sharing awards a percentage of the company's profits to each employee, usually in proportion to salary or wages. It is generally less motivationally effective than gainsharing because the payments are not clearly linked to any specific employee contribution to the result. Payment is also usually delayed until several months after the end of the fiscal year. Therefore, profit sharing is more often considered by employees to be an entitlement than a performance-based reward.

Employee stock ownership plans (ESOPs) allocate company stock to employees according to some predetermined formula. ESOPs increase employees' sense of ownership in the company, and provide them with a sense of having a real stake in the success of the company. However, like profit sharing, the reward value of ESOPs is often difficult for most employees to appreciate, since the stock distributions are rarely tied to any particular employee contributions.

Furthermore, because the financial rewards are usually quite long term, the real value of ESOPs lies in the ability of employees to actually participate in management. One company made its ESOP a success by treating employees like owners and soliciting their input into key management decisions.

Pay-for-knowledge is the practice of pegging base wages or salary to increased job knowledge and skills. Pay-for-knowledge is a relatively new concept in compensation, and is intended to encourage employee initiative in increasing knowledge and skill levels, presumably resulting in a more skilled and flexible workforce. Competency levels are established, and then correlated with pay rates. Employees work toward those rates by acquiring new skills.

Unfortunately, pay-for-knowledge has sometimes rewarded the accumulation of training credentials and the acquisition of unnecessary skills. Therefore, such plans should be implemented cautiously, and should never be used in place of other performance-based compensation arrangements.

As you can see, there are a great many innovative compensation options. When all the combinations and variations of these are considered, there is a virtually infinite number of ways to compensate employees. However, to be successful, any performance-based compensation arrangement must be built on a foundation of the kind of objective measurement discussed in the previous chapter.

Organizations no longer need to be locked into a traditional compensation system limited to base wages or salary with COLAs and annuity-like merit increases. SuperMotivating companies will be able to draw upon a wide variety of compensation approaches to create an optimal compensation system, tailored to the specific needs of the organization. In SuperMotivating organizations, pay checks will look a lot different from those most employees currently receive—including less base pay and more incentive pay.

SuperMotivating Compensation

The goal of compensation transformation should be to increase the positive motivational impact of financial rewards, with no cost increase, and preferably a reduction in total cost. In the future, SuperMotivating compensation systems will move organizations in the direction of rewarding excellence rather than attendance, and reduce costs at the same time.

Here are some important guidelines to consider so that your compensation approaches will have the maximum positive motivational impact:

• *Plan carefully.* Determine precisely what you want the compensation system to accomplish. Review past successes and failures. Determine what aspects of your current compensation system you are satisfied and dissatisfied with. Investigate compensation systems in other organizations, especially in those that are using nontraditional compensation arrangements.

• *Make sure that demotivators are being addressed.* Demotivators are always dangerous, but they can be especially hazardous when incentive compensation is being contemplated. In particular, unclear expectations, internal competition, dishonesty, and, of course, the perception of unfairness can turn even the best-intentioned incentive pay plan into a contentious battle between workers and management, among co-workers, and between departments—ultimately sabotaging the entire system.

• *Start small.* Don't overcommit resources to a compensation plan your organization can't afford. You certainly don't want to be put into the position of having to take away rewards you recently added. It is often a good idea to implement a pilot project before committing to a permanent compensation plan.

• *Provide an equitable base compensation package.* Your performance-based compensation plan should be built on a foundation of equitable base compensation. Employees should receive a decent wage or salary based on their job responsibilities. Failure to provide this will be a major demotivator.

The most important factor in determining base compensation should be the demands of the job, as established through a thorough job analysis. All organizations need to conduct a competitive analysis to ensure that base compensation is within the ballpark compared with that of other employers in your industry and in your area. However, remember that in most organizations, base compensation is viewed by employees as an entitlement rather than a motivator, so don't expect it to do much more than get employees to show up for work.

• *Emphasize performance-based compensation.* Increase the impact of financial rewards by maximizing the proportion of compensation that is truly performance-based. Today, only 13 percent of employees say they would personally benefit from increased production.[26] In the future, SuperMotivating organizations will be paying less for years spent on the job and more for *desired performance*—not only for production, but also for improvements in quality, cost savings, and increased safety.

• *Reward the right behaviors and results.* The importance of rewarding the right behaviors and results cannot be too strongly emphasized. Put your money where the payoff is! Determine the results *and* behaviors your organization needs in order to maximize its success, then make sure your compensation system rewards them. For example, if you want teamwork, reward team performance.

• *Make sure the link between performance and rewards is highly visible.* No compensation system will be effective unless employees can clearly see the relationship between their own specific actions and the rewards they receive. (As we saw earlier in this chapter, this is why profit sharing is rarely a successful motivator, whereas gainsharing generally is.) Furthermore, by making rewards (and the performance contingencies) as visible as possible, your organization will be sending a powerful message to employees that performance is important, and that it *will* be rewarded.

• *Never reward poor performers.* Poor performers should *never* be recipients of performance-based rewards. If you reward them, your organization will be sending entirely the wrong message, and it may negate many positive aspects of the compensation system.

• *Compensate promptly.* Promptness is another important feature of SuperMotivating compensation. The value of rewards is discounted by delay. Research findings are clear: Performance-based rewards should be paid *as soon as possible* after the performance they are rewarding. In one study, employees were asked their preference for $100 immediately or $500 in a year. Most employees chose the $100! This is why the most successful gainsharing programs pay employees monthly, rather than quarterly or annually.[27]

• *Use a variety of rewards.* Variety is another important success factor in compensation systems. There are basically two reasons why: First of all, employees can easily become habituated to "the same old rewards." And second, it is virtually impossible for one compensation arrangement to adequately reward everything desirable. Therefore, in SuperMotivating organizations, total compensation will consist of a wide range of rewards, both monetary and nonmonetary, allocated through a variety of compensation methods.

• *Ensure cost-effectiveness.* Nothing is more important to compensation in today's companies than cost-effectiveness. Effective compensation shouldn't cost *more;* it should cost *less.* Regularly reassess the cost-effectiveness of all reward programs. Redeploy your resources from traditional, wasteful, and ineffective compensation arrangements, and *invest* them in a SuperMotivating compensation system that will get the results your organization *really* wants.

• *Keep it simple.* Too many compensation plans are so complex that it takes a Ph.D. to understand them. The best compensation plan is simple enough to be understood by *everyone.* The understandability of any compensation plan is one of the most crucial determinants of its success. This issue will become increasingly important as employees' total pay comes from a variety of different plans.

• *Involve employees.* It is interesting that many great compensation ideas come from employees, but, alas, organizations are reluctant to ask for their help. If your organization wants to avoid a lot of future problems, solicit employee input into compensation system design. Involving employees in compensation planning will also increase their commitment to making the system work.

• *Ensure fairness.* Nothing will sabotage a compensation system like the perception of unfairness. More than anything else, employees want to be treated fairly. They want the recognition and rewards they feel they deserve, and have earned. And they want to make sure others don't receive more of the pie than *they* deserve.

The Japanese have long realized how important the perception of fairness is for motivating compensation. In Japan, reward criteria are almost always *explicit* and *objective*, and if pay cuts are ever necessary, management takes theirs first![28] It has been found time and time again: *In planning compensation, it is actually more important to be fair than to be generous.*

SuperMotivating Benefits

Benefits aren't usually considered to be part of a reward system, but in SuperMotivating organizations they ought to be.

For decades, American business has been the "gravy train" for millions of workers, who keep asking, "What has the company done for me lately?" As Judith Bardwick lamented in her book *Danger in the Comfort Zone,* "The real irony is that they're not grateful for what they get. Instead they want more."[29]

Benefits are no small proportion of total compensation, accounting, on average, for almost 40 percent of a company's total payroll. American companies spend more than $700 billion on employee benefits alone. Despite all this generosity, only 30 percent of all employees report feeling that their company has their best interests at heart![30]

Unfortunately, employee benefits, as currently constituted, are nothing more than extremely costly entitlements. Most companies have done little thinking about how to reduce benefits inflation and how to use benefits as an incentive to encourage improved employee performance.

Benefits include a bewildering array of subsidies and perks that provide a virtual welfare state for many employees. Common benefits include:

Social security	Health insurance
Vacations	Sick leave
Dental insurance	Educational assistance
Life insurance	Retirement plans
Disability insurance	Unemployment insurance
Stock options	Savings plans

Some organizations offer many more, but these are the core benefits. Peter Drucker has summed up the problem in this way: "Almost no benefits plan anywhere in the world was planned, designed *and* thought through."[31] Like most other aspects of the organizational reward system, benefits plans have just evolved—and at great cost. *The challenge of Super-Motivating benefits is to change the entitlement mentality into an earning mentality.*

In this section, we look at some of the ways in which employee benefits can be used to increase motivation on one hand, by reducing anxiety, worry, and other negative emotions, and on the other hand, by getting employees more actively involved in the benefits process. We explore ways to reduce costs, increase employee responsibility and choice, and increase the payoff for the employer. Believe it or not, there are benefits that can pay real dividends to the company, as well as to the employee. Benefits should be selected to positively affect work performance, not just provide a privately funded welfare program.

There is no doubt that benefits are needed, maybe more so today than ever before, but what is required is a *different mix of benefits.* Because of the increased diversity of today's workforce, employees have a much broader range of needs and wants, and they are not motivated by the same things as employees in the past. Therefore, organizations must be much more sensitive in the way they handle employee benefits.

Here are some ideas that can go a long way toward creating Super-Motivating benefits in any organization:

• *Educate employees about their benefits.* Most employees think benefits are free. They don't realize how much benefits cost the company. This is why organizations need to educate employees about the cost of their benefits, and how these costs affect the organization's bottom line.

One company gives all employees a quarterly report on their benefits (and how much they are costing the company). Supervisors are expected to discuss these benefits reports with each of their staff members. Employees are also informed about their total compensation (including benefits) with each pay check. Employees whose annual pay might be $25,000 are shocked to discover that their total compensation is really $40,000!

Another organization gives employees a "passbook" so that they can keep track of their contributions and accumulations in pension, profit sharing, and employee savings accounts.

Employees should also become better "benefits consumers." Some organizations offer benefits orientation sessions, so that employees will know exactly what benefits are available to them, how to select the most cost-effective options, and how to get the best results from the use of their benefits.

It is important for employees to understand any changes in their benefits program, and why these changes are being made. This way, changes are less likely to be interpreted as takeaways.

- *Eliminate all unnecessary and demotivating benefits.* Like the excessive rules discussed in Chapter 4, benefits, too, have tended to proliferate way beyond what is necessary. Therefore, all organizations should regularly review and "prune" benefits programs. What might have been appropriate ten years ago may no longer be viable today.

For example, one organization eliminated a half-dozen marginal benefits (including term life and accident/travel insurance), saving over $100,000 a year, and replaced them with a new wellness program costing less than $25,000. Although this was a takeaway, the negative impact was minimized by good communication and the addition of a more desired benefit.

Some organizations demotivate employees by offering benefits to some groups of employees and not to others. This unfair treatment has no place in a SuperMotivating organization. Some benefits are well intentioned but poorly conceived, such as the practice at one paper company of distributing its *defective* products to employees. Although motivated by generosity, this free "tissue issue" is greeted by employees with little gratitude and disparaging comments about all the poor-quality product the company produced!

- *Replace noncontributory benefits with contributory plans.* SuperMotivating organizations should view themselves as partners with employees. To consummate this partnership, employees should have some copayment responsibility for funding their benefits. Current thinking indicates that if they do, they will appreciate their benefits more, and take them more seriously.

There are many health insurance plans, retirement plans, and other benefits offering excellent protection with various levels of employee copayment. There are many great contributory retirement plans that are reducing the burden on employers, while making employees more active partners in their own retirement planning. Salary reduction plans (such as 401(k) programs) are justifiably popular today as both primary and supplementary retirement plans. Furthermore, smaller companies are discovering Salary Reduction Simplified Employee Pension plans that are simple to set up and are funded entirely through employee contributions. Other companies are offering stock *discounts,* instead of stock *gifts.*

Tuition assistance is another area that is ripe for change. Employees should contribute to their own educational expenses. Unfortunately, many companies are so generous that employees undertake educational programs they do not need, and some employees (at their employer's expense) even seek skills to help them go elsewhere to work! The most motivating tuition assistance plans are accompanied by career planning, and the amount of reimbursement given is contingent on grades earned.

Some companies offer employees discounts on products, rather than giving them free. For example, a publisher that used to give employees free books (most of which were never read) now offers them at a 50 percent discount. This has resulted in greater employee appreciation of the value of the products, and as an added benefit to the company, employees are becoming more knowledgeable about the entire product line. Another company negotiated excellent deals with suppliers, so that employees could purchase automobiles, computers, telephone services, and other such items at bargain prices.

Remember: Benefits don't have to be free to be benefits! In fact, totally free benefits are simply not realistic or desirable anymore.

• *Use more cost-effective health insurance options.* Nothing is doing more to undermine the competitive position of American industry than the well-publicized health insurance crisis. However, there are many ways in which businesses can provide comprehensive health insurance coverage for employees and still reduce the costs. Unfortunately, few companies compare all their options.

Well-run health maintenance organizations (HMOs) provide an excellent quality of care, with an emphasis on wellness, at lower prices than traditional plans. Preferred provider organizations (PPOs) can significantly reduce costs by negotiating more advantageous rates with health care providers. There are also great cost-saving opportunities through purchasing cooperatives, increasing deductibles and copayments, reducing coverage overlap, and cost controls (such as improved claims administration, case management, utilization reviews, and billing error detection). Some larger companies are even setting up their own in-house clinics to improve cost management, or opting for self-insurance. Still other companies are drastically cutting back on health benefits for retirees.

Companies are also addressing the problem of excessive sick leave by rewarding nonuse, having employees pay for the first few sick days, or some gainsharing arrangement. One company was able to cut its sick leave costs in half and virtually eliminate abuse by doubling employees' available paid leave, but making the employee responsible for the first two sick days.

However, probably the best *long-term* solution to high health care costs rests with prevention and wellness.

• *Promote wellness aggressively.* There is no excuse for the poor health of the American population, and employers need to take a more active role in addressing the problem. For one thing, unhealthy employees have much less energy than their healthy counterparts. Furthermore, did you realize that 7 percent of employees account for 70 percent of the average company's health care costs? *If employees expect to receive the best health benefits, they should also be willing to participate in health management efforts.*

To meet the challenge, many companies are offering innovative disease prevention and wellness programs, including:

Exercise	Nutrition counseling
Weight management	Back care
Accident prevention	Smoking cessation
Alcohol and drug treatment	Life risk analysis
Prenatal instruction	Cancer screenings
Blood pressure management	Cholesterol screenings
Stress management	Health resource centers

Other ways of increasing health consciousness include regular health education programs, employee assistance plans (EAPs), support groups, serving healthier foods in company cafeterias, and incentives for a healthier lifestyle. Some companies are including employees' families in wellness programs.

Incidentally, smaller companies are joining EAP consortia so that they can offer the same range of services that larger companies can.

• *Adopt low-cost, life-enhancing benefits.* In a recent survey, 72 percent of men and 83 percent of women reported "significant conflict between work and family."[32] One of the best ways for a company to contribute to its employees' well-being is to make life easier for them. This way, they can devote more productive energy to work, and less to worrying about outside-of-work concerns.

Almost every employee I talk with says that his or her major problem is lack of time. By increasing time flexibility, organizations can go a long way toward assisting employees, at hardly any additional cost. Flextime and unpaid maternity leave, paternity leave, and personal time off (even without pay) can greatly assist employees in coping with the rigors of everyday life. Other low-cost (or no-cost) benefits can include pretax spending accounts, telecommuting, job sharing, voluntary reduced workload, low-interest loans, purchase discounts, assistance in finding educational funding, legal services plans, and on-site after-hours education programs, among others.

Most employees would be happy to pay for some life-enhancing services, if their employers would just make those services more accessible.

Most employees I have interviewed say that they would be more than willing to pay for the convenience of on-site child care, sick-child care, elder care, counseling, financial planning (including tax preparation), fitness clubs, laundry facilities, cleaners, and other such services. Providing facilities like these on a fee-for-service basis makes life easier for harried employees, and costs employers little or nothing.

Organizations simply must show greater sensitivity to their employees, and the pressures they are under these days. One study indicated that one of the most important factors in reducing occupational stress was the supportiveness of supervisors concerning family issues.[33] And as Martin Yate said in *Keeping the Best,* "There's no limit to the commitment you can get from employees when they recognize that you look at business with their concerns in mind."[34]

• *Reduce paid time off.* As indicated above, time is one of the most valued rewards a person can receive in today's society. But some companies end up spending huge amounts of money on vacations and other time off. Not only is paid time off one of the most expensive benefits that any organization provides (accounting for an average of 13 percent of payroll), but it also does little to motivate.[35] In fact, many time-off programs are demotivating because they are perceived as unfair. In some companies, senior employees (regardless of performance) get up to six weeks' vacation a year, whereas many other employees get only two weeks.

More and more cost-conscious companies are beginning to reduce paid time off, and are moving toward the use of more flexible work schedules and offering leave without pay instead. Admittedly, great care must be taken when reducing paid time off, but companies can design time-off programs that are much more motivating than the costly entitlement programs that currently exist.

• *Let employees choose.* One of the most significant developments in benefits is the element of *choice.* Flexible benefits, or "cafeteria" plans, are revolutionizing the field. These plans let employees choose the benefits they want from a "menu" of options.

Benefits plans involving choice provide many advantages, including being able to tailor a benefits package to each individual employee according to his or her needs, and getting employees more involved in benefits decision making. Such involvement also reduces the problem of providing benefits many employees neither need nor want.

In SuperMotivating companies of the future, there will be a greater range of life-enhancing benefits, making it easier and less stressful for employees to work. In addition, employees will not mind contributing to the cost of these benefits, because they will feel more like business partners and less like hired help.

One final note is in order. Making any change in compensation or benefits is risky. As demotivating as the existing methods might be, they are comfortable to employees. Unless done sensitively and communicated effectively, such changes can, initially at least, be perceived as demotivating takeaways. Therefore, it is recommended that any compensation or benefits changes are well planned and are communicated using the suggestions provided in Chapter 8. Also, if you are taking pay or benefits away, *do it all at once!* Otherwise, the inevitable negative emotions will be needlessly prolonged.

Action Points

The following Action Points summarize ways in which the reward system in your organization can be motivationally transformed into the powerful, incentive-producing system it should be, so that employees feel energized, rather than just entitled.

How to Create SuperMotivating Recognition

- Recognize the right behaviors and results.
- Use creative ways of thanking employees for their extra efforts.
- Make "heroes" out of your employees.
- Celebrate successes, even the small ones.
- Recognize employees often.
- Recognize promptly.
- Make recognition easy.
- Involve all employees in recognition.
- Systematize recognition.
- Create a climate of recognition in your organization.

How to Design SuperMotivating Rewards

- Use low-cost rewards.
- Use symbolic rewards.
- Give thoughtful rewards.
- Personalize rewards.
- Use a variety of rewards.
- Tie rewards in with personal growth.
- Increase the longevity of rewards using point systems.

- Make rewards into a game.
- Give rewards with sincere appreciation.
- Choose rewards that remind employees of why the rewards were given.
- Don't let rewards become entitlements.
- Use creative promotion options:
  —Parallel career paths
  —Lateral career paths
  —Enrichment
  —Downward moves
  —Part-time status
  —External moves
- Develop personalized career plans.

How to Build a SuperMotivating Compensation System

- Plan carefully.
- Provide an equitable base compensation package.
- Emphasize performance-based compensation, such as:
  —Piecework
  —Performance bonuses
  —Gainsharing
  —Profit sharing
  —Employee stock ownership plans
  —Pay-for-knowledge programs
- Reward the right behaviors and results.
- Make sure employees see the link between performance and rewards.
- Never reward poor performers.
- Compensate promptly.
- Use a variety of rewards.
- Ensure cost-effectiveness.
- Make it simple.
- Involve employees.
- Maintain fairness.

How to Provide SuperMotivating Benefits

- Educate employees about their benefits.
- Eliminate all unnecessary and demotivating benefits.
- Replace noncontributory benefits with contributory plans.
- Use more cost-effective health insurance options.
- Promote wellness aggressively.

- Adopt low-cost, life-enhancing benefits.
- Reduce paid time off.
- Let employees choose.

Notes

1. G. Brim, *Ambition* (New York: Basic Books, 1992).
2. R. C. Huseman and J. D. Hatfield, *Managing the Equity Factor* (Boston: Houghton Mifflin, 1989).
3. S. Kerr, "On the Folly of Rewarding A, While Hoping for B," in *The Management of Organizations*, ed. M. L. Tushman, C. O'Reilly, and D. Nadler (New York: Ballinger, 1989), p. 174.
4. R. M. Kanter, "The Attack on Pay," *Harvard Business Review*, March–April 1987, p. 66.
5. R. H. Schaffer, *The Breakthrough Strategy* (Cambridge, Mass.: Ballinger, 1988).
6. D. Viscott, *Taking Care of Business* (New York: Morrow, 1985), p. 126.
7. S. W. Gellerman, *Motivation in the Real World* (New York: Dutton, 1992), p. 10.
8. G. Gallup and A. M. Gallup, *The Great American Success Story* (Homewood, Ill.: Dow Jones-Irwin, 1986).
9. A. Daniels, *Performance Management* (Tucker, Ga.: Performance Management Publications, 1989).
10. T. E. Kennedy and A. A. Deal, *Corporate Cultures* (Reading, Mass.: Addison-Wesley, 1982).
11. R. L. Hale and R. F. Maehling, *Recognition Redefined* (Minneapolis: Tennant, 1992).
12. E. Hatcher, "Positive Safety," *Training*, July 1991.
13. A. Daniels, *Performance Management* (Tucker, Ga.: Performance Management Publications, 1989).
14. Ibid.
15. Ibid.
16. S. C. Brandt, *Entrepreneuring in Established Companies* (New York: New American Library, 1986).
17. P. F. Drucker, *The Frontiers of Management* (New York: Dutton, 1986), p. 157.
18. C. E. Watson, *Managing With Integrity* (New York: Praeger, 1991), p. 33.
19. S. W. Gellerman, *Motivation in the Real World* (New York: Dutton, 1992).
20. J. R. Schuster and P. K. Zingheim, *The New Pay* (New York: Lexington, 1992).
21. F. Herzberg, "Conversations With Frederick Herzberg," in *Effective Management and the Behavioral Sciences*, ed. W. Dowling (New York: AMACOM, 1978).
22. E. E. Lawler, *Strategic Pay* (San Francisco: Jossey-Bass, 1990).
23. T. Peters, "Letter to the Editor," *Inc.* Magazine, *Managing People* (New York: Prentice-Hall, 1989).
24. For example, see W. E. Deming, *Out of the Crisis* (Cambridge, Mass.: MIT Press, 1986).
25. D. Ulrich and D. Lake, *Organizational Capability* (New York: Wiley, 1990).

26. B. Nelson, *1001 Ways to Reward Employees* (New York: Workman, 1994).
27. E. E. Lawler, *Strategic Pay* (San Francisco: Jossey-Bass, 1990).
28. J. C. Abbeggler and G. Stalk, *Kaisha: The Japanese Corporation* (New York: Basic Books, 1985).
29. J. M. Bardwick, *Danger in the Comfort Zone* (New York: AMACOM, 1991), p. 18.
30. M. Yate, *Keeping the Best* (Holbrook, Mass.: Bob Adams, 1991).
31. P. F. Drucker, *Management: Tasks, Responsibilities, Practices* (New York: Harper & Row, 1973), p. 297.
32. R. K. Cooper, *The Performance Edge* (Boston: Houghton Mifflin, 1991), p. 236.
33. F. S. Rodgers and C. Rodgers, "Business and the Facts of Family Life," *Harvard Business Review,* November–December 1989.
34. M. Yate, *Keeping the Best* (Holbrook, Mass.: Bob Adams, 1991), p. 35.
35. J. R. Schuster and P. K. Zingheim, *The New Pay* (New York: Lexington, 1992).

12

SuperMotivation: Making It Happen

In the preface of this book, I made the bold assertion that if you were to use just a small proportion of the concepts and principles presented in this book, you should be able to increase the effectiveness of your organization by at least 20 percent—and significantly reduce costs as well. Based on twenty years of experience in developing and using the SuperMotivation approach, I *know* that this statement is true. I hope that after having read the first eleven chapters of this book, *you* are also convinced that applying the SuperMotivation "technology" can dramatically increase motivation in your organization. And there is no limit to what a highly motivated organization can accomplish!

Although this is the last chapter in this book, the most important part still remains: *putting SuperMotivation into practice in your organization.*

Small-Scale SuperMotivation

While the focus of this book is on organization-wide motivational transformation, the SuperMotivation concepts and strategies can also be successfully used on a variety of other levels. If you feel that your organization is not yet ready for organization-wide SuperMotivation, or if you are not currently in a position to implement it organization-wide, the SuperMotivation approach can still prove extremely valuable when used *on a smaller scale.*

If you are a supervisor or middle manager, you can use most of the ideas presented in this book in your department or work area. Virtually every one of the hundreds of suggestions offered can be effective at increasing employee motivation.

For example, you might be intrigued by possibilities for increasing employee involvement in planning, improving communication, making training more effective and motivating, improving evaluation, or providing more cost-effective recognition. Review this book and select ideas that will immediately release motivation in your department, area, or work team.

If you are involved in designing a new project or initiative (such as safety, training, customer service, or quality management), applying elements of the SuperMotivation approach will greatly facilitate the effectiveness of your efforts. I have seen it happen time and time again: Many technically well-conceived projects fail because the motivational aspects were ignored. No initiative can ever be successful for very long if it isn't motivating.

I am sure that this book has already caused you to become more aware of the dangers that demotivators pose and the importance of building motivators into the context of work. Your efforts to remove demotivators and add motivators, whether on an organization-wide basis or on a smaller scale, will have a significantly positive impact on employee motivation, and consequently on organizational effectiveness.

Implementation Guidelines

If you decide to implement SuperMotivation on a broader organization-wide basis, considering the following guidelines will greatly enhance your efforts:

1. *Establish the need for SuperMotivation.* The decision to pursue SuperMotivation is one of the most important decisions your organization will ever make. If there's a motivation crisis in your organization, or even a desire to increase motivation in a particular area, make sure that senior management has formally acknowledged a *real need* for SuperMotivation and has made a sufficient commitment to its success.

The SuperMotivation Survey in Appendix B provides a simple but effective tool for helping to establish the need for SuperMotivation in your organization. This survey consists of sixty characteristics of a Super-Motivating organization drawn from this book. When taken together, the items in the survey provide a "vision," or operational definition, of SuperMotivation. Not only will you find the SuperMotivation Survey to be a valuable data collection tool, but it is also useful for communicating to others what a SuperMotivating organization might look like.

If you include a representative sample of managers, supervisors, and employees from various areas and at differing levels in the survey sample, the SuperMotivation Survey should provide a reliable measure of the current motivational climate in your organization. Preliminary interpretation guidelines are also provided in Appendix B.

2. *Select an auspicious time to begin.* It is usually best to begin implementing SuperMotivation when there aren't too many competing organizational improvement activities. Other priorities can sometimes divert attention from SuperMotivation. However, I have found that improvement in another area can also present an excellent opportunity for Super-Motivation. For example, one organization linked its SuperMotivation implementation with its Total Quality Management process and called it *Total Quality Motivation!*

3. *Ensure appropriate sponsorship.* In previous chapters, we discussed the importance of top management support. Choosing the right *sponsor* may be the most crucial implementation decision of all. The sponsor selected must be a highly credible leader within the organization. After all, the sponsor is the person who is ultimately responsible for driving the entire SuperMotivation process. Don't even consider starting without selecting such a person!

4. *Select the process leader.* In addition to the sponsor, there should also be a hands-on *process leader.* This person will lead SuperMotivation development on a day-to-day basis. The sponsor is rarely the process leader, but it is useful for the process leader to report directly to the sponsor. An effective working relationship between the process leader and the sponsor is vitally important.

5. *Build commitment throughout the organization.* To be successful, SuperMotivation must be perceived by all employees as a major organizational priority. But commitment throughout the organization starts with commitment at the top. Senior management must be willing to demonstrate its long-term commitment to SuperMotivation. Most employees will commit to almost anything if they see that upper management is *genuinely* committed.

All stakeholders should understand, accept, and buy into the Super-Motivation approach. The best way to accomplish this goal is to involve a "critical mass" of employees at all levels and in all areas. When building such a commitment, you should consider following the useful suggestions for participative planning presented in Chapter 6.

6. *Establish an advisory team.* One way to build commitment is through the use of an advisory team consisting of managers, supervisors, and rank-and-file employees at a variety of levels and areas of the organi-

zation. The involvement of diverse groups throughout the organization will make a big difference in the way the SuperMotivation process is perceived by employees.

Other employees will typically judge the credibility of the SuperMotivation effort on the basis of how well the advisory team is used. It is also important to involve key "system leaders," such as planners, production managers, communications people, training staff, human resources staff, and compensation and benefits experts either as members of the team or as advisors to it. When included in the process, these people can contribute valuable expertise and support.

7. *Create and maintain realistic expectations.* Nothing will kill Super-Motivation more quickly than unrealistic expectations. SuperMotivation must be viewed as an ongoing process, not a short-term "program." It must never be viewed as just another quick fix or panacea. Everyone should realize up front that striving for SuperMotivation will require both hard work and patience.

8. *Develop a strategic plan.* SuperMotivation requires a commitment of more than one year. I generally recommend that a two- to five-year strategic plan be developed. Although it should be regularly updated, such a plan will provide an overall guiding strategy and will serve as evidence of the organization's long-term commitment to SuperMotivation.

9. *Focus initial efforts.* Don't try to transform every system at once! Select one (or at most two) organizational system(s) to begin with. Sometimes initial enthusiasm for improvement leads companies to exceed their resources. Therefore, focus your efforts on one or two areas where they will have the greatest impact. Remember the old proverb: "A journey of a thousand miles begins with a single step."

10. *Begin with demotivator reduction.* As recommended in Chapter 4, demotivator reduction should begin before motivators are added. Start by selecting one or two demotivators for immediate reduction, then gradually expand your efforts to other demotivators.

11. *Use multiple motivators.* One of the key principles in this book is that no single motivator will ever be sufficient to motivate—at least not for long. Therefore, it is essential to add a variety of motivators to any organizational system you are attempting to motivationally transform. And additional motivators should be added from time to time to avoid the possibility of "motivator habituation" (referred to in Chapter 5).

12. *Develop your own SuperMotivation techniques.* Don't limit yourself to the ideas and suggestions provided in this book! Add to them. Enhance them. Customize them. Make SuperMotivation your own.

13. *Educate the organization.* Education is a vital component of Super-Motivation. Education should begin with the top management group, then expand to those who will be most active in the process, and finally flow down to other employees. This book can be used as the basic text-book for educating the organization about SuperMotivation.

14. *Communicate, communicate, communicate!* As you know, communication is essential to winning and maintaining support for any organizational change effort. The organization as a whole must be kept continually informed about *every aspect* of the SuperMotivation process. Explain *what* is going on—and *why.*

Use the suggestions presented in Chapter 8 to enhance your communication efforts.

15. *Model SuperMotivating behavior.* It is inevitable that employees will be watching closely and judging the organization's commitment to SuperMotivation. As one CEO recently told me, "I've discovered that employees are constantly watching my every move, to see if I am practicing what I am preaching." SuperMotivation should become an integral part of everyday managing. Make SuperMotivation a way of life in your organization!

16. *Celebrate accomplishments.* It can never be stressed too often or too strongly that recognizing accomplishments is a key to success in any area of human endeavor. Therefore, I'll say it again: Look for the positives; celebrate *all* motivational improvements!

17. *Stick with it long enough.* SuperMotivation requires constancy of purpose. Ironically, early success can sometimes be the greatest enemy of organizational improvement because of the complacency that often results. When you do achieve early success, resist the temptation to rest on your laurels. Make sure that your organization sticks with the SuperMotivation process long enough to ensure that the changes are truly systematized.

A New Perspective on "Motivating Leadership"

As we saw in Chapter 1, the traditional dependence on individual programs (including quick fixes and panaceas) has distracted managements from looking deeper into real solutions to the problem of motivation in the workplace. Another major obstacle to organization-wide motivation has been the tendency to depend on individual managers and supervisors to motivate others.

When we think of *motivating leaders,* we tend to think of charismatic personalities like Washington, Jefferson, Roosevelt, Churchill, Patton, Kennedy, Rockne, King, and Iacocca. However, the real leaders in most organizations are more likely to be ordinary people. Although these people may be very effective technical managers, they may not be particularly inspiring! The fact is that most of those who are promoted to leadership responsibilities in organizations are not particularly motivating—*nor should we expect them to be.* (How many *truly motivating* leaders have you worked with, or for, in your career?) With all the pressures on managers and supervisors today, motivation shouldn't be one of them.

This book provides a powerful and reliable alternative to the practice of *individual motivating leadership* by showing that the long-term solution to organizational motivation lies in *systems leadership.*

I am not suggesting that individual leadership isn't important. On the contrary, effective leadership *at the top* is still the most important single factor in business success. However, few middle managers and supervisors are equipped to be motivators.

The beauty of SuperMotivation is that because "motivators" are built into the work context itself, individuals no longer need to be the primary motivators in any organization. Therefore, managers and supervisors can concentrate on the tasks they perform best.

One supervisor whose company recently began implementing SuperMotivation thanked me profusely. For years, he had suffered because managers expected him to single-handedly motivate his staff. Now, all he has to do is "work the system." When motivation is built into organizational systems, *all* organizations will be able to become SuperMotivating.

The Economics of SuperMotivation

Philip Crosby chose *Quality Is Free* for the title of his well-known book on quality management. His reasoning was that improving quality doesn't really cost anything, because, ultimately, quality becomes a major source of increased profits. Similarly, this notion underscores what I believe about SuperMotivation: *SuperMotivation is free!* And it is free in more ways than one.

Not only does SuperMotivation increase productivity and profit, but it won't add a penny to your total costs. You may find that you will invest a little money in a few areas, such as employee involvement and training. But you will find this cost more than offset by even larger savings—by reducing, for example, unrewarding rewards and benefits that don't really benefit your employees. The point here is that, no matter how you analyze it, there will be *no net cost increase* by implementing SuperMotivation—and the financial and nonfinancial value to your organization will be large and enduring.

The Final Word

Given the new breed of employees who populate most organizations, and the increasingly competitive global economy, I'm sure you will agree that employee motivation has never been more important than it is today.

I hope you are becoming motivated about the prospect of "SuperMotivating" your organization.

There is no doubt in my mind: World-class organizations need world-class motivation—and the most successful organizations in the future will be *SuperMotivated!*

Appendix A

Demotivator Identifier

___ Politics
___ Unclear expectations
___ Unnecessary rules
___ Poorly designed work
___ Unproductive meetings
___ Lack of follow-up
___ Constant change
___ Internal competition
___ Dishonesty
___ Hypocrisy
___ Withholding information
___ Unfairness
___ Discouraging responses
___ Criticism
___ Capacity underutilization
___ Tolerating poor performance
___ Being taken for granted
___ Management invisibility
___ Overcontrol
___ Takeaways
___ Being forced to do poor-quality work

Other demotivators:

___ _____

___ _____

Motivator Planner

__ Action
__ Fun
__ Variety
__ Input
__ Stake sharing
__ Choice
__ Responsibility
__ Leadership opportunities
__ Social interaction
__ Teamwork
__ Using strengths
__ Learning
__ Error tolerance
__ Measurement
__ Goals
__ Improvement
__ Challenge
__ Encouragement
__ Appreciation
__ Significance

Other motivators:

__ _____
__ _____
__ _____

Appendix B

SuperMotivation Survey

In the space to the right of each statement below, please place a number (from 1 to 5) indicating *how true* the statement is *about your organization,* using the following rating scale:

1 = Not true at all
2 = True to a small extent
3 = True to some extent
4 = Mostly true
5 = Completely true

1. Employees in this organization are energetic and enthusiastic. _____
2. Employees are highly productive. _____
3. Employees have positive and optimistic attitudes. _____
4. There is little or no wasted effort. _____
5. The organization is highly customer focused from top to bottom. _____
6. Unsafe conditions are identified and promptly corrected. _____
7. Employees are made to feel like true business partners. _____
8. Employees have a strong sense of organizational identity. _____
9. Employees are very careful about how they use the organization's resources. _____
10. Employees have a clear understanding of the organization's mission, vision, and values. _____
11. Employee input into organizational strategic planning is solicited and used. _____
12. Employees are encouraged to make significant choices and decisions about their work. _____

13. Employees are involved in making key production decisions. _____
14. Employees are empowered to improve work methods. _____
15. Employees are encouraged to work closely with their internal customers and suppliers. _____
16. There is a no-fault approach to problem solving in this organization. _____
17. A concerted effort is made to identify and use the full range of abilities employees bring to work. _____
18. Employees are challenged to strive for ambitious goals. _____
19. Obstacles to effective employee performance are promptly identified and eliminated. _____
20. Personnel decisions are perceived to be fair and consistent. _____
21. There are few, if any, unnecessary policies and rules. _____
22. Effective communication is a high organizational priority. _____
23. Employees throughout this organization are well informed. _____
24. Management explains to employees the rationale behind all important decisions. _____
25. There is frequent communication between employees and management. _____
26. Senior managers regularly visit employees' work areas. _____
27. No secrets are kept from employees. _____
28. Meetings are well led and highly productive. _____
29. Company publications are informative and helpful. _____
30. Management is highly responsive to employees' needs and concerns. _____
31. Employees feel that management has their best interests at heart. _____
32. When labor-management conflicts arise, they are promptly and constructively resolved. _____
33. Management is quick to take personal responsibility for its mistakes. _____
34. Employees are encouraged to assume leadership responsibilities. _____
35. Employees receive a great deal of encouragement and recognition. _____
36. Outstanding performance is always recognized. _____
37. Both individual performance and team performance are appropriately rewarded. _____

38. Poor performance is never rewarded. _____
39. Creativity is encouraged and rewarded. _____
40. Employees consider their pay to be fair and equitable. _____
41. Employees are willing to pay part of the cost of their benefits. _____
42. Employees feel that their ideas and suggestions are genuinely welcomed by management. _____
43. Employees' suggestions receive prompt and constructive responses. _____
44. Everyone in the organization is committed to continuous improvement. _____
45. There are no barriers between departments or units. _____
46. There is a high level of trust between workers and management. _____
47. There is excellent teamwork throughout the organization. _____
48. There is a high level of interdepartmental communication and cooperation throughout the organization. _____
49. Management views problems as opportunities for improvement, rather than as obstacles to success. _____
50. Learning is a high priority in this organization. _____
51. Employees are encouraged to learn from one another. _____
52. There is consistent follow-up after training. _____
53. Employees are involved in making training decisions. _____
54. Employees are involved in determining performance requirements, measures, and standards. _____
55. Employees view performance evaluation as a positive developmental process. _____
56. Self-evaluation and peer evaluation are integral components of performance appraisal. _____
57. Discipline is perceived to be fair. _____
58. Employees consistently give extra effort. _____
59. Tardiness, absenteeism, and turnover rates are extremely low. _____
60. Employees are excited about working in this organization. _____

Your organization's score: _____
(add all item responses)

Your organization's percentage score (divide by 300) _____%

Preliminary Survey Interpretation

Add all your responses. This is your organization's score. A perfect score would be 300 (based on a maximum response of 5 for each of the 60 items on the survey). When you divide your organization's score by 300, you will obtain an overall percentage score. The lower an organization's score, the more urgently it needs to apply the SuperMotivation strategies presented in this book.

Here are some preliminary guidelines for helping you interpret your organization's overall percentage score:

90–100 percent	Congratulations! Your organization has already attained SuperMotivation status.
80–89 percent	Your organization is well on its way to Super-Motivation.
70–79 percent	Your organization has some aspects of Super-Motivation.
60–69 percent	Your organization has a slightly above aver-age* motivational climate
50–59 percent	Your organization has an average* motiva-tional climate.
Below 50 percent	Your organization has a below average* moti-vational climate.

*Based on national norms for this survey.

References

Abeggler, J. C., and G. Stalk. *Kaisha: The Japanese Corporation.* New York: Basic Books, 1985.

Albrecht, K., and R. Zemke. *Service America.* New York: Warner Books, 1986.

Armstrong, D. *Managing by Storying Around.* New York: Doubleday, 1992.

Aubrey, J. A. *Love and Profit.* New York: William Morrow, 1991.

Augustine, N. *Augustine's Laws.* New York: Penguin, 1987.

Bardwick, J. M. *Danger in the Comfort Zone.* New York: AMACOM, 1991.

Basso, B., and J. Klosek. *This Job Should Be Fun.* Holbrook, Mass.: Bob Adams, 1991.

Bennett, A. *The Death of the Organization Man.* New York: Simon & Schuster, 1990.

Blake, R. R., and J. S. Mouton. *Productivity: The Human Side.* New York: AMACOM, 1981.

Blanchard, K., and S. Johnson. *The One Minute Manager.* New York: Berkley Books, 1983.

Block, P. "Reassigning Responsibility." *NSPI News & Notes,* October 1994.

––––––. *The Empowered Manager.* San Francisco: Jossey-Bass, 1987.

Blohowiak, D. W. *Mavericks!* Homewood, Ill.: BusinessOne Irwin, 1992.

Bongiorno, L. "A Case Study in Change at Harvard," *Business Week,* November 15, 1993.

Bowles, J., and J. Hammond. *Beyond Quality.* New York: Berkley Books, 1991.

Boyatzis, R. E. *The Competent Manager.* New York: Wiley, 1982.

Brandt, S. C. *Entrepreneuring in Established Companies.* New York: New American Library, 1986.

Brassard, M. *The Memory Jogger Plus.* Methuen, Mass.: GOAL/QPC, 1989.

Brim, G. *Ambition.* New York: Basic Books, 1992.

Byham, W. C. *Zapp! The Lightening of Empowerment.* New York: Harmony Books, 1988.

Caggiano, C. "The Profit-Promoting Daily Scorecard." *Inc.,* May 1994.

Chusmir, L. H. *Thank God It's Monday.* New York: New American Library, 1990.

Clemmer, J. *Firing on All Cylinders.* London: Piatkus, 1991.

Clifford, D. K., and R. E. Cavanagh. *The Winning Performance.* New York: Bantam, 1985.

Clifton, D. O., and P. Nelson. *Soar with Your Strengths.* New York: Delacorte Press, 1992.

Colson, C., and J. Eckerd. *Why America Doesn't Work*. Dallas: Word Publishing, 1991.

Coonradt, C. A. *The Game of Work*. Salt Lake City: Shadow Mountain, 1984.

Cooper, R. K. *The Performance Edge*. Boston: Houghton Mifflin, 1991.

Corning, P., and S. Corning. *Winning with Synergy*. New York: Harper & Row, 1986.

Cronin, M. P. "Meaningful Meetings." *Inc.*, September 1994.

Crosby, P. B. *Running Things*. New York: Mentor, 1989.

———. *Quality Without Tears*. New York: McGraw-Hill, 1984.

———. *Quality Is Free*. New York: New American Library, 1979.

Csikszentmihalyi, M. *Beyond Boredom and Anxiety*. San Francisco: Jossey-Bass, 1975.

Daniels, A. *Performance Management*. Tucker, Ga.: Performance Management Publications, 1989.

Davidow, W. H., and B. Uttal. *Total Customer Service*. New York: Harper & Row, 1989.

Davis, S., and B. Davidson. *2020 Vision*. New York: Simon & Schuster, 1991.

Deal, T. E., and A. A. Kennedy. *Corporate Cultures*. Reading, Mass.: Addison-Wesley, 1982.

Deci, E. L. *Intrinsic Motivation*. New York: Plenum Press, 1975.

Delbecg, A. L., A. H. Van de Ven, and D. H. Gustafson. *Group Techniques for Program Planning*. Glenview, Ill.: Scott, Foresman, 1975.

Deming, W. E. *Out of the Crisis*. Cambridge, Mass.: MIT Press, 1986.

———. *Quality, Productivity, and Competitive Position*. Cambridge, Mass.: MIT Press, 1982.

DeVille, J. *The Psychology of Leadership*. New York: New American Library, 1984.

Dowling, W. *Effective Management and the Behavioral Sciences*. New York: AMACOM, 1978.

Drucker, P. F. *The Frontiers of Management*. New York: Dutton, 1986.

———. *Management: Tasks, Responsibilities, Practices*. New York: Harper & Row, 1973.

Duncan, J. "Clerical Work Needs Engineering." *The Office*, July 1969.

Edelston, M., and M. Buhagiar. *I-Power*. Fort Lee, N.J.: Barricade Books, 1992.

Emery, G., and P. Emery. *The Second Force*. New York: Dutton, 1990.

English, G. "How About a Good Word for Meetings?" *Management Review*, June 1990.

Executive Committee, The. *Small Business Survey*. San Diego: T.E.C., 1993.

Fisher, K., S. Rayner, and W. Belgard. *Tips for Teams*. New York: McGraw-Hill, 1995.

Frankl, V. *Man's Search for Meaning*. New York: Pocket Books, 1963.

Freud, S. *Complete Psychological Works of Sigmund Freud*. London: Hogarth Press, 1968.

Fritz, R. *The Path of Least Resistance*. New York: Fawcett Columbine, 1989.

Gallup, G., Jr., and A. M. Gallup. *The Great American Success Story*. Homewood, Ill.: Dow Jones-Irwin, 1986.

Gallwey, W. T. *The Inner Game of Golf.* New York: Random House, 1981.

Gardner, J. W. *Self-Renewal.* New York: Perennial Library, 1963.

Garfield, C. *Second to None.* Homewood, Ill.: BusinessOne Irwin, 1992.

———. *Peak Performers.* New York: Avon, 1986.

Garfield-Schwartz, G., and W. Neikirk. *The Work Revolution.* New York: Ramson Associates, 1983.

Gellerman, S. W. *Motivation in the Real World.* New York: Dutton, 1992.

Gerber, M. E. *The Power Point.* New York: HarperBusiness, 1991.

———. *The E-Myth.* Cambridge, Mass.: Ballinger, 1986.

Gilbert, T. F. *Human Competence.* New York: McGraw-Hill, 1978.

———, and M. B. Gilbert. "Performance Engineering: Making Human Productivity a Science." *Performance and Instruction,* January 1989.

Grensing, L. *Motivating Today's Work Force.* North Vancouver, B.C.: Self-Counsel Press, 1991.

Hale, R. L., and R. F. Maehling. *Recognition Redefined.* Minneapolis: Tennant Company, 1992.

Hall, J. *The Competence Process.* The Woodlands, Tex.: Teleometrics International, 1980.

Hammer, M. "Reengineering Work: Don't Automate, Obliterate." *Harvard Business Review,* July–August 1990.

Hammer, M., and J. Champy. *Reengineering the Corporation.* New York: HarperBusiness, 1993.

Handy, C. *The Age of Unreason.* Boston: Harvard Business School Press, 1990.

Hatcher, E. "Positive Safety." *Training,* July 1991.

Helmstetter, S. *What to Say When You Talk to Your Self.* Scottsdale, Ariz.: Grindle Press, 1986.

Herman, S. M. *A Force of Ones.* San Francisco: Jossey-Bass, 1994.

Herzberg, F. "Conversations with Frederick Herzberg." In *Effective Management and the Behavioral Sciences.* Ed. W. Dowling. New York: AMACOM, 1978.

———. *Work and the Nature of Man.* New York: World Publications, 1966.

Hickman, C. R., and M. A. Silva. *The Future 500.* New York: New American Library, 1987.

Hill, N. *Think and Grow Rich.* New York: Fawcett Crest, 1960.

Hughes, C. L. *Goal Setting.* New York: American Management Association, 1965.

Huseman, R. C., and J. D. Hatfield. *Managing the Equity Factor.* Boston: Houghton Mifflin, 1989.

Imai, M. *Kaizen.* New York: McGraw-Hill, 1986.

Izard, C. E. *Human Emotions.* New York: Plenum Press, 1977.

Jacobs, G., and R. McFarlane. *The Vital Corporation.* Englewood Cliffs, N.J.: Prentice-Hall, 1990.

James, W. *The Principles of Psychology, vol. 1.* New York: Henry Holt, 1890.

Johnson, W. B. *Workforce 2000.* Indianapolis: Hudson Institute, 1987.

Juran, J. *Juran on Leadership for Quality.* New York: The Free Press, 1989.

Kahn, R. L. "Productivity and Job Satisfaction." *Personnel Psychology,* vol. 13, 1960.

Kanter, R. M. *When Giants Learn to Dance.* New York: Simon & Schuster, 1989.

———. "The Attack on Pay." *Harvard Business Review*, March–April 1987.

———. *The Change Masters*. New York: Simon & Schuster, 1983.

Katz, S. J., and A. E. Liu. *Success Trap*. New York: Ticknor & Fields, 1990.

Katzenbach, J. R., and D. K. Smith. "The Discipline of Teams." *Harvard Business Review*, March–April 1993.

Keller, M. *Rude Awakening*. New York: Harper Perennial, 1989.

Kennedy, T. E., and A. A. Deal. *Corporate Cultures*. Reading, Mass.: Addison-Wesley, 1982.

Kerr, S. "On the Folly of Rewarding A, While Hoping for B." In *The Management of Organizations*. Ed. M. L. Tushman, C. O'Reilly, and David Nadler. New York: Ballinger, 1989.

Kidder, T. *The Soul of a New Machine*. Boston: Little Brown, 1981.

Kilmann, R. H. *Beyond the Quick Fix*. San Francisco: Jossey-Bass, 1984.

Kirkpatrick, D. L. "Performance Appraisal: When Two Jobs Are Too Many." *Training*, March 1986.

Kohn, A. *Punished by Rewards*. Boston: Houghton Mifflin, 1993.

———. *No Contest: The Case Against Competition*. Boston: Houghton Mifflin, 1986.

Kolbe, K. *The Conative Connection*. Reading, Mass.: Addison-Wesley, 1990.

Kouzes, J. M., and B. Z. Posner. *Credibility*. San Francisco: Jossey-Bass, 1993.

Krueger, D. W. *Emotional Business*. San Marcos, Calif.: Avant Books, 1992.

Land, G., and B. Jarman. *Breakpoint and Beyond*. New York: HarperBusiness, 1992.

Larean, W. *Conduct Expected*. Piscataway, N.J.: New Century, 1985.

Lawler, E. E. *The Ultimate Advantage*. San Francisco: Jossey-Bass, 1992.

———. *Strategic Pay*. San Francisco: Jossey-Bass, 1990.

LeBoeuf, M. *GMP: The Greatest Management Principle in the World*. New York: Berkley Books, 1985.

Lee, C. "The Vision Thing." *Training*, February 1993.

Levering, R. *A Great Place to Work*. New York: Random House, 1988.

Levinson, H. *The Great Jackass Fallacy*. Boston: Harvard University, 1973.

Lowen, A. *Bioenergetics*. New York: Penguin Books, 1975.

Maccoby, M. *Why Work?* New York: Simon & Schuster, 1988.

Mackenzie, R. A. *The Time Trap*. New York: McGraw-Hill, 1975.

Maltz, M. *Psycho-Cybernetics*. New York: Pocket Books, 1969.

Manz, C. C., and H. P. Sims. *SuperLeadership*. New York: Berkley Books, 1989.

Maslow, A. *Motivation and Personality*. New York: Harper & Row, 1954.

McClelland, D. C. *Human Motivation*. New York: Cambridge University Press, 1987.

McGill, M. E. *American Business and the Quick Fix*. New York: Henry Holt, 1988.

McGregory, D. *The Human Side of Enterprise*. New York: McGraw-Hill, 1960.

Menninger, K. A. "Work as Sublimation." In *Human Life Cycle*. Ed. W. C. Sze. New York: Jason Aronson, 1975.

Miller, L. M. *American Spirit*. New York: Warner Books, 1984.

Naisbitt, J., and P. Aburdene. *Reinventing the Corporation*. New York: Warner Books, 1985.

Nanus, B. *Visionary Leadership*. San Francisco: Jossey-Bass, 1992.

Neff, W. S. *Work and Human Behavior.* New York: Aldine, 1985.

Nelson, B. *1001 Ways to Reward Employees.* New York: Workman, 1994.

Nohria, N., and J. D. Berkley, "An Action Perspective: The Crux of the New Management." *California Management Review,* Summer 1994.

Odiorne, G. S. *The Human Side of Management.* Lexington, Mass.: Lexington Books, 1987.

Pascale, R. T. *Managing on the Edge.* New York: Simon & Schuster, 1990.

———, and A. G. Athos. *The Art of Japanese Management.* New York: Warner, 1981.

Pascarella, P. *The New Achievers.* New York: The Free Press, 1984.

Payne, T. *From the Inside Out.* Albuquerque, N.M.: Performance Press, 1991.

Pelton, W. J., S. Sackmann, and R. Boguslaw. *Tough Choices: The Decision-Making Styles of America's Top 50 CEOs.* Homewood, Ill.: Dow Jones-Irwin, 1990.

Peters, T. "Letter to the Editor," *Inc.,* April 1988.

———. *Thriving on Chaos.* New York: Knopf, 1987.

———, and R. H. Waterman. *In Search of Excellence.* New York: Harper & Row, 1982.

Prince, G. M. *The Practice of Creativity.* New York: Collier Books, 1970.

Pryor, F. *The Energetic Manager.* Englewood Cliffs, N.J.: Prentice-Hall, 1987.

Putman, H. D. *The Winds of Turbulence.* New York: HarperBusiness, 1991.

Quick, T. L. *Successful Team Building.* New York: AMACOM, 1992.

Rifkin, J. *Entropy.* New York: Bantam Books, 1981.

Robbins, A. *Awaken the Giant Within.* New York: Summit Books, 1991.

———. *Unlimited Power.* New York: Fawcett Columbine, 1986.

Rodgers, F. S., and C. Rodgers. "Business and the Facts of Family Life." *Harvard Business Review,* November–December 1989.

Rosen, R. H. *The Healthy Company.* Los Angeles: Tarcher, 1991.

Rosenbluth, H. F., and D. M. Peters. *The Customer Comes Second.* New York: William Morrow, 1992.

Rummler, G. A., and A. P. Brache. *Improving Performance.* San Francisco: Jossey-Bass, 1990.

Ryan, K. D., and D. K. Ostreich. *Driving Fear Out of the Workplace.* San Francisco: Jossey-Bass, 1991.

Rydz, J. S. *Commonsense Manufacturing Management.* New York: Ballinger, 1990.

Schachter, S. *The Psychology of Affiliation.* Stanford, Calif.: Stanford University Press, 1959.

Schaffer, R. H. *The Breakthrough Strategy.* Cambridge, Mass.: Ballinger, 1988.

Schein, E. H. *Organizational Psychology.* Englewood Cliffs, N.J.: Prentice-Hall, 1980.

Schmidt, W. H., and J. P. Finnigan. *The Race Without a Finish Line.* San Francisco: Jossey-Bass, 1992.

Schneider, C. E., R. W. Beatty, and L. S. Baird. *The Performance Management Sourcebook.* Amherst, Mass.: Human Resource Development Press, 1987.

Scholtes, P. R. *The Team Handbook.* Madison, Wis.: Joiner Associates, 1990.

Schonberger, R. J. *Building a Chain of Customers.* New York: The Free Press, 1990.

Schuster, J. R., and P. K. Zingheim. *The New Pay.* New York: Lexington Books, 1992.

Seligman, M. E. P. *Learned Optimism.* New York: Knopf, 1991.

Senge, P. *The Fifth Discipline.* New York: Doubleday, 1990.

Sibson, R. E. *Increasing Employee Productivity.* New York: AMACOM, 1976.

Sirota, D., and A. D. Wolfson. "Pragmatic Approach to People Problems." In *People: Managing Your Most Important Asset.* Cambridge, Mass.: Harvard Business Review, 1983.

Skinner, B. F. *About Behaviorism.* New York: Vintage Books, 1976.

Sloma, R. S. *No-Nonsense Planning.* New York: The Free Press, 1984.

———. *No-Nonsense Management.* New York: Bantam, 1981.

Spitzer, D. "Training: What It Is and How to Use It Appropriately." *Performance and Instruction,* September 1991.

———. "The Best Performer: Sharing the Secrets of Success." *Performance and Instruction,* December 1986.

———. "Five Keys to Effective Training." *Training,* September 1986.

———. *Improving Individual Performance.* Englewood Cliffs, N.J.: Educational Technology Publications, 1986.

———. "But Will They Use Training on the Job?" *Training,* September 1982.

Sprouse, M. *Sabotage in the American Workplace.* San Francisco: Pressure Drop Press, 1992.

Srikanth, M. L. "For Performance, Think Nontraditional." *Industry Week,* July 6, 1992.

Stack, J. "The Great Game of Business." *Inc.,* June 1992.

Stayer, R. "How I Learned to Let My Workers Lead." *Harvard Business Review,* November–December 1990.

Terkel, S. *Working.* New York: Avon, 1975.

Ulrich, D., and D. Lake. *Organizational Capability.* New York: Wiley, 1990.

Viscott, D. *Taking Care of Business.* New York: William Morrow, 1985.

Vough, C. F. *Tapping the Human Resource.* New York: AMACOM, 1975.

Waitley, D. *The Psychology of Winning.* New York: Berkley Books, 1984.

Walton, W. B. *The New Bottom Line.* New York: Harper & Row, 1986.

Waterman, R. H. *Adhocracy: The Power to Change.* New York: Norton, 1990.

Watson, C. E. *Managing with Integrity.* New York: Praeger, 1991.

Weiss, A. *Managing for Peak Performance.* New York: Harper & Row, 1989.

Welles, E. O. "Lost in Patagonia." *Inc.,* August 1992.

White, R. W. "Motivation Reconsidered: The Concept of Competence." *Psychological Review,* vol. 66, 1959.

Whiteley, R. C. *The Customer-Driven Company.* Reading, Mass.: Addison-Wesley, 1991.

Whyte, W. H. *The Organization Man.* New York: Simon & Schuster, 1956.

Yate, Martin. *Keeping the Best.* Holbrook, Mass.: Bob Adams, 1991.

Young, P. T. *Motivation and Emotion.* New York: Wiley, 1961.

Zaleznik, A. *Executive's Guide to Motivating People.* Chicago: Bonus Books, 1990.

Zemke, R. "Is Performance Appraisal a Paper Tiger?" *Training,* December 1985.

Ziglar, Z. *Top Performance.* New York: Berkley Books, 1987.

Zuboff, S. *In the Age of the Smart Machine.* New York: Basic Books, 1988.

Index